The Pursuit of Local History

Readings on Theory and Practice

AMERICAN ASSOCIATION FOR STATE AND LOCAL HISTORY BOOK SERIES

Series Editor

Sandra Sageser Clark
Michigan Historical Center

Editorial Advisory Board

Robert R. Archibald, Missouri Historical Society
Lonnie G. Bunch, Smithsonian Institution
Debbie Kmetz, State Historical Society of Wisconsin
George F. MacDonald, Canadian Museum of Civilization
Philip Scarpino, Indiana University-Purdue University, Indianapolis
George L. Vogt, South Carolina Department of Archives and History

About the Series:

The American Association for State and Local History Book Series publishes technical and professional information for those who practice and support history and addresses issues critical to the field of state and local history. To submit a proposal or manuscript to the series, please request proposal guidelines from AASLH headquarters: AASLH Book Series, 530 Church Street, Suite 600, Nashville, TN 37219. Telephone: (615) 255-2971. Fax: (615) 255-2979.

About the Organization:

The American Association for State and Local History (AASLH) is a nonprofit educational organization dedicated to advancing knowledge, understanding, and appreciation of local history in the United States and Canada. In addition to sponsorship of this book series, the association publishes the periodical *History News*, a newsletter, technical leaflets and reports, and other materials; confers prizes and awards in recognition of outstanding achievement in the field; and supports a broad educational program and other activities designed to help members work more effectively. Current members are entitled to discounts on AASLH Series books. To join the organization, contact: Membership Director, AASLH, 530 Church Street, Suite 600, Nashville, TN 37219.

The Pursuit of Local History

Readings on Theory and Practice

■

edited by
Carol Kammen

ALTAMIRA
PRESS

A Division of Sage Publications, Inc.

Walnut Creek ■ *London* ■ *New Delhi*

Published in cooperation with the
AMERICAN ASSOCIATION FOR STATE AND LOCAL HISTORY

For information contact:

AltaMira Press
A Division of Sage Publications, Inc.
1630 North Main Street, Suite 367
Walnut Creek, California 94596 U.S.A.

Sage Publications Ltd.
6 Bonhill Street
London EC2A 4PU United Kingdom

Sage Publications India Pvt. Ltd.
M-32 Market
Greater Kailash 1
New Delhi, 110 048 India

PRINTED IN THE UNITED STATES OF AMERICA

Library of Congress Cataloging-in-Publication Data

Kammen, Carol
    The pursuit of local history: readings on theory and practice / edited by Carol Kammen.
        p.   cm. — (American Association for State and Local History book series)
    Includes bibliographical references.
    ISBN 0-7619-9169-7 (pbk.)
    1. United States—History. Local. 2. Local history. I. Kammen, Carol, 1937– . II. American Association for State and Local History. III. Series.
E160.987   1996
p73—dc20
96-9947

Production Services: Carole Bernard
Editorial Management: Denise M. Santoro
Cover Design: Denise M. Santoro
Cover Photo: car in front of Shulman's market on "N" at Union Street S.W., Washington, D.C. Louise Rosskam, 1910– , photographer
Library of Congress, Prints & Photographs Division, FSA-OWI Collection, LC-USF351-636 DLC

Published in cooperation with the American Association for State and Local History

Contents

About the Editor

Carol Kammen is a graduate of The George Washington University. One of the foremost scholars in her field, Kammen has researched, written about, and taught local history for over twenty years. Presently a Senior Lecturer in history at Cornell University, Kammen focuses on the nature and practice of local history, as well as on the regional history of upstate New York.

Carol Kammen is a regular contributor to the American Association for State and Local History's magazine *History News* and to *The Ithaca Journal*. She also has written numerous books and plays on local history. These include *On Doing Local History: Reflections on What Local Historians Do, Why, and What It Means* (which won a special award from the Center for Historic Preservation at Mary Washington College in 1989), *The Peopling of Tompkins County: A Social History* (which won the Regional Council of Historical Agencies Award for Social History in 1986), and most recently "Flight to Ithaca" (a drama in two acts about the Fugitive Slave Act and the Underground Railroad).

Kammen has served on a number of AASLH committees and is a member of the National Humanities Faculty.

Acknowledgments

Over the years, a number of people have aided in this project. My husband Michael Kammen has always interested himself in the concerns of those of us who do local history. I have learned from Raymond Starr and appreciate our many collaborations. Bob Archibald, long a friend and currently president of AASLH, has been most generous in helping me with this book; conversations with him are a pleasure.

I am most grateful to all those who have granted permission to reprint the essays included here.

I would like to thank many former and current staff members of the American Association for State and Local History: Martha Strayhorn and her staff were most helpful, as were LuAnne Sneddon, Patricia Hogan, and John-Paul Richiuso, and, currently, Terry L. Davis.

Mitch Allen and Denise Santoro of AltaMira Press have been cordial collaborators and I appreciate the care and patience with which they regarded this project. I am indebted especially to Sandra S. Clark of the AASLH Publications committee for her careful reading of the manuscript and her insightful suggestions.

No book is the product of any one person, this book least of all. *The Pursuit of Local History* creates, I believe, a community of those of us—past and present—who care about doing local history.

Carol Kammen

For all those local historians
and students from whom I have learned.

The second day was dedicated to Clio, the Muse of History.
At this point the philosopher Callisthenes participated, too, giving a speech in which he explained how he imagined history should be written.
"What is meant by Truth?" he said.
"To believe in what you see.
What is meant by Myth?
To believe in what you do not see.
What is history? The daughter of Truth and Myth."
—Nikos Kazantzakis, *Alexander the Great: A Novel*

Introduction

Local History—in Search of Common Threads

When I began work as a local historian, some years ago, I dug into the records of my community, wrote several books and many articles, and spoke frequently to all sorts of groups about the history of my area. These activities were similar to those of other local historians: we are all miners, each in our own sphere, burrowing for information to enrich the life and times of our own places. Over the years, I read a good deal of local history produced by others and I attended exhibits and visited historical sites and societies. Because I live near a fine research library, I also looked up the literature of local history, expecting to find in it a discussion of what local history is all about.

What I discovered, instead—to my surprise—was that there is scant literature about local history. Some books are listed under the "Local History" heading, but most are manuals purporting to tell amateurs how to write local history, and the majority of these were written in England. Of the articles I finally tracked down in journals or printed as separate pamphlets, some were written by professional historians who had researched local history themselves, and some were by scholars who had not. Few local historians, though, have written about what it is that they do.

It is natural, of course, that local historians address history as a kind of quest, rather than writing about their methods. But is seems to me that some consideration of the field within which we work is important and necessary. Local history is a popular pursuit of a great many people, but they rarely consider it as something that has or needs an overriding rationale, a set of principles, a shared set of readings, a concern for consequences—or even a common agenda. Out of my interest in local history came *On Doing Local History* and a series of articles in *New York History*[1] on what local historians do, why, and what it means. Of concern to me is that local historians continue to enjoy what they do while being aware of the tradition in which they work, the innovations and new currents in historical interests, and the importance of their craft.

To that end I began to collect articles about local history that I found most interesting. There were not so many, after all, and—because of their date or their place of publication—a number of them are inaccessible to most people. Therefore, this book is made up of a representative selection, as an offering of statements about local history—how it should be done, what local historians might look for, how local history can be thought about and researched, written, and exhibited. These articles offer some guidelines for the pursuit of local history and contain suggestions that may help local historians join in common cause.

During the course of my reading about local history, I came across an issue of the *Alabama Historical Review* in which Margaret Pace Farmer offers an article entitled "History as Hobby."[2] Farmer gives a long list of reasons explaining why local history is an ideal hobby. Some of these are that local history is entertaining, that it can be inexpensive—in a period of ten years, she spent $30.42 on books of a historical nature—and that it is engaging, for "the more you know the more you want to know," and a "life span is not [time] enough" for a local historian to do all that he or she might want. These are probably true enough, especially if the local historian uses interlibrary loans and works closely with reference collections in a library or historical society. Farmer also says that history has prestige and that "if you love history you are apt to be praised by your fellow man for your high-minded industry." The local historian, insists the author, gets credit from his or her townspeople for being serious-minded, intellectual, and diligent. She adds that history has variety, it is enlightening, it is creative, and it is an escape.

Despite Farmer's list of reasons supporting the notion that history is a hobby, I insist upon the opposite. Whereas a hobby is an engrossing pursuit to which one constantly reverts, or an occupation or interest to which one gives spare time,[3] local history has too many community implications to be regarded simply as something to do on a rainy Tuesday night. A stamp collector has a hobby: the individual stamp collector who keeps his or her stamps in good condition, neatly organized and inserted in envelopes, affects his or her own interest, as does the stamp collector who keeps stamps housed carelessly in cigar boxes. The public interest is not involved. If a collector of paperweights is missing a key item from a set, or if a genealogist cannot find Great Aunt Sarah's death date, as upsetting as that may be, there is not, in either case, a wider, public consequence.

But local history is different. Exhibited poorly, conceived with a narrow focus, written to establish a particular code of behavior or an assumption about the community, local history has an impact beyond the personal. A carelessly written local history can lead the public to believe that history is boring or not worth doing well. Local history that is incorrect passes misleading information or generalizations into the general culture of a community. Inaccurate history or biased history moves into the culture of a place and is excised only with great difficulty —if at all. Local history has too many implications for too many people for it to be regarded as a hobby. To consider local historical activity as having no consequences but personal ones is to sell short what we do—and also to sell short the public's needs and interests.

Because of the importance of local history—to those of us who practice it and to the public at large—it is important that local historians consider what they do in some larger context. Some have claimed that local history is not a field of study; others have said that local history is not teachable because the facts of one place are not the same as the facts of another place, and who, after all, would be interested? But local history has common aspects that transcend the particularities of one community or another. And it is those common threads that local historians need to grasp. They must understand that the history of Portland, Oregon, or Pocatello, Idaho, fits into a regional and national context, either as part of a pattern or as apart from that pattern. They must realize that questions of one place can be asked of other localities, thereby creating comparative history. And they must appreciate that local historians have common problems concerning the documents they use, their research methods and strategies, and their presentation. We have a commonality of interest that draws us together.

In the 1950s and 1960s, the English attempted to direct the writing of local history by devising an approach for all to follow. To counter the fact that much English local history was a "heap of all facts that could be discovered without order or art or method" and with no discrimination between the trivial or the relevant, Professor H. P. R. Finberg, and others, devised a schema for local history.[4] Rather than study the successions of important people and families, Finberg and his colleagues suggested that local historians look at the community in terms of its origin, growth, and decline. Writing at the same time, W. G. Hoskins complained that, in the past, local history in England had presented a lopsided view with excessive attention given to manorial history while the village itself was neglected. There had been, he asserted, a preoccupation with land, landed classes, pedigrees, and heraldry. Local history in the mid-twentieth century, he insisted, was little better, because it was "preoccupied with facts and correspondingly unaware of problems."[5] Hoskins stated that local history should be about the nature of society and the way a community solves its basic problems. Although a few writers disputed these ideas, they guided English local history for a time.[6]

In the United States, some writers have suggested topics for local historians to consider, but their ideas have not received much attention and local historians have gone merrily on their own separate ways. So, too, have our museums, historical societies, and historic sites. In 1987, however, the American Association for State and Local History, the American Association of Museums, and others held a conference to determine the needs and problems faced by the many historical museums in North America. Their goal was to understand the problems of exhibiting history and those of storing and organizing historic materials, and then to set about addressing those problems. Participants at the conference believed that a common language—in this case, one about collection categories—might aid museums in exchanging information with each other and in making known the holdings of each of these repositories. "By defining a standard, museums will have a basis for developing or reviewing their own collection management systems," states a special AASLH report, "and they will also have a means to communicate or share data whether they choose to adopt the standard for their own records or not."[7] Thus, the Common Agenda was born. It seeks to regularize the language of the many history museums in this country, to give them a set of procedures that each might follow in order to make information intelligible and accessible from one place to another. This is happening on a very practical level, and it has great potential.

Should local history follow the same path? Can there be stated themes that local historians might wish to address? And would they? I believe that local history is an individualistic affair and that it would be unrealistic to expect all local historians to study the same problems. But we might ask whether there are some common concerns that could guide the efforts of local historians and be considered as suggestions of ways of organizing research and presenting local history.

The idea of themes for local historians to consider is attractive, just as the Common Agenda is a step in the direction of regularizing museum nomenclature and, in some instances, museum practices. My concern, then, is not to tell local historians what to do or what not to do, but to suggest valid and attractive ways of communicating historical information about their communities.

Local historians might want to consider some of the following broad topics:

- Population change over time. This corresponds with the English idea of origin, rise, and decline of communities, but it is less mechanistic. The demography of a locality is important, and once it has been charted other questions of a social, political, and economic nature will follow automatically.

- Decision making. At what points in a community's life were decisions needed, what forced those decisions, who made them, and how did they affect the total population? This line of inquiry might look at a community in the face of a natural disaster, such as a flood; or at a community improvement, such as the creation of a public water system or the placement of rail lines; or at a challenge, such as economic stress when businesses fail or threaten to move away. On what basis were decisions made? At what point did public boards develop to cope with perceived public need? And what was the effect of a decision on all or many parts of the population? This is a theme that can be studied for one event or for a series of events over time.

- Domestic life and culture. The family has long been considered one of the building blocks of our national life; however, except for special old and important families, family life is often ignored or by-passed in local history. We should look at the uses a family makes of a community—the demand for schools and libraries; the development of bus transportation; the origin and development of orphan asylums, poorhouses, homes for unwed mothers, prisons, courts; and public charity. This theme can be expanded to include changes in the family due to technological advances, from new sewing machines, changes in foodways, to new modes of birth control. Family life and family culture can reveal trends in leisure activities, reading, and popular culture.

- Community competition. America's home towns coalesced, but they also competed with each other for population and economic development as a way of creating community identities. Today, there are development officers in many of our towns and cities. In the past, there were often committees that sought to entice new industries to a place; there were newspaper accounts about the healthiness of one town and the unhealthy aspects of another. There were also people who promoted one place over another. Communities actively sought country seats or the honor and importance of becoming a state capitol: there is even a folklore theme called "stealing the country seat." How our communities competed with each other, and why, is a story that is often neglected but it is central to how places regarded themselves and how they functioned regionally.
- Community activism. Over time, in every community, people have helped others, and they have helped themselves. Sometimes that help was freely given, as to a church fund or mission works. Sometimes that help took the form of taxes to maintain poor relief or to keep orphans from the community in a nearby home. Sometimes, community activism takes the form of philanthropy; at other times, culture is the desired result. We have organized for a variety of purposes. Throughout time, there are political groups, and there are unions, insurance societies, and fraternal organizations.

There are, of course, many other themes worth mentioning, but these are the ones that particularly interest me. They provide a start at forming a common agenda for local historians; other people, and some of the writers in the collection, have added and will continue to add to this beginning.

* * * *

The local historian does not work in a vacuum. At any given time, others are engaged in researching and presenting local history—they constitute our community of scholars. Local history also has a past, which gives us a common language, some traditions to avoid, and others to emulate. One of the things that we have inherited from the past is a body of literature—little known perhaps and little read—that challenges us to know what we are all about and joins us in a common enterprise.

The selections in this volume do not include all the essays about local history that I have been able to find, but these are the liveliest ones, and the ones from which I learned the most. They offer some important points for local historians to consider. Gathered in this book are twenty essays about local history. From them, some common themes emerge. Most of the writers expect American local history to be inclusive—to have a broad and representative cast of characters, rather than to focus on the few. Even the earliest essays, those from the nineteenth century, assert that local history should reflect the lives of ordinary people and that it should consider the causes and consequences of events. These essays call for local historians to seek the reasons behind the facts, the emotions experienced by a range of characters, and the culture of the people of each place.

The writers share a vision of local history as needing to be broadly based, to address subjects beyond the institutional and political. Professors A. Theodore Brown and Richard Wohl describe the diverse histories to be found in one place and they demonstrate the importance of listening to varied voices.

These authors also expand upon the topics that a local historian might consider. In 1846, James Davie Butler asked where women's voices and popular songs were to be found. Paul Leuilliot offers a whole set of topics for the local historian that are worth considering. Constance McLaughlin Green elaborates on the types of subjects local historians might research.

The nineteenth-century essays discuss history as having moral lessons, an interest not present in the twentieth century. Recent authors are more inclined to stress the importance of knowing what historical trends are current, so that local history might expand its repertoire.

The authors in this collection display some differences. Hermann Ludewig is interested in American exceptionalism and patriotism, whereas later essayists are more interested in broadening the scope of local history and in seeing local history reflect a balanced view of what happened. Among the more recent historians, there is a trend toward seeing the applicability of local history to our modern problems.

The book is divided into six sections, and except for minor copyediting, the articles appear as they were originally published. In the first section, the local historian is considered, and a range of local history activities are suggested. David Russo's article is a preview of *Keepers of Our Past: Local Historical Writing in the United States. 1820s–1930s* (New York, 1988), a book that traces the history of local history.

The second section presents three nineteenth-century views of local history. Here, Salma Hale surprises us with the modernity of his approach. One wonders what sort of reputation local history might have if Hale had been widely read and his ideas about local history followed. Hale is also quoted by Hermann Ludewig and by Whitfield Bell.

The third section of the book, "The Nature of Local History," deals with the reasons for local history's popularity in the past and reasons for its practice. Constance McLaughlin Green asks local historians to consider a fresh range of topics and a new rigor. She calls local history the life history of a community.

"Thinking Anew about Local History," the fourth section, discusses new ways of considering local history. These are bold essays that challenge local historians to go beyond the old and tired subjects often presented in filiopietistic accounts of the past. In a second essay, Green asks us to consider what major subjects we have to deal with when thinking about a community. She does not emphasize the origins, rise, and decline of a locality, but rather the institutions that make a community work, the physical environment as part of local history, and the changes that evoke new responses from the people living there.

A. Theodore Brown and Richard Wohl look for the forgotten or unheard history of a place, and Paul Leulliot offers a manifesto calling for bold histories, carefully created, about a number of specific topics reflecting the interests of French historical scholarship during the past forty years.

Over time, some writers have listed dos and don'ts for local historians. The fifth section of this reader is a cautionary tale, told in a sprightly manner; it consists of the proscriptions and antidotes for many of the local historian's worst ills.

The final section written by Robert Archibald calls for empathy, sympathy, and knowing in the doing of history. The French historian Marc Bloch commented that "the scholar who has no inclination to observe the men, the things, or the events around him will perhaps deserve the title . . . of a useful antiquarian. He would be wise to renounce all claims to that of a historian."[8]

There has never been a collection of local history material of the sort presented here. There are complex reasons for this; among them is that local history customarily has not been considered a separate field of endeavor by academic historians or even by local historians. Publishers, too, have not found in local history a market great enough to sustain such a collection. The time, I believe, is right for *The Pursuit of Local History*: there are many practitioners of local history; there is interest in the field among the public at large and in people who are generally interested in history; and there is academic interest, with more and more universities and colleges offering courses in local history and in its adjacent field, public history. There is also community interest in history, reflected in concerns about cultural tourism.

This book pulls together some of the threads of a local historian's self-knowledge. It defines local history's past and points to the future. It examines what local historians do; it offers suggestions; it cautions; and it recommends some guidelines. If local history is more to each of us than a hobby, as I believe it to be, these essays will help challenge us to be thoughtful practitioners of Clio's art.

NOTES

1. Carol Kammen, *On Doing Local History: Reflections on What Local Historians Do, Why, and What It Means* (Nashville: AASLH Press, 1986) and "On Doing Local History in New York State," a regular feature in *New York History*, January 1985 through November 1988. These essays have been reprinted in *Plain as a Pipestem: Essays about Local History* (Interlaken, NY: Heart of the Lakes Publishing, 1989).

2. Margaret Pace Farmer, "History as Hobby," *Alabama Historical Review* 15 (July 1962): 163–73.

3. *Webster's New Collegiate Dictionary* (Springfield, MA: G & C Merriam Co., 1960), Ed., s.v. "hobby."

4. H. P. R. Finberg, *The Local Historian and His Theme* (Leicester, England, 1954), especially p. 15; and H. P. R. Finberg, *Local History in the University: An Inaugural Address* (Leicester, England: Leicester University, 1964): 8.

5. W. G. Hoskins, *Local History in England* (1959; London: Longman, 1972), 14–16, 26–27.

6. W. R. Powell, "Local History in Theory and Practice," *Bulletin of the Institute of Historical Research* 31 (1958): 41–48. Powell questions how anyone can determine when a community has reached any of the stages in this triad. He offers his own list of topics to be considered by local historians. They include topography, architecture, public service, population study, folklore, social life, customs, and "worthies"—ownership of land, aspects of agrarian history, industries, the church, school and government, and charities. The most important of these, he asserts, is ownership of land, with lord of the manor being the key to a community's history.

7. "The Common Agenda Museum Information Survey," *History News* 43 (July/August 1988): 17–28.

8. Marc Bloch, *The Historian's Craft* (Manchester: The University Press, 1954), 44–45.

PART I

The Local Historian

. . . the self-styled local historian, the gently agitated mole grubbing through our Masurian past. He invites me to delve into the abundant bog with my blue and yellow shovel; he teaches me, if not reverence, then awe for the eloquent relics of our early times; in the course of years of fanatical collecting, he has transformed his house into a museum of regional history, and there I learn that any understanding of the world must begin at home—or end there.

—Siegfried Lenz, *The Heritage*

Chapter One

The Amateur Historian

Introduction

Whitfield J. Bell, Jr., in his essay "The Amateur Historian," notes that much of the history we venerate has been written by amateurs. Bell relates the various activities of local historians—collecting and preserving local materials, compiling and writing local chronicles of all sorts and of all qualities, and searching through materials often ignored by historians who write about the nation as a whole. He writes that an amateur historian has a tradition to uphold, a future of greater cooperation with academic or professional historians, and an increase of topics that will interest both.

Whitfield Bell was born in 1914 in Newburgh, New York. He has been an historical editor, working on the papers of Benjamin Franklin, and for many years was librarian at the American Philosophical Society in Philadelphia, Pennsylvania.

His essay, "The Amateur Historian," was presented as the keynote address at the Annual Meeting of the New York State Historical Association in Cooperstown on July 9, 1971, and was published originally in *New York History* 53 (July 1972): 265–81. It appears here by permission of the New York State Historical Association.

* * * *

Everyman, Carl Becker reminded us, forty years ago, is his own historian—remembering, recounting, recording things he has done and said and seen. He reflects on the day's little events, calls on yesterday's experiences to organize and enlighten today's problems, even adds to his daily satisfactions by relating the adventures and achievements of bygone years. In such simple, natural ways, Everyman is indeed something of a historian. But he is also a historian on a higher, less personal level. From his own observations, experience, and reading, from the observations and impressions of his fellows, Everyman composes, almost

---

Whitfield J. Bell, Jr., "The Amateur Historian," *New York History* 53(3) (Summer 1972): 265–81.

subconsciously, an image of the past that may serve or solace him—whether of Betsy Ross sewing her flag or of mine-owners locking out the workers. When he discusses world politics with his neighbor, Everyman can draw on his personal historical office to tell his adversary just what history teaches.

But it is not of men as natural historians (if I may use that term) that I want to speak, but rather of men as historians in the conventional sense: of men who consciously record events and collect the records of events—in print, unpublished manuscripts, pictures, or artifacts—and sometimes fashion from them a historical narrative or description. A whole profession is, of course, committed to just these kinds of business—including 15,000 dues-paying members of the American Historical Association, with professional chairs, quarterly journals, seminars, institutes, students, disciples, and deeply cherished opinions about compensation and tenure.

Professional historians, however, are no major part of my tale; nor are those who, without formal historical training, make their living by writing history, not a little of it sound history indeed, as witness the work of Cecil Woodham-Smith, Irving Brant, Barbara Tuchman, and Catherine Drinker Bowen. I propose to speak instead of the amateur historian; of those for whom history is an intellectual avocation, who can court Clio—they should never use that pretentious phrase—only from inclination and not at all as a business. Such men and women are every-where—as no one in this audience needs to be told. They read everything they can find on the topic of their interest; they bring their special skills and knowledge to its study; they collect books, manuscripts, and artifacts; spend all the hours they can spare or decently take to cull data from basic records or make toilsome expeditions to see things for themselves; write articles and sometimes volumes; and are often turned to in disputes over some obscure fact in their community's past.

In an age of specialization and professionalism, the word *amateur* has an invid-ious connotation (it is in fact essentially a word of the nineteenth century); but I use it here most emphatically without disparagement or condescension. Amateurs are not always ineffectual dabblers (nor are professionals necessarily more expert). After all, our earliest historians were all "amateurs"—how oddly the word sounds when applied to them—whose works beginning graduate students have been known to disparage as unscholarly because they lack bibliography and footnotes! From the seventeenth century to the present day, nonprofessionals have been producing historical works of the first importance and quality. To illustrate the point, one need only recite the names of William Bradford, who recorded the history of Plymouth Colony so faithfully and movingly; Cadwallader Colden, a physician, natural philosopher, public official, and historian of the Five Indian Nations; and the Reverend Dr. Samuel Miller, one of the ministers of the United Presbyterian churches of New York City, who wrote a comprehensive two-volume survey of the age of the Enlightenment, a work still too little-known and appreciated, called *A*

Brief Retrospect of the Eighteenth Century. Nor were any of those professionals who, inspired by the American Revolution, produced some of the earliest state histories. The Reverend Mr. Jeremy Belknap of New Hampshire, the Quaker schoolmaster Robert Proud of Pennsylvania, the physicians Hugh Williamson and David Ramsay of North and South Carolina, respectively, were simply men of good general education, searching curiosity, and untiring industry.

The truth of the matter is that the professionalization of American historiography began only at the end of the nineteenth century. Although Jared Sparks was named professor of modern history at Harvard in 1838 and offered a course on the American Revolution the next year, his was a pioneering effort, and no institution followed Harvard's example. In 1872, President Andrew Dickson White of Cornell complained to his board of trustees that an American had to go to Paris or Berlin to learn the history of his own country. Not until nine years later did Cornell get a chair of American history—it was the first in the country.

Professional historians made national history their theme and national statesmen their cast of characters. They wrote about constitutional history, politics, diplomacy, and finance; about Jefferson, Jackson, Webster, Adams. Since the tendency of American history seemed to be from colonial diversity and multiplicity to federation and national unity, these preferences were self-justifying; and moreover, they had strong psychological and even aesthetic appeal. To many professionals, it appeared that the history of the states ended in 1776; everything after that was local history, unworthy of—and irrelevant to—the grander national themes they studied, and best left to antiquarians and genealogists. Local history, which was once nearly all there was in America, was now supplanted in rank and esteem; the very term was almost pejorative.

Yet local historiography has a long, strong tradition, with no mean accomplishments to its credit. Though it might be ignored by the professionals, it did not die. It may, in fact, have been stimulated by the neglect. Addressing themselves increasingly, even exclusively, to national generalizations, the professionals overlooked or obscured local variations, often got local facts wrong, and by their default unwittingly encouraged knowledgeable amateurs to tell the story as it really happened. The establishment of state and local historical societies, the publication of histories of local institutions, the magnificent series of colonial records issued under state auspices, were some expressions of this concern. More than this—as not a few persons came to realize, as they read the splendid narratives of national history—much of the common life of the people found no place in the writings of the professionals. The latter paid scant attention to education, poor relief, church history, popular thought, manners, and similar matters. Local history and many aspects of social life thus came to be studied—if at all—by the nonprofessional. Local history and the amateur historian became linked and almost interchangeable.

The result is well known. The historical guild was divided, with the professionals dismissing local history as second-class history and amateur historians as second-rate historians. The amateurs usually accepted the designation without demur; though occasionally one would retort with extravagant claims for the discovery of facts that professionals could be charged with having neglected or suppressed. The gap continues to widen, until today the American Historical Association is almost exclusively a union of professionals, while state and county historical societies, and those devoted to special interests like church history, are manned largely by amateurs. Each group is poorer for the absence of the other. Your association, to its glory be it said, has not fallen into *that* trap, but has succeeded to an outstanding degree in uniting all the historical interests of its area into our common enterprise.

To a greater extent, and perhaps more successfully than their professional brethren, amateur historians have discovered, collected, and preserved the original materials of history that survived outside official offices and archives. One thinks of Mrs. Deborah Norris Logan, sorting the papers she found in the garret at Stenton, laboriously arranging and copying in her neat hand the correspondence of William Penn and James Logan, answering inquiries of John Fanning Watson and others, and in old age discussing with Charles Thomson, secretary of the Continental Congress, the great events which both had observed and passed through. Eventually she gave those papers to the then newly established Historical Society of Pennsylvania. The core of the Wisconsin Historical Society is the great collection of books, manuscripts, and notes assembled by Lyman C. Draper. No year passes that some library does not receive a collection made by some enthusiast for history. My own, for example, has just received by bequest a collection on Thomas Paine, of staggering size and incalculable scholarly worth, that is virtually a library of the history of the American and French Revolutions and the English radical and reform movements, with subsidiary collections on theology and atheism.

Such collections, it should be obvious, are among the principal contributions that anyone can make to the study and writing of history. The materials Draper assembled at Wisconsin, to take but one example, contained many of the raw data on which young Frederick Jackson Turner pondered and based the frontier hypothesis, which has been such a fruitful interpretation of American history. Important collections will be made in the future, as many have been made in the past, by amateur historians, even by some who will disclaim the name of historian. A good deal can be done today to collect for the future needs of history, on even a modest scale. Visitors to Cooperstown are surrounded by evidences that such collecting is important. A year's assemblage of all the second- and third-class mail one receives, for example—advertisements, bills, and receipts, appeals to charity, birthday, Christmas, and Father's Day cards, personal letters, postcards—will provide the historian fifty years hence not only with intriguing illustrations for exhibition but with basic materials from which to write on several aspects of social or economic history. A dozen photographs made each year of the main streets and principal buildings of any town or city—with the traffic, shopping crowds, throngs leaving church or a high school football game—will provide a visual record of actual life in later twentieth-century America as important to the historian in 2100 as Lewis Miller's sketches of York, Pennsylvania, and its citizens are to us today. The American past is composed of pictures of San Francisco, New York, Omaha, Boston, Leadville, New Orleans, Syracuse, Oneonta, and a thousand more. And what would we not give for more annotated printed programs like one I saw of the dedication exercises of the Bunker Hill battle monument in 1825: on it, the young woman who carried it characterized Webster's appearance—a noble countenance; recorded the wry but cheerful hail of a gnarled veteran in the crowd—"Take a good look at us, ma'am—we won't be here much longer"; and noted that the clergyman was so overcome by heat or patriotic emotion that he collapsed, was carried from the platform, and never pronounced the benediction at all. And would that more men and women with a sense of history kept diaries. Whether as full and thoughtful as Sydney George Fisher's in Philadelphia and George Templeton Strong's in New York, or as short, plain, and honest as those which provided subjects for Wallace Notestein's *English Folks*, they would form valuable records for the historians of subsequent generations.

In addition to collecting, amateur historians have compiled the annals of their communities and familiar institutions. Anniversary histories of towns and counties, histories of churches, roads, academies, professions, businesses, and the like, rest most firmly on careful reading of old minutes and account books, tireless culling of newspapers, letters, and court records, persistent seeking out of informed survivors, and a determination to present a truthful record. Despite the thoroughness of their searches, not a few authors of such works have presented their findings with diffidence. John F. Watson, author of *Annals of Philadelphia in the Olden Time*, explained, "I have chiefly aimed to furnish *the material* by which better, or more ambitious, writers could elaborate more formal History—and from which as a Repository, our future Poets, Painters, and Imaginative Authors could deduce their themes, for their own and their country's glory." Like that of other amateur historians, Watson's achievement was greater and more lasting than he could have hoped, for the *Annals of Philadelphia* continues, after 130 years, to furnish material to other, but not necessarily better, writers of history.

As early as 1846 Hermann E. Ludewig, a bookish lawyer recently come from Germany to practice in New York, found no fewer than 1400 titles of books and articles to list in his bibliography of the *Literature of American Local History*. Had Ludewig lived forty years to publish a second edition of his bibliography, he could have included several score county and city histories, like Justin Winsor's *Memorial History of Boston* and Scharf and Wescott's *History of Philadelphia*. Though some bear the marks and suffer the limitations of their commercial origins, these volumes constitute a remarkable achievement, not least because they required the effective cooperation of a number of local historians to compile. Though the American county histories of the 1800s seldom examine any single topic as exhaustively as do England's *Victoria County Histories*, which some persons would call the finest achievements of amateur and local historians, they are likely to offer researchers an introduction to a greater number of aspects of community life. And no list of authoritative models of local history by amateur historians should fail to include, among others, Charles Francis Adams, Jr.'s history of church and town government in Quincy or Andrew D. Melick's *Story of an Old Farm*, which began as a family genealogy but grew into the annals of a community and the picture of a period.

We may be sure that amateur historians will continue to compile and publish the annals of local communities, of their principal events and institutions, of churches, lodges, schools, professions, and customs. We should wish that they will prepare themselves for the task, and thus ensure greater usefulness for their narrative, by taking into account the larger questions of national history and social conduct which professional historians, other scholars, and publicists are interested in. Consider, for example, voluntary associations of every kind, by which much of society's work has been done. In them men learn to join with others to pursue a common objective, to accept the majority's will and respect the minority's rights, and to govern themselves and their affairs by rules of law. These are things men have to learn. Most of us today (but not all, as contemporary disturbances in community, church, and university life make clear) have learned these required lessons of democracy, learned them so long ago we can scarcely remember the circumstances. In the eighteenth century, however, the lesson was taught and learned by many for the first time. At least, that is what the by-laws of societies and clubs seem to mean, for they often contained such specific injunctions as that no member might interrupt another speaking or lay violent hands upon him for expressing contrary opinions. One Masonic lodge in central Pennsylvania broke up and lost its warrant in 1802 because its members would not submit to the rudiments of decent discipline at their meetings. The citizens may very well have learned the purpose and methods of self-government first of all in scores of churches, societies, clubs, lodges, and other institutions in their local communities. It is noteworthy, one should remark in passing, that small voluntary associations and a liberal democratic national government have reciprocally supported one another, while centralized, autocratic governments arise most easily where such groups are few and weak; in fact, they move swiftly to suppress or control them.

In addition to local history, however, amateur historians have sometimes written works of history and biography of the first order. Neither Parkman nor Prescott was a professional, nor were Motley and Bancroft; while a magisterial work on the Inquisition of the medieval Roman Catholic Church was produced by a Philadelphia publisher, Henry Charles Lea—a most unlikely subject for the son of a Quaker father. James Ford Rhodes, who wrote on the United States between the Compromise of 1850 and the end of Reconstruction in the South, was a retired Ohio industrialist; Charles Francis Adams, Jr. was a railroad president; Douglas Southall Freeman, a newspaper editor; while John Bach McMaster was a civil engineer when he wrote the first volume of *The History of the People of the United States*, which gave American history a fresh perspective.

McMaster's achievement is significant. Turning to history with only a layman's interest, intelligence, and understanding, he asked what the life of the people was like in the past; and he found the answers, or many of them, in newspapers and journals of travel. Like McMaster, other amateur historians studied topics traditionally neglected by the professions. They made the history of churches, agriculture, education, and social life their special province. They peopled their historical canvas with the nameless common people, who settled new lands, cleared the forests, fought the Indians and weather, established schools and libraries and kept them open. Before Richard H. Shryock gave us an interpretive scheme, almost everything we knew about medicine in America came from amateur historians, usually physicians, like James Thacher of Plymouth, Massachusetts; George W. Norris and Francis R. Packard of Philadelphia; Joseph M. Toner of Washington; and Wyndham B. Blanton of Richmond, Virginia. William B. Sprague's *Annals of the American Pulpit* is still indispensable to any historian of early American churches and religion; while their taste for the quaint should not obscure the scholarship and continuing usefulness of the volumes of Alice Morse Earle on manners and customs of colonial America. In addition to presenting facts about areas neglected by the professionals, the best of the amateur historians thought deeply about the meaning of the processes of American history. Edward Eggleston, for example—Methodist circuit-rider and novelist-turned-historian—titled his extremely significant book on aspects of the cultural life of colonial New England *The Transit of Civilization*. Decrying "drum and trumpet history," he appealed for studies of "the history that underlies history," and himself examined what he called "the mental outfit" of the colonists. Eggleston's viewpoint has informed a growing library of books ever since.

I knew an amateur historian who displayed many of the best characteristics of the type. Signor D'Agostino, whom I met during World War II in Italy, was a member of an ancient family of Chieti Province in southern Italy. He was a lawyer, an old-fashioned liberal who had political ambitions and held public office; but when opposition to the Fascist regime became impossible, and men like Count Sforza were exiled or fled, he retired to the village of Pollutri to live with his family and his books. Signor D'Agostino protested that he was only a dilettante, but his methods and achievement belie his self-deprecation. For years he had kept several series of scrapbooks in which he filed and annotated letters, pamphlets, newspaper clippings, and pictures—one for political events in Italy, one for the history of foreign countries, one for medicine, another for manners and customs, another for literature, and so on. During the First World War, when Italy wavered between the Allied and Central Powers, he compiled a little pamphlet of extracts from the thoughts on foreign policy held by Napoleon, Bismarck, Cavour, and George Washington. He wrote a pretty good history of the town of Casalbordino, a market town on the next hill from Pollutri two miles away, whose records run back a thousand years; and he was the author of a biography of a nineteenth-century liberal, a native of the region, who was the teacher of Benedetto Croce. Now, during World War II, when the Germans occupied Pollutri in the late summer and early fall of 1943, Signor D'Agostino commenced a daily journal of their activities. When the men whom the Germans impressed to work on the Sangro River defenses returned home, he interviewed them all, about fifty in number, recording their stories in what may one day be discovered to be an unspectacular but valuable source of information on the war and on social life in Italy—as important for its time and place as Eliza Andrews's eyewitness account of Sherman's march through Georgia, or the diary Sally Wistar kept during the British occupation of Philadelphia.

The amateur's opportunities for historical research are many and various and can be stimulating and rewarding if he makes his investigations with reference to the significant questions that can be put to the past. To the answering of these questions many an amateur brings impressive qualifications. A patient, laborious investigator, content to accumulate his data by bits and scraps over a long period, not driven by demands to publish and extend his bibliography, the amateur often acquires an exhaustive knowledge of sources, local events, and terrain, which few professionals can match. One recalls the tireless inquiries of Merriman Smith, a Washington newspaper reporter, into the amusing, yet not entirely irrelevant history of the first White House bathtubs; and of Max Hall, another journalist, into the origins and printing history of Polly Baker's Speech, one of Franklin's most successful and long-lived hoaxes. How many professionals who have written on Indian relations in colonial America have ever retraced the Indian's trails, as did Paul A. W. Wallace, who came to history from a career in English literature? The publications of these men might appropriately be required reading in any graduate seminar in methods of historical research.

Professionals, especially those who must generalize for purpose of instructing their students, find it necessary, even easy, to speak of American history as though most of that history had not been played out on a thousand local stages, with local characters speaking in their local vernacular. But historians ought never to forget that many aspects of our national history, such as education, poor relief before 1933, religion, and manners, have hardly any national history at all. The amateur who chooses to study American local history has the opportunity of examining the roots of American action, of throwing light on accepted generalizations of American history, and, perhaps, sometimes even of modifying those generalizations by presenting the grass-roots, local history of the events on which those generalizations rest.

This may be illustrated by almost any general account of the antislavery movement. The chapter on this subject in one college text presents the story in terms of a succession of individual events: the murder of Elijah Lovejoy at Alton, Illinois; the burning of the mails at Charleston, South Carolina; the opening of Oberlin College in Ohio to Negroes; the enactment of a "personal liberty" law in Pennsylvania and its subsequent overturn by the United States Supreme Court; the founding of the *Liberator* by William Lloyd Garrison at Boston in 1831; the operations of the Underground Railroad through Kentucky, Virginia, and Maryland into Ohio and Pennsylvania; the abolition of slavery in the British West Indies in 1833. Each of these events occurred in a specific local community, and each had its local causes as well as its national significance.

The author of this account of the abolition movement might also have included a reference to the McClintock Riot at Carlisle, Pennsylvania, in 1847. Two fugitive slaves from Maryland, apprehended in Pennsylvania, were ordered by the county court to be returned to the custody of their owner; a riot ensued; and when it was over, the Negroes had been spirited away, and their owner was found dying in a pool of his own blood. Professor John McClintock of Dickinson College, apparently the best-known figure present in the abolitionist crowd, together with eighteen free Negroes, was indicted for riot and assault and battery. This much appeared in the Philadelphia and Baltimore papers. Readers might reasonably have inferred that detestation of slavery was deep and widespread in Carlisle, if an otherwise inoffensive professor of Latin and Greek in a little Methodist college risked reputation and freedom to aid escaping slaves. Yet the truth was something else, as the local history of the case makes clear. Professor McClintock's friends besought the aid of the abolitionist lawyer Thaddeus Stevens, who agreed to represent the professor but warned that he would pitch the defense on the ground of the higher law. The argument, Stevens conceded, might have no effect on a Pennsylvania jury, but it would present the issue squarely, even though McClintock went to jail. With no stomach for a cell of martyrdom, Professor McClintock declined Stevens' aid with thanks and retained instead eminent counsel from Philadelphia. The latter took no exalted view of a man's moral duty to defy an unjust law and so gained their client's freedom. There was an aftermath: the "best people" in town, of which McClintock was certainly one, regretted the whole episode and, though the president of the college defended the professor's right as a citizen to hold what opinions he wished and to act on them, McClintock withdrew from the college the next year—a decision that reflected local disapproval of his alleged conduct. In short, a careful examination of the McClintock Riot would require the general historian to modify the conclusion that he might have fairly inferred from the original newspaper report.

I have said enough to indicate that I regard history as indivisible, a single whole that is portioned out only for practical reasons of analysis and study; and I believe historical inquiry is an enterprise to which many persons may and should and do make essential contributions. History is not the exclusive province of professional historians, but an undertaking in which, especially in the United States, all the citizens are deeply interested. I wish that all historians of every sort shared this view and, sharing it, would ignore arbitrary and restrictive distinctions between national and local history, professional and amateur historians. There are a few hopeful signs that some do and more will.

In the first place, the New York State Historical Association—to take one example—has demonstrated how professionals and amateurs, professors and students, historians and laymen may all work together to their mutual benefit and the advancement of historical knowledge. Taking a broad view of what history is, welcoming everyone at all historically inclined, the Association has both supported impeccably scholarly research and made scholarly history popular in the best sense. No intellectual or social snobbishness has been allowed here to raise a barrier between Everyman and his history. Experience won in associations like this and the knowledge and confidence gained under its auspices should encourage its members to participate in other historical institutions of every kind and so bring to an end the estrangement of general from local history, of professional from amateur historian.

In the second place, an increasing number of young historians are exploring topics, and employing new methods in the process, that should lead them to seek the collaboration of local and amateur historians. In modern studies of social history—movements of populations, composition of classes, processes of the melting pot, for example—the professionals use mathematics and computers. They compile, analyze, and interpret raw data preserved in census returns, court records, tax lists, mortality tables, membership rolls, statistics of every kind. Although not everything that comes out of a computer is either sound or useful to historians, their careful tabulations and correlations are suggesting new insights and conclusions of considerable interest. The materials the historical quantifiers require are, of course, precisely the kinds which local historians often use and know well. A collaboration of the two kinds of historian should prove mutually profitable. The professional's questions would put the local historian's work in a larger frame; while the local historian not only knows where the local records are, but can usually offer helpful comments on their meaning, value, and limitations. One professor I know might have spared himself and a graduate student much time and distress in a project to identify the wealthy members of the community from tax lists had he consulted a knowledgeable local historian or genealogist, who would have told him that the annual returns he required do not survive, and, in any case, that those that do exist list only obvious wealth, like houses, land, cattle, and servants, not mortgages, bills of credit, inventories, ships—the real measure of wealth in a mercantile community. More than this, the cliometricians, as the quantifiers call themselves, will also discover that some amateurs are quite familiar with the notion of statistics: every good historian has always counted cases, as Charles Francis Adams, Jr. did for his inquiry into aspects of sexual morality in early New England; and as Roger Thabault did in the remarkable history of his village Mazières-en-Gatine, in which the quality of soil, tax returns, religious affiliations, roads, schools, and national laws were all woven into an analytical history of the rise of the village and its emergence into the nineteenth century.

Thirdly, still other opportunities for joint efforts by general and local historians are likely to be provided by the forthcoming celebrations of the Bicentennial of Independence. Though the professional cadre is much larger today than it was in 1876, when also the historical interests of the nation were enlisted in a common enterprise, today's plans for historical enterprises are also more numerous and more extensive. One of these projects is a biographical dictionary of the American Revolution, a multivolumed work that would contain biographical sketches of five to six thousand principal figures of the Revolutionary generation. Obviously, most of these men were persons of second and third rank—back-country farmers who served a term or two in the legislature, political preachers, leaders of the local Sons of Liberty, printers, colonels of militia. Indeed biographies of such men are the principal reason for the project; we do not need a dictionary for Washington, Jefferson, Baron Steuben. Manifestly the great majority of these sketches will have to be written, if they can be written at all, from local records—deeds, wills, letters, even gravestones —and by local historians. Should this project be inaugurated (and this association has gone on record as favoring it), it will inevitably enlist a small army of local and amateur historians in willing and equal cooperation with the professionals and their graduate students. And when the task is completed, American historians will not only have raised together a monument to American historical scholarship, but will also have removed distinctions separating some historians from others.

In the early days of the republic the historian filled an important public role. His opportunity and obligation were to discover and present the true story of the founding of the nation and of the principles and processes by which freedom, happiness, and prosperity were spread to ever-increasing numbers of people. This was no easy assignment, for nothing like the discovery and settlement of a new world had ever happened before. Salma Hale, author of a once-popular history of the United States, developed the idea in an address to the New Hampshire Historical Society almost a century and a half ago. The histories of other countries furnished no model for Americans, Hale began. America stood in "a new and different era."

The foundations of society have been broken up, and its elements have been arranged and combined anew. The whole surface has been brought nearer to a level. The ruler and the warrior have sunk in the estimation of their fellow men, and the private and peaceful individual has assumed a higher and more dignified station. . . . His virtues and his vices, his habits and his wants, have acquired an importance unknown to former times, and force themselves upon the attention of all who look abroad upon the world to survey its aspect. America, and especially our own country, has been the first and principal theatre of this political and social revolution, and a corresponding change in the duties of a historian has become necessary. He cannot satisfy himself, and still less can he satisfy others, by performing the easy task of reciting the actions of men in power, and at the head of armies, and recording those events, which for the time, produce astonishment and alarm. He must bring other and far more numerous actors upon the scene; he must trace events to different and more recondite causes; he must sketch the character, not of a prominent individual only, but of society in the aggregate, and of the age; he must describe the progress of intellect, the fluctuations of opinion, the discoveries of science, the state of morality, or religion, and the laws. He must gather facts which the mere annalist disdains to record; he must note circumstances which the superficial observer disregards; and to give to his history that interest which brilliant incidents lend to the narratives of others, he must endure the more painful labor of making a proper selection and just arrangement of his multifarious materials, and of imparting to his style that purity, precision and force, which is indispensable to compensate the sacrifice of the attractive, but inappropriate and cheaper ornaments of pompous diction and splendid imagery.

That is still an honorable challenge to the historians of America; a challenge which, it seems to me, the amateur historian, no less than his professional brother, is equipped by temperament, tradition, and opportunity to take up.

Chapter Two

Some Impressions of the Nonacademic Local Historians and Their Writings

Introduction

David J. Russo spent a year surveying the local history that has been produced in this country, reading extensively in the local history collection of the Library of Congress. He believes that local history was nurtured most especially in Massachusetts and New England. Within the genre, Russo has found wide variety. He concludes, however, that local history has been the story of the successful, by the successful, and for the successful—"an account of old-stock America."

Now a professor of American history, David Russo grew up in Deerfield, Massachusetts. In his book *Families and Communities: A New View of American History*, published by the American Association for State and Local History in 1974, Russo presents an innovative way of viewing the history of America. That is, he focuses upon the "small town as the most important community Americans have lived in, until our own century."

"Some Impressions of the Nonacademic Local Historians and Their Writings" is reprinted by permission from *Local History Today: Papers Presented at Three 1979 Regional Workshops for Local Historical Organizations in Indiana* (Indianapolis: Indiana Historical Society, 1980), 4–20. Russo's book is *Keepers of Our Past: Local Historical Writing in the United States. 1820s–1930s* (New York, 1988).

David J. Russo, "Some Impressions of the Nonacademic Local Historians and Their Writings," *Local History Today: Papers Presented at Three 1979 Regional Workshops for Local Historical Organizations in Indiana* (Indianapolis: Indiana Historical Society, 1980), 4–20.

* * * *

During this past school year, I have examined hundreds of volumes of local history; and out of this work, I have formed some impressions of the amateur town and city historians and their histories. I'd like to emphasize that what I'm about to say is impressionistic and that any number of these tentative observations may well be revised in the future as a result of further research. I believe that a progress report on current projects has a place in a gathering of this kind, however.

I decided to work from the West Coast to the East Coast, state by state: west to east, because I felt that, since much of the best historical scholarship in the field of American local history has been focused on the eastern states, especially on New England, I should avoid the charge that what I have to say is restricted to, say, eastern Massachusetts; and state by state, because I felt that, since much scholarship involves a small sampling of states or regions, I should try to avoid the charge that my conclusions are based on material that is somehow uncharacteristic or atypical. Though I've become bleary-eyed in the process, I'm glad, in retrospect, that I chose the method just outlined: there really is no substitute for looking at the whole thing, especially when you can do so from a single vantage point—in this case, the local history collection of the Library of Congress in Washington.

My first observation is that nonacademic town and city histories are very unevenly distributed across the country. It would be misleading and an exaggeration to claim that such writing is largely a New England phenomenon; but there is only one area in the union where there has been an almost geographically continuous production of town and city histories, and that area is New England, especially Massachusetts—something that, ironically, supports the geographic imbalance in historical scholarship I mentioned a moment ago. Cities everywhere have been the subject of amateur histories, but not towns. Indeed, the farther away from Massachusetts a small community is, the less likely it is that someone has written its history, though the populous West Coast is somewhat of an exception to this rule.

Why some local communities are the subject of histories and others are not is something I cannot answer at present, but there undoubtedly are many answers. In fact, generalizations of any kind on this overall topic are hard to come by—for the antiquarians, it seems, had little sense of themselves as a group, were certainly without any formal organization beyond the state level; and though there have been widely recognized models of good local history, the amateur historian has never felt compelled to imitate slavishly anyone else's work. The whole enterprise has been a loosely structured one, something entirely in keeping with the fact that these histories have been focused on particular towns and cities, on that which makes a place Hoboken, New Jersey, or Eureka, California, and no other place on earth.

I should amend my earlier remark about towns without histories, to some extent: most towns have had historical sketches written about them, sketches that have appeared in county histories. I have not yet examined this other form of local historical writing because I—perhaps myopically—have until now fixed my gaze on full-scale town and city histories. At least in its heyday—from the Civil War to World War I—the county history, with its town-by-town sketches, was certainly produced with greater geographic uniformity across the country than the histories to which I've paid attention.

That the full-scale local history was nurtured in New England, and particularly in Massachusetts, is indisputable, I think. Why this was so has everything to do with the earlier history of that area, so that to comment intelligently on the question of origins, one needs to be familiar with the overall history of colonial New England. One needs to know, in short, about the context within which this particular genre of writing emerged.

Towns were a very special human creation for the Puritans. The original white settlers of each township in colonial Massachusetts pledged to form a community dedicated to and in the service of God. Puritan ministers later wrote histories of these settlements, placing them within the wider framework of a divine drama involving God and his chosen people.[1] It was a natural development for Congregational ministers to write the earliest recognizably secular histories in the 1820s, 1830s, and 1840s, though the timing of such a shift cannot be easily explained. Drawing on relatively well-kept church and town records, these pioneering antiquarians presented a series of "civil" and "ecclesiastical" accounts of various Massachusetts towns, fanning out from Boston.

My state-by-state survey has turned out to be quite sensible, in that the origins and development of local historical writing, I've found, varied considerably from state to state, even in the case of adjoining states with similar periods of initial white settlement. Sometimes individuals presented themselves as the pioneer, with varying degrees of fanfare and self-advertisement. Frances Caulkins maintained that her *History of Norwich* (Connecticut), published in 1845, "is not founded on previous histories—it has no predecessor . . . it is an independent, original work."[2]

In other cases, local, county, or state historical societies were instrumental in fostering the earliest projects in a given state. For example, in Vermont, the Historical Society of Middlebury in 1846 appointed a committee to investigate the feasibility of finding people to write histories of the various towns in the county. This committee appointed competent agents in the several towns and sent to them circulars, embracing the plan recommended by the society.[3]

In states such as Massachusetts, New Jersey, Pennsylvania, Maryland, Wisconsin, and Washington, it is clear that the state historical society played a key role in the early development of local historical writing, providing a repository for material, a forum for the publication of pieces shorter or narrower than full-scale histories of towns or cities—and even of officials, who themselves became well-known antiquarians for certain communities (like Mayer Brantz of Baltimore, John Watson of Philadelphia, Clarence Bagley of Seattle, or Clarence Burton of Detroit).

Even though there has always been a considerable variety in the overall format and design of amateur local historical writing, certain basic forms have been at least typical of certain periods of time, though there has always been considerable overlapping.

The first form to typify this genre of writing was the annals—that is, a listing or description of events presented in chronological order, year by year. Some of the earliest recognizably secular histories assumed this form.[4] Though I can't prove or demonstrate the connection, it seems to me that these annals evolved out of the efforts of colonial printers to provide a chronology of events on a daily or weekly basis in their early journals or newspapers. Just as the pioneering journalists tried to provide what they called a history of their times, so too did the annalists try to provide a retrospective collection of events extending over a long period, arranged much as they had been in the colonial press, but with one crucial difference: the early journalists ordinarily did not focus on local happenings, whereas the annalists, of course, did—exclusively so.

But the "annals" form did not typify local historical writing for very long; and in Massachusetts, during the 1830s, 1840s, and 1850s, Congregational ministers developed the quasi-civil, quasi-ecclesiastical histories already referred to—histories still characterized, it should be added, by descriptive references to particular events—as was done in the annals. By the time of the Civil War, and especially in the two decades following that conflict, another basic form evolved, which was really an amalgamation of more specific kinds of local historical writing that had developed separately since the 1820s.

One element in the new synthesis derived from the genealogical compilations and group biographical sketches that reflected the growing interest of "old" families in their ancestral backgrounds. Another element was closely related to the increasingly popular gazetteers, atlases, and directories—that is, compendia of information about various communities, whether towns, cities, counties, or states. As Charles T. Greve put it, in his *Centennial History of Cincinnati* (1904): "A history of a city should be neither a directory, a guide book, nor a chronological table, and yet it is hard to avoid giving to it some of the qualities of all these valuable methods of treatment."[5]

Still another element descended directly from the annals and other even more specialized narrative, descriptive accounts, such as the quite common military histories.

The resulting amalgamation consisted of three parts: first, a series of chapters arranged as a narrative in a chronological sequence and focused on the early years of the community, its settlement, and initial growth; second, another series of chapters organized topically and dealing descriptively with many different facets of the community's life, everything from its clubs and parks and water or sewer works to its government, its arts, and its commerce; and third, a final, separately designed section consisting of biographical sketches of the individuals or families who were either prominent in the community or who had lived there from the beginning. This merging of families and communities, as it were, was sometimes defended in prefaces as natural and appropriate. Biographical or genealogical sketches of the old and prominent were added, in the words of an early annalist, "to perpetuate their good fame, and with it, the salutary influence of their examples," or, according to a later author, "are admirably calculated to foster local ties, to inculcate patriotism, and to emphasize the rewards of industry dominated by intelligent purpose."[6]

These were the essential elements of the most mature form of nonacademic local historical writing ever developed in America. It was far more likely that the history of a city, rather than the history of a town, would be presented in this mold; but some of the more ambitious antiquarians of smaller settlements—once again, especially in New England—put together histories that came close to matching the great variety of subjects to be found in the histories of their urban brethren.

Beginning at about the time of World War I and increasingly during the 1920s and 1930s, another form emerged: the narrative history. Sometimes written by a professional writer, often about a town or city that was widely known as distinctive or unusual in some way or other, narrative histories were presented to the general public almost as a form of travel literature. Ralph Birdsall, in his *The Story of Cooperstown* (1917), aptly summed up what such an account consisted of:

> The ensuing narrative is a faithful record of life in Cooperstown from the earliest times, except that the persons and events to be described have been selected for their story-interest, to the exclusion of much that a history is expected to contain. The dull thread of village history has been followed only in such direction as served for stringing upon it and holding to the light the more shining gems of incident and personality to which it led. . . . The effort has been made to exclude everything that seemed unlikely to be of interest to the general reader.[7]

At this point, let me repeat: generalizations on this subject are risky, so varied has the enterprise under scrutiny been, so individualistic have those involved in it been. I cannot give an explanation for the timing and durability of the basic forms local historical writing has assumed since its secularization in the early nineteenth century any more than I can say why some communities have histories and others do not. All that I can provide is the kind of information the antiquarians themselves disclose in their prefaces as to how their books came into being.

Some books started as lectures, delivered at the request of varied groups—and just grew into book-length treatments. Others began as edited versions of earlier histories and were turned into new histories amalgamated with the old. Still others were written at the invitation of town or city committees and were presented as centennial or bicentennial histories.[8] At least one state historical society, that of

New Hampshire, appointed a Committee on Histories of the Towns.[9] During the national centennial year of 1876, the federal government got into the act, when Congress adopted a resolution in March, "recommending that in every town the delivery of a historical sketch of the place from its foundation should be part of the local celebration."[10]

And, indeed, some authors of local histories that appeared in the years following the centennial referred to that resolution as at least partial justification for their efforts.[11] Sometimes would-be subscribers initiated the process, with one writer admitting that the appearance of his history was "in some degree due to the solicitation of influential citizens."[12] Finally, several publishers who had a special interest in producing books on local history—firms such as Lewis and S. J. Clarke—sometimes made contracts with individuals who agreed to serve as authors or editors for the history of certain communities.[13]

I also want to be cautious about making generalizations concerning the identity of those who have written town and city histories. It is clear that many were professional people—clergymen, lawyers, doctors, journalists, politicians, authors— people with the perspective, awareness, and at least some practice as writers; people who, above all, had leisure time, in their later years, to undertake what often was a very time-consuming task. But others, not of this background, have presented histories because of a deep and sustained interest in their community and its past. I'm thinking particularly about women authors and scions of pioneering families. The only common denominator seems to have been age: the typical local historian has always been someone in his or her later years.

Why did they write? What motivated them? One of the earliest, Emory Washburn, summed it up rather well:

> We have been prompted to this, more from feelings of local interest and attachment, than from any hope of literary reputation or, much less, of profit. The graves of our fathers are here; and we felt a curiosity to trace, not only their histories, but also those of all who were their contemporaries, and acted and suffered with them. We felt desirous of snatching from oblivion, events connected with the history of our country, and preserving the names of men whose merits deserve a place on its pages.[14]

Another, William Little, said that the writing of his history "has not been a labor. It has been a pleasant pastime, a source of amusement—good fun." And Silas Farmer asserted that "[time], patience, discrimination, and large expenditures of money have been essential factors in the preparation of the volume; I, however, have had no regrets, for the work has been a labor of love, and I have been increasingly glad that it was my privilege to write the history of my birthplace."[15]

Perhaps the most common statement involving motivation was that the author wanted to preserve for future generations existing records and the reminiscences of pioneers before such evidence was forever lost.

What was the purpose of writing such histories? I shall again generalize, even though aware of much variety. Simply put: the pioneering or initial histories of communities in any part of the country typically were written in honor of the original settlers and constitute a record of their deeds—that is, of their successful creation of the communities their descendants inhabited. These communities were sometimes built with much hardship, whether produced by nature or by a hostile native population, and the early histories were often a celebration of pioneering hardiness, sturdiness, and persistence. In essence, this was history as a form of ancestral worship. As villages grew into towns and towns into cities, later histories were typically focused on a community's growth or progress, and sometimes ended with optimistic statements concerning the future. Local history with this emphasis became a kind of "booster" literature, and its practitioners were to some extent publicity agents for fast-growing, progressive communities, whose future, it was assumed, would match their past.[16]

In sum, local history was the story of the successful, by the successful, and for the successful—an account of old-stock America—of heroic ancestors and their early settlements, grown prosperous and secure through the years. Such writings provided an important means by which the durable, stable element in the American population retained a sense of place and continuity. In such a success story, there was not space for community conflict or for recent foreign immigrants. In 1866, Charles Brooks articulated what many others must have felt in one form or another when he said: "These registers of early families in New England will contain the only authentic records of the true Anglo-Saxon blood existing among us; for, if foreign immigration should pour in upon us for the next fifty years as it has for the last thirty, it will be difficult for a man to prove that he has descended from the Plymouth Pilgrims."[17]

By the 1920s, writers like John M. Killits had a somewhat different reaction:

> We note, perhaps with regret, that, in some parts of the country, men of alien lineage and habits of thought are taking over places hallowed with memories of early struggles in the development of our American commonwealth. . . . Wherever historical associations . . . make up local atmosphere, we may look for beneficial results when residents of any extraction are brought under their influence.[18]

Those who at first produced local histories sometimes thought of themselves as just "compilers," especially when they assembled and reproduced documents of various kinds in some sort of chronological sequence.[19] But by the time of the Civil War, at least some writers claimed the title historian outright, as did Charles Hudson, when he asserted that "I could have made it [my history] more flattering; but I chose to appear in the character of a historian, rather than in that of a eulogist."[20]

And, indeed, perhaps the most frequently repeated assertion in prefaces and introductions is that the author seeks to be factually accurate. There was less agreement on the desirability of trying to be impartial or objective, however. And, though doubtless all could agree in principle with Augustus Gould and Frederic Kidder, who said "to 'say nothing of the dead except what is good,' is an ancient and most charitable maxim; but it is by no means one which can be admitted in impartial history," many could also appreciate Dwight Goss's comments on the difficulty of achieving impartiality. It would appear that William Boyd adopted a less popular position when he stated that:

> . . . it has been my intention not to give anything in this work, to reflect upon the charactor [*sic*] of persons, or hurt the feelings of their descendants. Should there be an instance of that kind in the book, I humbley [*sic*] ask their pardon from unintentionly [*sic*] doing them an injury.[21]

The sources local historians used varied, according to the availability of documents as well as the interest and persistence of the author. One common type of source was the oral or printed memoir, something especially common in areas west of the Appalachians, where the pioneers were often still living at the time the first history was written.[22] Another often-used source was the newspaper, though as I point out in another study just completed, American newspapers did not contain regular local news columns until the middle decades of the nineteenth century; this meant that, once again, the farther west a community is, the more likely it is that its historians have had access to newspaper files covering the early and formative years. Large-scale city histories were also based on council records, directories, county records, state laws, federal censuses, reports of a great array of private and public organizations, annals of area historical societies, and earlier histories of the city.[23]

Though on occasion, through the nineteenth century, local historians referred with obvious approval to the growing popularity of town and city history,[24] the fact is that in many cases the amateur historian either supported himself while preparing his history or went after other townspeople to act as subscribers, and, indeed, some volumes contain lists of subscribers.

David Noyes unashamedly told the citizens of Norway, Maine, that "should you be pleased to liberally patronize the present work, it will greatly serve to smooth the down-hill of life, which I am fast descending." J. W. Hanson of Gardiner, Maine, "hopes his fellow citizens will encourage his effort by buying his book, and being pleased with it." E. M. Ruttenber of Newburgh, New York, was equally candid: "Indeed, our expenditures upon the work are far in advance of the income which we have already derived from its publication, or that we may anticipate in the future."[25] Though such early writers as James Thacher of Plymouth, Massachusetts, and John Watson of Philadelphia could boast in prefaces to second editions that the first had been completely sold out,[26] the only alternative to personal expenditures or subscription guarantees for most of the amateur historians was the financial support of a town or city committee or a contract from publishers like Lewis or S. J. Clarke, who raised money from those whose biographical sketches appeared as the final section in the city histories these firms produced after the turn of the century—a practice that led critics to dub such tomes "mug-books."

As early as 1887, the publishers of W. Scott Robison's *History of the City of Cleveland* indicated that:

> . . . [in] endeavoring to profit by the experiences of the publishers of the histories of other cities, it was deemed most judicious to produce a book that could be sold at a price considerably less than that of the average local work of this kind. Voluminous and elaborate local histories, with their proportionately high cost, have not proved commercial successes. So large is the amount that one must read in these days to keep up with the times, that the majority of people find it necessary to select condensed treatments of subjects.[27]

By the 1930s, condensed or shorter histories were typical, and William Bruce's defense of them was much more familiar: "The general public is not inclined to delve exhaustively into local history, . . . elaborate studies serve the research student and statesman rather that the average reader. . . . [The present volume] is intended for popular reading rather than for extensive study."[28]

Whether profitable or not, local historical writing was difficult to produce. The litany of complaints resonates through the introductory pages of hundreds of volumes like a long moan: records were scarce or incomplete; previous works were almost nonexistent; townspeople were uncooperative; the author's health was impaired; the enterprises cost too much.

With such hardship everywhere apparent, it is a tribute to the antiquarians that they, in fact, wrote so much history, especially since some of them believed that what they were doing had no value or interest to anyone beyond the inhabitants of the community they wrote about.[29] Many referred almost disparagingly to their "trivial" facts. But others argued that the collective study of particular communities provided much information on how people actually lived, in contrast to national history, which was centered on the activities of a distant federal government. Both kinds of history were important; both had value. In this way, some local historians invested their work with a significance that went beyond the preservation of the past in given towns and cities.

Others thought that such work provided its own justification, however. As Alonzo Lewis aptly put it:

> There is something so natural in enquiring into the history of those who have lived before us, and particularly of those with whom we have any connexion [*sic*], either by the ties of relation or place, that it is surprising any one should be found by whom this subject is regarded with indifference. . . . To trace the settlement and progress of our native town—to read the history of the playplace of our early hours, and which has been the scene of our maturer joys—to follow the steps of our fathers through the course of centuries, and mark the graduation of improvement—to

learn who and what they were, from whom we are descended—and still further, to be informed of the people who were here before them, and who are now vanished like a dream of childhood; and all these in their connexion [sic] with the history of the world and of man—must certainly be objects of peculiar interest to every inquisitive mind.[30]

Similarly, John Watson wrote that:

. . . [our] love of antiquities—the contemplation of days by-gone is an impress of Deity. It is our hold on immortality. The same affection which makes us reach forward and peep into futurity prompts us to travel back to the hidden events which transpired before we existed. We thus feel our span of existence prolonged even while we have the pleasure to identify ourselves with the scenes or the emotions of our forefathers.[31]

Local historical writing of the kind I've been speaking about is still being written, of course. But, as far as I am able to discern, no new forms have emerged since the period between the two world wars, when the short narrative was developed. As of now, I can only guess at the reasons for this general lack of vitality and change. Many older communities have stopped growing. The sort of people who used to write such histories—professional people—have been far more mobile in recent decades than they were in the nineteenth and early twentieth centuries and are, therefore, less rooted—have less of a sense of place. More broadly, the patterns of American life have become nationalized; little is now organized on a purely local basis; towns and cities are losing their distinctiveness, are becoming more and more alike and subjected to common national influences.

In the last decade, academic historians have become increasingly interested in the study of local communities. (I myself will introduce a course to be called "The Town in U.S. History" at my university next year.) This development has been sudden, and the reasons for it are not yet clear. Academic local historical writing focuses on developments affecting local communities generally, features statistical evidence that measures certain features of the lives of urban and rural populations, and is organized around concepts or models or themes, often borrowed from the social sciences. Scholars of local history shun the study of particular communities for what is unique about them—offer evidence, not interesting details; present analysis or arguments, not description or narrative; study all the inhabitants, not just prominent families; and search for common patterns in the large mosaic of rural and urban life.

What concerns me most about the dramatic entrance of academic scholars into the field of local history is that those interested in the study of the American past are now, as never before, divided into two quite separate groupings—the academic and the nonacademic. There was a common audience for national and local historical writing in the nineteenth century in the United States. The emergence of academic historical study, with its emphasis on conceptual analytical thinking, on statistical evidence, and on technical terminology, has meant that a small intel-ligentsia has had the means to study our history that others do not—perhaps cannot—share. And now academic history has moved into—poached upon—the territory long occupied by the amateur alone: the family and the local community. But the study of the past is too important, too fundamental, to become the preserve of specialists. What will the long-term effect for a society be when its intellectuals and its general population lose the capacity to view a common past in a common way? What dangers lurk there? I wonder. I wish I knew.

NOTES

1. On this point, see Peter Gay, *A Loss of Mastery; Puritan Historians in Colonial America* (Berkeley: University of California Press, 1966).

2. Frances Caulkins, *History of Norwich* [Connecticut] (Norwich: T. Robinson, 1845), v.

3. Samuel Swift, *History of the Town of Middlebury* [Vermont] (Middlebury: A. H. Copeland, 1859), 5–6.

4. For example, Thomas W. Griffith, *Annals of Baltimore* (Baltimore: Printed by W. Wooddy, 1824); John F. Watson, *Annals of Philadelphia* (Philadelphia: E. L. Carey & A. Hart, 1830); Jacob B. Moore, *Annals of the Town of Concord* [New Hampshire] (Concord: J. B. Moore, 1824); and Nathaniel Adams, *Annals of Portsmouth* [New Hampshire] (Portsmouth: C. Norris, 1825).

5. Charles T. Greve, *Centennial History of Cincinnati* (Chicago: Biographical Publishing Co., 1904), "Preface."

6. Moore, *Annals of the Town of Concord*, "Biographical Notices," 53; William M. Rockel, ed., *20th-Century History of Springfield* [Ohio] (Chicago: Biographical Publishing Co., 1908), "Preface."

7. Ralph Birdsall, *The Story of Cooperstown* (Cooperstown: The Arthur H. Crist Co., 1917), "Foreword."

8. An example of the kinds of books that grew from a lecture series is John Daggett's *Sketch of the History of Attleborough* [Massachusetts] (Dedham: H. Mann, Printer, 1834). Samuel G. Drake's *The History and Antiquities of the City of Boston* (Boston: L. Stevens, 1854) illustrates the edited version of an earlier history. Typical of those written for civic committees, to serve as centennial or bicentennial histories, are *The Centennial History of the Town of Dryden* [New York], George E. Goodrich, ed. (Dryden: J. G. Ford, Printer, 1898) and *History of the Town of Marlborough* [Massachusetts], by Charles Hudson (Boston: Press of T. R. Marvin & Sons, 1862).

9. Charles J. Fox, *History of the Old Township of Dunstable* [New Hampshire] (Nashua: C. T. Gill, 1846), 3.

10. John S. Hittell, *A History of the City of San Francisco* (San Francisco: A. L. Bancroft & Co., 1878), 5.

11. See especially W. Scott Robison, ed., *History of the City of Cleveland* (Cleveland: Robison & Crockett, 1887), ix.

12. William Bache, *Historicial Sketches of Bristol Borough* [Pennsylvania] (Bristol: [W. Bache, Printer], 1853), "Preface."

13. There is an unusually full statement on the arrangements one author made with S. J. Clarke in Thomas W. Lewis, *Zanesville and Muskingum County, Ohio* (Chicago: S. J. Clarke Publishing Co., 1927), v–vi. Another example is J. Thomas Scharf, *History of Baltimore City and County* (Philadelphia: L. H. Everts, 1881), vii; Scharf said his history was "undertaken at the request of Major Lewis H. Everts, the enterprising publisher." Still another example is David L. Pierson, *History of the Oranges* [New Jersey] *to 1921* (New York: Lewis Historical Publishing Co., 1922), "Foreword." Pierson comments on the role of the Lewis Publishing Company.

14. Emory Washburn, *Topographical and Historical Sketches of the Town of Leicester* [Massachusetts] (Worcester: Printed by Rogers & Griffin, 1826), 3.

15. William Little, *History of the Town of Warren* [New Hampshire] (Concord: Steam Printing Works of McFarland & Jenks, 1854), iii–iv; Silas Farmer, *The History of Detroit and Michigan* (Detroit: S. Farmer & Co., 1884), v.

16. General statements concerning the character of the settlers in certain areas and their villages can be found in concluding statements and—more briefly—in prefaces in various early town histories. For example: Erastus Worthington, *The History of Dedham* (Boston: Dutton and Wentworth, 1827), 146; James Thacher, *History of the Town of Plymouth* (Boston: Marsh, Capen & Lyon, 1835), 299–300; Edwin M. Stone, *History of Beverly* (Boston: J. Munroe and Co., 1843), 306–309; Herman Mann, *Historical Annals of Dedham* (Dedham: H. Mann, 1847), "Casual Remarks," 131–34; John M. Weeks, *History of Salisbury* [Vermont] (Middlebury: A. H. Copeland, 1860), 346–50. Examples of later histories focused on community growth and progress include Neville B. Craig, *The History of Pittsburgh* (Pittsburgh: J. H. Mellor, 1851), ch. 15: William H. Miller, *The History of Kansas City* [Missouri] (Kansas City: Birdsall & Miller, 1881), "Preface" and chs. 1 and 18; Frederic J. Grant, *History of Seattle* (New York: American Publishing and Engraving Co., 1891), 303–305; and William Griffith, *History of Kansas City* [Missouri] (Kansas City: Hudson-Kimberly Publishing Co., 1900), ch. 8. The latter four books contain uncharacteristically explicit statements on the nature of urban expansion. In most histories, the theme of growth and progress is implicit, something understood, but seldom directly referred to.

17. Charles Brooks, *History of the Town of Medford* [Massachusetts] (Boston: J. M. Usher, 1855), vi.

18. John M. Killits, *Toledo and Lucas County, Ohio* (Chicago and Toledo: The S. J. Clarke Publishing Co., 1923), iii.

19. For example: Abiel Abbot, *History of Andover* [Massachusetts] (Andover: Flagg and Gould, 1829), advertisement; and Bache, *Historical Sketches of Bristol Borough*, "Preface."

20. Hudson, *History of the Town of Marlborough*, viii.

21. Augustus A. Gould and Frederic Kidder, *The History of New Ipswich* [New Hampshire] (Boston: Gould and Lincoln, 1852), viii; Dwight Goss, *History of Grand Rapids* [Michigan] (Chicago: C. F. Cooper & Co., 1906), "Preface"; William P. Boyd, *History of the Town of Conesus* [New York] (Conesus: Boyd's Job Printing Establishment, 1887), 7.

22. The more sophisticated local historians were careful to point out the distinction between such reminiscences and their own efforts, however. As Mary L. Booth put it: "It had

been the fashion to tell of personal reminiscences and entertaining gossip concerning leading families and familiar landmarks, but these, while affording most valuable material to the historian, were not history." *History of the City of New York* (New York: E. P. Dutton & Co., 1880), 3.

23. A good example is Samuel P. Arth, *A History of Cleveland, Ohio* (Chicago: The S. J. Clarke Publishing Co., 1910), 8–10.

24. Early statements are those of Stone, *History of Beverly*, iii, and Gould and Kidder, *The History of New Ipswich*, vii.

25. David Noyes, *The History of Norway* [Maine] (Norway: The Author, 1852), v; John W. Hanson, *The History of Gardiner* [Maine] (Gardiner: W. Palmer, 1852), iv; Edward Manning Ruttenber, *History of the Town of Newburgh* [New York] (Newburgh: E. M. Ruttenber & Co., Printers, 1859), "Conclusion."

26. Thacher, *History of the Town of Plymouth*, iii; and John Watson, *Annals of Philadelphia*, 2nd ed. (Philadelphia: The Author, 1844), iii.

27. Robison, *History of the City of Cleveland*, ix–x.

28. William G. Bruce, *A Short History of Milwaukee* (Milwaukee: The Bruce Publishing Co., 1936), vii–viii.

29. Daggett, *Sketch of the History of Attleborough*, 3, made this point well.

30. Alonzo Lewis, *The History of Lynn* (Boston: Press of J. H. Eastburn, 1829), 4–5.

31. Watson, *Annals of Philadelphia*, v.

<hr>
Chapter Three
<hr>

Local Historians
and Their Activities

Introduction

In 1919 and 1947, New York State enacted laws mandating that all communities with a population greater than 400, and all counties, appoint a local historian to collect and preserve its history. The laws suggested that cities might also appoint historians and many did. Judith Wellman, at a gathering of some of these appointed officials, spoke about local history. She said that the field was "in a state of flux, caught between old paradigms and new." She explored reasons for local history's recent popularity and looked at implications for the emergence of "the new social history," with its emphasis on ethnicity, gender, family, and community. Referring to adjacent fields that have benefited from local history's new popularity—historical societies and museums, genealogy, and archives—Wellman also spoke of local historians' activities: collection, preservation, education, and organization.

"Local Historians and Their Activities" appeared originally in *Historians' Guide: A Handbook for Local Historians*, published in 1982 by the State Education Department of the University of the State of New York, Albany, and appears here by permission.

* * * *

During the last ten years, local history in one of its many guises—community history, historic preservation, museum studies, genealogy, urban history, ethnic studies, and interest in local records of all kinds—has captured the imagination of Americans. As individuals, local historians certainly share in the nationwide

<hr>

Judith M. Wellman, "Local Historians and Their Activities," in *Historian's Guide: A Handbook for Local Historians* (Albany, NY: State Education Department, 1982), 11–26.

excitement. But what roles do local historians as a group play in this drama? More specifically, what are the roles of the municipal and county historians in New York State?

Local historians work in a field whose very name is deceptive. At first, local history seems easy to define. One might reasonably argue that it is the study of life at a local level. Yet what is local? Is it state, region, town, village, crossroads, or house? To what extent do people in the locality define themselves and thus generate unique cultural forms? To what extent do their thoughts, words, and deeds reflect forces outside the locality? Local history encompasses life in its most personal form—life bounded by death and embracing love and work, and every variation imaginable on those intertwining, inescapable essentials. What explains this field's continuing fascination for so many people? The seeming simplicity of the term local history camouflages immense complexity.

Books that are classified as state, local, or regional histories often are very like other kinds of history books. John Williams, who surveyed material on state history written during the twentieth century, concluded that state history was not really a field, since it lacked what he called a "coherent and bounded character." In terms of methods, topics, and sources, state history resembled any other kind of history. It was what any particular historian chose to make it. Others have argued along similar lines, concluding that the study of state and local history today lacks both a conceptual framework and a workable methodology. The whole field is in a state of flux, caught between old paradigms and new. At this point, there is no real agreement on appropriate questions, much less on answers.[1]

Local historians have little to guide them. The New York state law that established the office is an old one. The volume of published material directed specifically at local historians is slim. There is not enough feedback or organized action by those who know most about the job—other local historians. And there is not enough interaction between local historians and those people in colleges and universities who are becoming more and more interested in local history and in local records. Given the complexity of this field and the wide variety of personal interests and personal styles, we can best begin by asserting that in diversity there is strength. Grassroots action, personal commitment, high standards of respect for evidence, and a genuine desire to be of service have carried individual local historians forward for a long time. Perhaps these will continue to be the prime sources of effectiveness.

Nevertheless, there is also virtue in trying to see some broader patterns amid this rich texture. We need to sit down together to assess the current situation and attempt to define problems and identify priorities for the future. That is not the end of the process, for there are no definitive answers. But we do have some thoughts on how to more clearly define the questions. Why are Americans so caught up in their local history? How has this interest affected groups such as archivists, preservationists, the museum community, academic historians, and genealogists? How have local historians responded to the demands of new audiences? What resources are available to provide further insight? What can local historians do to define their own objectives and to get the resources they need to carry them out? And finally, what are some possible priorities for coordinated action?

Like running and religion, local history is now a national passion. Intellectual curiosity is a compelling motivation. The study of local and family history in its purest sense is a fascinating mental exercise. Like historical studies of any kind, local history offers a never-ending series of tantalizing mysteries. Each solution leads to another question, the answer to which may lie, literally, in the lay of the land, in the character of local buildings, in printed or manuscript sources, or in the lives and memories of local people. Although all these sources may contain clues, they remain silent and uninformative without the active and inquiring mind of a historian. The historian picks and chooses the pieces that seem to fit the particular puzzle and describes the picture that seems to emerge, filling in the blank spaces with insight and empathy, to produce a plausible reconstruction of a part of the past, always remembering that it is just that: a reconstruction, not the reality.

Yet intellectual curiosity alone does not explain the attraction. Why do people choose to study history? Part of the answer lies in the overall pattern of the present world, a pattern that most of us perceive only dimly, if at all. Hindsight provides better vision. Looking back through time, certain ages seemed to be turning points in terms of economic organization, political and social structures, and patterns of thought. New problems or questions generated new excitement, new movements, and a creative search for new solutions. They also generated new tensions, new anxieties, and new questions about the relationship of individuals to institutions, of process and structure, of what Frederick Tonnies described in 1887 as *gemeinschaft*—a kind of folk and communal mentality—versus *gesellschaft*—a world-view that emphasized more formal institutions and earned, rather than ascribed, status. The mid-nineteenth century in the United States was such a time of churning and change. Some argue that the present is also such a time. Interestingly, both periods produced the two main peaks of popular interest in local history.

Whatever the underlying causes of this public enthusiasm for local history, it has had a strong impact on the related fields of archives, historic preservation, and museums; on the writing and teaching of history; and on genealogy. Archivists are paying increasing attention to records and manuscripts relating to family and community history. And local public records themselves will benefit from a new awareness of their importance. Historic preservation has been one of the fastest-growing areas of local history. Not only does preservation involve historians, but it has made a significant impact on urban planning and on the physical appearance of our communities. Enthusiasm for local history has rejuvenated many local historical societies as well. In 1977, the [New York] State Museum surveyed cultural organizations across the state. More than 70 percent of the 620 agencies that responded identified themselves as history museums. Most were small local or regional organizations.[2]

Concern for local history also has made a profound impression on the output produced by historians at work as scholars and teachers. In 1978, for example, one-fourth of the papers given at the annual meeting of the Organization of American Historians dealt in some way with community history. The primary biographical index to articles and books in American history—*America: History and Life*—includes state and local history as one of its largest sections. And family history and community studies are by far the largest categories in the New York State's Division of Historical and Anthropological Services' annual bibliography.

Many of these historical works deal with what became the dominant concerns of academically trained American historians during the 1970s—social history, women's history, black and ethnic history, family history, and community history. Many of these studies have been locally focused. But most are quite different from the local history that local historians traditionally have produced. They are also different in some ways from the work that most academically trained social historians produced before the mid-twentieth century. Indeed, they are so different that some people have called them the "New Social History."

The new histories are focused on people, events, or processes, rather than on the institutional development of local areas. Often they deal with large numbers of people or with a total population instead of a selected few. To do so, they often rely on quantification and statistics. The new histories tend not to be simply narratives or collections of anecdotes, as were many nineteenth-century local histories—instead, they focus on a theme, often dealing with only one part of community life such as economics or social mobility, work, or the family, and they usually include analysis and narrative.

During the 1970s, scholars used well-known material in new ways and searched for nontraditional sources. Diaries, letters, newspapers, local histories, and literary sources of all kinds retain their immense value. But historians have supplemented—and sometimes even supplanted—such sources with nonliterary evidence, particularly all kinds of lists: church members, participants in local elections, signers of antislavery petitions, members of local temperance societies, passengers on ships, factory workers, family members, taxpayers, and town residents. Unlike literary materials, lists are usually inclusive. They will include all the members of a family (as in a genealogy), or all the residents of a town (as in a census), or all the tax-payers (as in an assessment roll). Historians call this comprehensive type of information systematic data.

Using systematic data as evidence, and borrowing techniques and theories from many social sciences, the new historians have looked at questions ranging from whether American immigrants generally have experienced upward mobility (a qualified yes); to whether extended families changed to nuclear families as part of the process that some people have called modernization (not really); to whether American women consistently have produced about the same number of children per woman at different times in American history (definitely not).

Local historians are familiar with these materials because, traditionally, such materials have been important to genealogists. Indeed, many genealogists themselves have been caught up in the new history. Genealogists who once thought it most important to trace their families back to some well-known personage, for example, now are more involved in tracing their families forward through history. Samuel Hays has argued that, in many ways, "the new social history is simply the new genealogy writ large." And "when the social historians begin to work with family history and to focus on a broader network of kinship relationships over time, and [when] the genealogist begins to spend time and effort in indexing the same manuscript census returns that historians use, it is time for the two groups to examine their common ground."[3]

That common ground belongs not only to the genealogist and the academic historian, but also to the archivist, the museum curator, and the preservationist. Most importantly, that common ground belongs to the local historian. Suddenly, many people, both locally and across the nation, are interested in this material. Thus, the local historian is confronting a whole array of new audiences with new kinds of questions and with new needs.

How should local historians act? There are two levels of answers to this question. One is individual. How will each historian choose to define the job? This level is where most local historians operate, whether by necessity or by choice. The other level is collective. How will historians, as members of the body of officially appointed historians in New York State, choose to define their jobs? Both levels are important.

Combining personal predilections with the perceived needs of the audience, local historians have accomplished the following. They have written both scholarly and popular books and articles. They have answered queries from local government officials and local residents. They have responded to mail from genealogists and history buffs across the country. They have spoken to local groups. They have organized historical societies, clubs, and preservation groups. They have accumulated artifacts, photographs, printed materials, and manuscripts. They have developed card files about local people and local events. They have participated in surveys of buildings and of local records. They have recorded information from cemeteries. They have written articles for the local newspaper, kept newspaper clippings, and have indexed newspapers. They have presented local history programs to school and adult education groups. They have attended historical meetings of all kinds, including those with other local historians. Sometimes they even managed to get their annual reports in on time. In short, responding to observed public need and to the texture of the historical record in each locality, local historians have carried out their function as keepers of our collective past in whatever ways they saw fit.

In so doing, most have received no pay and only a minimal budget for supplies and equipment. Lucky ones might have money for travel to official meetings. But most have done their work primarily because they loved to do it, both for its intellectual rewards and because it enabled them to do real public service. Thus, the historians themselves have been the only people, to date, able to define the scope and fabric of their activities. These activities are diverse, but most of the local historian's duties and responsibilities fall into four basic categories:

First, most local historians have seen themselves, at least in part, as preservationists. They have attempted to collect, preserve, and protect local historical materials, whether public records, manuscripts generated by individuals or organizations, current newspaper clippings, genealogical files, or even artifacts. Historians have done this so that the past will not be lost. Local historians have kept their own files at their offices or at home. They have encouraged public officials to provide adequate storage and access in public facilities for public records. They have led the fight to save and restore their community's historic buildings. And they have worked with local museums and libraries to provide care for manuscripts and artifacts generated by nongovernmental sources.

Second, most local historians have been active as scholars, both as researchers and as writers. The best ones have upheld high standards of gathering and evaluating evidence, making thoughtful and appropriate generalizations, writing well-organized and readable narratives, and sharing their work with others through the most appropriate mediums. These two functions—those of preservationist and scholar—form the core of any local historian's work.

However, local historians often go beyond these two basic functions. Many reach out actively and enthusiastically as teachers and public educators. Through lectures and exhibits, they work directly with students and civic groups to promote knowledge of and interest in local history. Finally, many act not only as educators, but also as organizers. Not content to respond to requests for help from existing groups, many historians have created new organizations devoted to local history. Among those are historical societies, historic preservation groups, and Yorker clubs.

Of these four categories, the first two functions (of preservationist and scholar) are the scholarly side of a local historian's work. The second two functions (of educator and organizer) are the activist side. Depending on local needs and personal interests, most local historians emphasize some of these categories more than others. However, all these functions are important. It is appropriate for one historian to write well-researched articles on local history and for another to organize a local preservation group.

If many local historians have found ways to carry out their jobs effectively, most have not been successful in defining and defending their own interests as a group. But they have made some important beginnings. In 1967, the county historians of New York State formed their own organization. Village, town, and city historians followed in 1971, with the formation of Municipal Historians Association. Some of the MHA's regional affiliates hold regular meetings and publish short newsletters. Still, when searching for a discussion of priorities for coordinated action, one finds little. The Historian's Law offers a broad functional outline. Publications from the state history office also offer some help. And regional and national historical associations can provide assistance in specific areas. Unfortunately, all of them have their limits. None really provides the kind of dialogue that local historians need in this time of rapid change.

New York State passed the first Historian's Law in 1919. With slight modification, it remains in force today. What does it encompass? First, each historian has been authorized "to collect and preserve material relating to the history of the political subdivision for which he or she is appointed, and to file such material in fireproof safes or vaults in the county, city, town, or village offices." Also, the historian is empowered to "examine into the condition, classification and safety from fire of the public records of the public offices of such county, city, town, or village, and shall call to the attention of the local authorities and the state historian any material of local historic value which should be acquired for preservation." Finally, the historian is required to make an annual report to the appointing officer and to the State Historian and, upon leaving office, to turn over all materials and correspondence to a successor.[4]

The law provides a general description of the historian's function. However, it raises as many questions as it answers. Must all material relating to local history be collected, or only a part? Must everything collected be filed in local government offices, even if those offices have no facilities to protect such material? Should some of it be kept at home? Logically, it might seem best to store such material where it could be best cared for and made most accessible to the public—perhaps in the local historical society or the local college library.

Unspecified by the law, perhaps publications by the state of New York itself will clarify some of these issues. The state history office did produce several short guides specifically for local historians. Some looked generally at the overall mission of local historians. Two of the most helpful of these are "A Quiz for Local Historians," printed in mimeograph form in 1961; and Margaret C. McNab's "Ethics for a Town Historian," delivered originally as an address at the annual meeting of the Municipal Historians Association in 1972.[5] Both are thoughtful and thorough and both deserve consideration. Neither, however, raises all the questions that need to be asked. When complete, this *Historian's Guide* should provide the basic explanation of and curriculum for the local historian's activities.

The serious seeker of knowledge about the function of the local historian will turn finally to national historical associations. None speaks directly to the issues. But the American Association for State and Local History comes close. Three-quarters of its members are paid professionals and most of them are employed in local history agencies or museums. But AASLH's resources, including the journal

History News, technical leaflets, and instructional books, are valuable resources for any local historian.

In New York State, organizations such as the Regional Conference of Historical Agencies (RCHA) and the Federation of Historical Services (FHS) serve a parallel function.[6] The National Trust for Historic Preservation, genealogical societies, archival groups, the New York State Studies Group, and the New York State Historical Association also organize helpful activities.

An introduction to scholarly research in American local history requires some effort, but is not impossible. Donald Parker's *Local History: How to Gather it, Write it, and Publish It* has been republished recently. Thomas Felt's *Researching, Writing, and Publishing Local History* is an introduction to techniques written especially for local historians. David Russo's *Families and Communities: A New View of American History* provides a basic overview of American local history from the nineteenth century to the present. Thomas Bender's *Community and Social Change in America* presents a sophisticated and thoughtful assessment of theories about community. The Newberry Library in Chicago has developed a program in state and community history and has carried out extensive workshops in this field. Finally, David Gerber, in "Local and Community History: Some Cautionary Remarks on an Idea Whose Time Has Returned," asks us to transcend a narrow parochialism and to focus not only on epic events in a community's history, but also on social process.[7]

These are only a few of the many methodological and conceptual introductions to local history. In addition, specific studies of particular communities or regions will provide ideas on specific types of sources, methods, and conceptual frameworks. New York State is rich in this kind of material, but most of it has not reached an audience outside of the university. Alan Kraut's article on Liberty Party voters in the town of Smithfield in Madison County, for example, uses poll lists, newspapers, census reports, and printed local histories to develop a collective biography of political abolitionists in a small upstate community. Such collective biography techniques can be applied to any group of people by using simple descriptive statistics. Paul Johnson's work on Rochester revivals makes creative use of church records, tax lists, and city directories to explore the effect of the Finney revival of 1831. Philip White's study of the Clinton County community of Beekmantown makes thorough use of many sources, including legislative journals. Mary Ryan's discussion of evangelical religion in nineteenth-century Utica makes a contribution not only to the history of religion, but also to women's history. Ronald Formisano's and Kathleen Smith Kutolowski's work on Antimasonry in western New York explores the regional roots of a major movement in American politics.[8]

However, local history guides and scholarly writings speak to only some of the responsibilities of local historians. These sources can provide helpful ideas. But none deal specifically with the local historian's unique function. Nor do they try to identify the questions that are most important to historians as a group. Should the historian therefore retreat to the community dooryard and do—if not what comes naturally—at least whatever does come along? Certainly not. For too long, local historians as individuals have risen to the challenges posed by their constituencies. Given the renewed interest in archives, historic preservation, museums, genealogy, and history in general, the historian's job is more important than ever. Historians need to be able to rely on each other as they have in the past—as individuals with a high sense of purpose, high standards of scholarship, and a genuine concern for public service. We need to rely on our local historians for mutual support for our common goals—preserving the evidence, upgrading library collections, promoting historical organizations, and writing accurate, readable, and useful historical works.

Yet, historians labor under almost impossible circumstances. Not only do most not get paid; they often do not even get money for stamps or file cabinets. (This encourages some to become hoarders and not promoters of history.) Public records, for which the historian has some legal as well as moral obligation, are frequently lost or destroyed because a town board did not consult its historian before sending them to the dump. Researchers impose upon historians. And those who ought to ask them for help (such as local government officials) often do not. When historians turn for assistance to the law that established them, or to the (New York) State Education Department that guides them, or to other historical organizations, or even to other historians, they may feel like the elephant that the blind men touched. Everyone has a different idea about what historians are and what they should be. All of these sources describe parts of the job. None define it fully. None speak for the local historian.

Now is the time for local historians to speak for themselves. Like the many varieties of grasses that grow in a meadow historians have great diversity, and in diversity there is strength. But they also have much in common, and in unity there is also strength. Individual historians have developed effective activities at the grassroots level. However, there are many problems that cannot be solved alone. Historians must now pool their collective wisdom to define their own goals, to identify their own problems, to begin to work together toward solutions that cannot be attained as well, or at all, by isolated individuals. The public needs the local historian's services very much.

The task breaks itself down into a series of questions. Who is the audience? What are the historian's objectives? What can be done to achieve those objectives? What resources are needed to carry out essential activities? And how will historians get those resources? Too many historians start with the last question, decide they do not have enough money, and never get around to asking the first questions. On the other hand, after deciding on the "what," one often can find some resources to support the actual work.

Some of these points require more discussion. What constitutes the historian's constituency? Obviously, the local historian must provide service to the local government and to people who live within the community. But how responsive need one be to the genealogist who writes from California? What are a historian's obligations to the consulting firm hired by the town government to prepare a cultural resources study? And must the historian serve all constituents equally? What about the student who wants to use the historian as the sole source for term paper? Flattering, perhaps, but is it ethical? How prepared are local historians to deal with a black or Hispanic migrant worker who asks for information about the history of labor camps in the local fruit industry? Should the historian ever charge for services? What is the historian's interest in schoolchildren, women's groups, labor unions, and senior citizens in a locality? Local historians usually respond enthusiastically to people who ask them questions. But are the people who seek them out the ones they really want to reach? Even the town government, which should know enough to consult its historian, often does not. A simple check with a local historian might reveal, as it did in one upstate county, that place names on new road signs did not always correspond to the official names of streets and villages.

Working with the constituency, the historian must define the most important goals. Will it be simply to respond to inquiries? To educate people more broadly about history? To preserve records? To develop a genealogical collection? To save local landmarks? All of these are legitimate, and all are within the historian's legal mandate. At various times, local historians have been involved in all of them. But are there certain priorities on which most historians might agree?

The preservation of local records is an area that deserves immediate and consistent action—statewide. Nothing is more important to all interested in local history than record preservation. Yet, in 1980, storage conditions for local records in New York State ranged from very good to absolutely deplorable. And the decision on whether particular records should receive one kind of treatment or another has been independent of any pressure exerted by historians. Deeds, for example, generally are kept in reasonable condition because they still are important for buying and selling property. Assessment records, which are just as important for historical purposes, often are stored in abysmal surroundings. Even worse than storing records in poor condition is not keeping them at all. Local government officials may decide, without consulting their historian, that some of their nineteenth-century materials are fire hazards and should be taken immediately to the dump. This is not a wild and fanciful nightmare. It has happened in several places.

But rather than condemn local officials—who, after all, are not historians—those who do care about such records and who do know how valuable they are for historical purposes have a special obligation to work toward their safekeeping. Such attention is needed desperately, and it is also part of the local historian's legal mandate. Working with the New York State Archives, historians in every city, town, and village are the best group of people available for a task that, in many localities, has reached the crisis point. But this task needs to be done with a concerted plan for united action.

In terms of local history writing itself, a simple overview of recent literature on New York communities would be helpful. The local historian also might suggest topics that might be especially important to study in many different localities. The historian could develop guidelines for these topics, along with a review of relevant literature, suggested themes, possible sources, and appropriate methodology. These "cookbooks" could be prepared on a variety of topics, such as how to analyze changing birth and death rates, how to write a study of a Greek Revival farmhouse, or how to use simple statistical techniques. Over time, several studies might be produced and thus build a base for the comparative analyses that are very much needed.

As the historian begins to define goals and priorities, new questions will be raised. What, for example, is the historian's relationship to local historical organizations? Consider records preservation. In attempting to collect and preserve historical materials that are not generated by the local government, is the historian theoretically or actually in direct competition with the local historical society or the local public library? Should historians actually collect the material themselves? Or, rather, should the historian's goal be to place the historical evidence wherever it can receive the best protection and be most accessible? Sometimes the best place for it is a dining room table. Usually, however, other facilities are more appropriate.

Once priorities have been decided, what resources are needed to carry them out? Where will those resources come from? As town officers, what resources do town historians need from towns? What resources do they actually receive? Are they adequate? Do historians receive postage money? Do they have the fireproof vault that they are legally obligated to use but that the town is not legally obligated to provide? Should records be stored in fireproof vaults when other storage facilities might do just as well? Here again, perhaps it is time to rethink the legislative mandate. Should the town provide equipment? Membership in the AASLH? A reference library? What resources might the state of New York provide? Would workshops be helpful? On what topics? More in-service training? More regional meetings? Are more "how to" publications needed?

In turn, how can the historian best help the state of New York provide service to the historical community? The Division of Historical and Anthropological Services is attempting to serve its constituents in the best ways possible. Its training organization, the Institute for Local Historians, at which this essay originally was delivered, is one of many examples of that effort. Yet the division, as part of state government, has severe financial limitations. What kind of feedback and support can historians provide for worthwhile programs?

If county and municipal historians in New York State decide to undertake this kind of planning, they might begin by appointing a committee made up of their most knowledgeable and creative people. Such planning will take money and time, and the first task of this committee might well be to seek financial support. Funding agencies may be able to provide money for travel expenses and for consultants who could share their own perspectives from experiences elsewhere in the country. With minimal financial support, such a committee could begin to get extensive feedback from local historians in the field and from their allies in related areas.

One result of this solid assessment might be a positive and well-publicized statement outlining needs and goals. Call it a local historian's manifesto, or a declaration of sentiments, or a statement of rights and privileges. But let it reflect what historians define as their own obligations—a kind of historian's Hippocratic Oath—and what they perceive to be their own legitimate needs. And mince no words. Historians deserve recognition. They deserve support. Their constituents— many of whom also are enthusiastic fans—stand ready to lend that support. The historian's job is too important not to give it the serious consideration that it deserves.

Robert Frost once said that poetry is a way of taking life by the throat. Historical studies also are a way of taking life by the throat. A culture that exists without a sense of its own rich past fails in very real ways to confront its present. Local historians are important keepers of our collective past. May all who practice the art and science of history practice it wisely and well, with commitment, integrity, and a high sense of the importance of our collective responsibilities, our collective mission.

NOTES

1. John Alexander Williams, "Public History and Local History: An Introduction," *The Public Historian* 5 (Fall 1983): 8–16; Mark Friedberger and Janice Reiff Webster, "Social Structure and State and Local History," *Western Historical Quarterly* 9(3): 297–314.

2. *Survey of Museums and Historical Societies in New York State* (Albany, NY: The State Education Department, 1979).

3. "History and Genealogy: Patterns of Change and Prospects for Cooperation," *Prologue* 7(2): 81–84.

4. "State Education Law," Section 148.

5. See also Leslie Hayes, *The Historian and Local Public Records* (Albany, NY: The State Education Department, 1969); Edgar Leaycraft, *New Directions for Local History* (Albany, NY: The State Education Department, 1969); and Edmund J. Winslow, *Historical Societies and Other Historical Agencies in New York State* (Albany, NY: The State Education Department, 1975).

6. One especially useful article in this context is Margaret Hobbie's "The Work of the County Historian," in the newsletter *Regional Conferences of Historical Agencies* 10(7). See also Carol Kammen's "New York's Municipal Historians," *New York History* 69(2) (April 1988): 202–15, published in *Plain as a Pipestem: Essays about Local History* (Interlaken, NY: Heart of the Lakes Publishing, 1989).

7. Donald Dean Parker, *Local History: How to Gather It, Write It, and Publish It* (New York, 1974); Thomas E. Felt, *Researching, Writing, and Publishing Local History* (Nashville: American Association for State and Local History, 1976); Carol Kammen, *On Doing Local History: Reflections on What Local Historians Do, Why, and What It Means* (Nashville: AASLH Press, 1986); David J. Russo, *Families and Communities* (Nashville: American Association for State and Local History, 1974); and Thomas Bender, *Community and Social Change in America* (New Brunswick, NJ: Rutgers University Press, 1978); D'Ann Campbell and Richard Jensen, "Community and Family History at the Newberry Library: Some Solutions to a National Need," *History Teacher* 11(1): 47–54; and David Gerber, "Local and Community History: Some Cautionary Remarks on an Idea Whose Time Has Returned," *History Teacher* 13(1): 7–30. [Reprinted in this volume as Chapter 19, pp. 216–37.]

8. Alan M. Kraut, "The Forgotten Reformers: A Profile of Third-Party Abolitionists in Antebellum New York," in *Antislavery Reconsidered: New Perspectives on the Abolitionists*, edited by Lewis Perry and Michael Fellman (Baton Rouge: Louisiana State University Press, 1979), 119–48; Paul Johnson, *A Shopkeeper's Millennium* (New York: Hill and Wang, 1978); Philip White, *Beekmantown, New York* (Austin: University of Texas Press, 1979); Mary P. Ryan, "A Woman's Awakening: Evangelical Religion and the Families of Utica, NY, 1800–1840," *American Quarterly* 30(5); 603–23; Ronald P. Formisano and Kathleen Smith Kutolowski, "Antimasonry and Masonry: The Genesis of Protest, 1826–27," *American Quarterly* 20(2): 139–65.

PART II

Nineteenth-Century
Views of Local History

In 1844 . . . the day of the amateur historian came to a close. Local historians henceforth would defer to the professional. Many scholars of the older generation, like Julian Winsor, welcomed the new group and into their hands gladly relinquished the future of historical studies.

—David D. Van Tassel, *Recording America's Past*

Chapter Four

An Address Delivered Before the New-Hampshire Historical Society

Introduction

Salma Hale was born in 1787, in New Hampshire. At the age of thirteen, he was apprenticed to a printer; the following year, he published an English grammar. He went on to become an editor, a lawyer, an author. His books include a popular history of the United State and a book of local history, published in 1826: *Annals of the Town of Keene, N.H.*, about his home town.

Hale's address, delivered at the Annual Meeting of the New-Hampshire Historical Society in 1828, is surprisingly modern. He complains about the paucity of historical materials being preserved, and cautions about the motives of writers of history.

Hale believed that our history is too often biased, and that people "ought to be placed in the foreground." He commented that there were no acceptable models of history suitable for Americans to follow, for the American historian must bring into the story numerous and nontraditional actors, besides men of power. "He must trace events," urged Hale, "to different and more recondite causes: he must sketch the character . . . of society in the aggregate."

"An Address: Delivered Before the New-Hampshire Society, at the Annual Meeting, 11th June, 1828," is reprinted from *Collections of the New-Hampshire Historical Society* 3 (Concord, NH, 1832): 123–39.

* * * *

The utility of History has been the theme of writers of all ages, and all classes. It has been termed philosophy teaching by example. It has been called the instructor

Salma Hale, "An Address Delivered Before the New-Hampshire Historical Society," *Collections of the New-Hampshire Historical Society* 3 (1832).

of politicians, the guide of statesmen, and the school of virtue. Commanders have resorted to it to acquire perfection in the art of war; moralists to give a sanction to their precepts; orators to embellish and illustrate their harangues; and poets to give dignity to their effusions. It has, by common consent, been placed highest on the list of useful and liberal studies, and an acquaintance with it has been deemed indispensable to the citizen, the scholar, and the magistrate.

Such, in truth, is the elevated rank to which history would be entitled, had the writers of history possessed the means and the talent to impart to it all the interest, and all the usefulness, of which it is susceptible; and had they, which is still more important, been always actuated by that honesty of purpose which impels, and that entire freedom from prejudice which permits, an author to seek for truth and to relate it, whatever may be its influence upon the country or party to which he belongs. Its lessons would then have the highest of all human authority—that of long and varied experience; and, receiving undoubted credit, would exercise an influence over the actions of men, but little less imperative than the precepts of inspiration. It would disclose the operation of the invariable laws impressed by our creator upon man, enable us to foresee the inevitable consequences of every action, and to trace back effects to their true and appropriate causes. It would exhibit the influence of outward circumstances upon society, account for all its changes, instruct us how to guard against the approach of evil, and point to that course which would lead us onward, in the career of improvement, until we had reached the highest elevation of human felicity and grandeur.

But no historian has ever had the means to do full justice to his subject. Few materials are preserved; those which escape destruction are dispersed, hidden, or forgotten; and the efforts of a single individual are insufficient to discover and collect them. And even when the means are in his power, the disposition to use them as he ought is too seldom felt. The motive which impels him to write, and which afterwards guides his pen, is too often the desire to elevate one country, or one sect, or one party, at the expense of another, or to defend one that has, in his view, been misrepresented; and this is the principal cause why so few histories have been written to which entire credit should be given. Most of them are made the medium of error rather than of truth, and none so much as those which aspire to the character of philosophic or speculative histories, and, from a partial knowledge of facts, presumptuously speak of the causes of events, and of the motives of men.

The single circumstance of want of materials, would, in the absence of all other reasons, justify us in receiving with extreme distrust, the narratives of the earliest historians. Before the art of printing was invented, but few documents existed, and tradition furnishes almost the only materials for history. How much falsehood tradition gathered in its progress, and how much truth, modifying and almost changing the aspect of the truths it transmitted, was lost on the way, could only be the subject of conjecture.

. . .[H]istory gives also moral as well as political lessons. No man can read it, when written as it ought to be written, and fail to be convinced that, in regard to nations, communities and individuals, there is a close and indissoluble connection between virtue and happiness—between guilt and suffering. It cannot lift the veil and show the rewards, whether for good or for evil, dispensed in the world to come—that is the province of inspiration—but it can show, and it does show, the operation, in this world, of those moral laws which have the same relations to human actions that physical laws have to the material world.

A consideration of the uncertainty of all, and the falsity of most of the histories of former times; of the high importance, in a political and moral view, of preserving the memorials of the events which marked the infancy of our existence, for the use of the future historian, led to the institution of this society. I can speak without indelicacy of the laudable motives of its founders, for none of the merit is mine. They were aware that time, with restless motion, was constantly sweeping from the stage, the actors in the great drama which has recently closed, and burying in the grave the memory of events and principles, which do honor to our state, to our country, and to human nature. They were unwilling that our future fame should be left at the mercy of any one who might, to inculcate other principles, misrepresent those of their ancestors. They were sensible that individual exertion could do little, and that the zeal of many, concentrated upon one object, could do much, to accomplish their praise-worthy purpose. They were sensible too of the utility of attracting public attention to this purpose, and thus drawing from neglected repositories, fugitive and occasional publications, personal memoirs and journals, and the correspondence of individuals in official and private stations, which, more than public documents and labored performances, display the spirit of the times, disclose the secret springs of action, and lay bare the motives of men. Procuring the sanction of the government, they established this Society, and the collections they have made, and the volumes they have published, shew the ardor and continuance of their zeal, and the value of their labors.

The first establishment of historical societies is of recent date. They may justly be classed among the distinguishing features of the age. They show that enlightened men have become sensible, that history is too important to be entrusted, and the task of writing it too difficult to be left, to individual exertion; that the only method of imparting to it all utility of which it is susceptible, and which it has heretofore been supposed to possess, is to make facts, and all the facts the basis of the narrative; and that it is the duty of men, who love their country and cherish its fame, to lay up treasures for the historian who comes after them, that may facilitate his labors, and restrain him from substituting conjectures for facts.

Upon the members of these societies, important duties devolve. In assuming the station to which they have been called, they incur obligations to collect and impart all the materials within their power that may assist and guide the historian. These materials are far more abundant, even in this state, than is generally supposed. They consist not solely of facts fixing the date or the place of great events—designating the actors—disclosing their motives—and ascertaining the naked result. These important events are produced, and their effects modified, by a thousand circumstances which, at the time, appeared to have none, or at most a very remote connection, with them, or with each other. The mighty Nile is composed of small tributary streams, whose sources have, for ages, been the object of painful research, in order to discover the cause of the fertilizing properties of its waters. So a combination of minutiae produce the great events which stand prominent in the pages of history; and a knowledge of the parts is essential to a just conception of the whole. These minute events are found in the histories of our towns, of our churches, of our interior legislation, and in the biography of individuals who have risen to any degree of political or professional eminence. How much light must it cast upon the character of this people, to trace the progress of one of these towns, from the time when the sound of the axe was first heard within its limits until its fields were covered with flocks and verdure—until its surface was studded with buildings and intersected with roads, and school houses and churches had risen in all their appropriate places. The mere fact that such a town had sprung up, as it were, out of nothing, without aid, or fostering care, and that no striking event had marked its progress, giving it a forward impulse, would be a forcible commentary upon the free institutions of modern times, which, leaving the powers of man unshackled, permit them to exert all their energies in the pursuit of wealth and happiness. How instructive, too, must be the biography of an individual, who starting from a humble station, rises, struggling through difficulties, to eminence—instructive not merely in a moral, but in a political view, and affording an insight into the character of the age and people.

But to furnish materials for the history of his country is the duty also of every citizen. Every man owes something to his country, and he, whose fortunate situation enables him to enlarge the stock of historical information, cannot in a more useful or honorable mode, discharge his obligations. Gratifying indeed would it be, could our library present, to those who might choose to visit it, every publication, stating or elucidating facts, or expressing the feelings and opinions of the people, which has appeared since the first landing of the adventurers on Strawberry bank; and could our collections contain historical notices of all our towns and biographical sketches of all our citizens, who have been distinguished for their attainments, or usefulness. In the perusal and study of these, the citizen would be inspired with just sentiments, and be led to adopt right principles—the future historian would be carried back to the times of which he was writing; he would feel himself in presence of those whose deeds he recorded; he would be awed by the majesty of their virtues; he would imbibe their spirit, understand and appreciate their motives, and his pages would present, not merely a dry narrative of events, but a correct impress of the different periods which passed successively under his review—he would be animated by the same spirit and infuse the same sentiments into the bosom of the reader.

And if it be, as it doubtless is, the duty of legislators to secure to the people the advantages of education, is it not a corresponding duty to enable them to acquire that species of instruction which is derived from the study of a full and correct History of their country. Of little use is the boast that every American can read, if the opportunity be withheld of reading what, next to the volume which contains the doctrines and precepts of our holy religion, is more important than all others. Some at least of the states of this union, witnessing and applauding the disinterested efforts of individuals, have made munificent donations to their historical societies, enabling them to enlarge their libraries and to publish their collections. Of such munificence, history will not fail to speak in terms of merited praise; and what must be far more grateful to the patriot, the encouragement afforded will ensure the transmission to posterity of many honorable names, and many virtuous deeds, which time would otherwise leave behind in its course; and will embalm in glowing language, sentiments and principles which, so long as they are remembered, will preserve in all their purity, those free institutions which are the pride and boast of our country.

Chapter Five

Deficiencies in Our History:
An Address Delivered Before the
Vermont Historical and Antiquarian Society
at Montpelier, October 16, 1846

Introduction

James Davie Butler, Jr., was born in 1815 in Rutland, Vermont. He attended school there, graduated from Middlebury College in 1836, and from Andover Theological Seminary in 1840. He taught at Norwich University in Vermont and later at Wabash College and the University of Wisconsin.

"Deficiencies in Our History" is the address he presented before the Vermont Historical and Antiquarian Society in 1846, the year that society was created.

Butler's concern that Vermont get credit for its activities during the Revolutionary War turns much of this piece into a tirade against historians crediting only Massachusetts or New York for Revolutionary War exploits in which Vermonters participated. In the process of redressing the record, however, Butler calls for state and local history that is imaginative, responsive to the people, and sensitive to the effects of events. He believed that history should include those usually ignored or forgotten, that it should record expectations, conditions, and—when writing of war—the home front, as well as the outcome of military engagements. He calls for history that includes face-to-face details, lest it be "like the Pope . . . never to be seen except gorgeous with trailing robes."

Because of the specific nature of Butler's excoriations, a few of his more stinging comments have been deleted here, leaving only the principal commentary, which reflects his ideas about the subject of local history.

James Davie Butler, Jr., *Deficiencies in Our History: An Address Delivered Before the Vermont Historical and Antiquarian Society at Montpelier, October 16, 1846* (Montpelier: Eastman & Danforth Publishers, 1846).

This essay is reprinted from James Davie Butler, Jr., "Deficiencies in Our History: An Address Delivered before the Vermont Historical and Antiquarian Society at Montpelier, October 16, 1846" (Montpelier: Eastman & Danforth Publishers, 1846).

* * * *

Fellow Citizens of Vermont:

The life of old nations is memory. In the old world travellers daily behold great events and the scenes of them—not only commemorated by monuments, but canonized by chapels and altars.

Young nations live in hope rather than in memory. (While pressing forward to those things which are before, they forget those which are behind.) This truth finds many exemplifications in our history.

A circular was recently sent to every town in Vermont that was incorporated when our State independence was declared, requesting information concerning the 71 signers of that declaration. It was vouchsafed only one answer. Our declaration of State independence was never published in this State until last summer, and then only in fugitive newspapers. The papers of our first and most memorable Governor were sold to a pedlar with paper rags.

The cannon taken (in defense of our frontier) at Bennington lie unclaimed at Washington. The maps, captured at the same place, were used as curtains until all, save one, perished. The grenadiers' arms and drum there taken, and presented as a trophy to our State council were received with a promise that, according to the donor's request, they should be kept in the council-chamber as a memorial of the glorious action fought at Wallumscoik. But this trophy has been vilely thrown away.

Properly speaking we have no rostrum. A rostrum is a speaker's stand begirt with memorials of vanquished foes. We have none.

Facts such as these prepare us to expect a universal apathy in regard to our history, and move our special wonder that we can boast so many historians, and several worthy of no common praise.

It is no great discredit to our historians that they are in many respects deficient, since they were forced to make brick without straw, the collections needful for the adequate execution of their task, which are still imperfect, not having been fairly begun, when most of our chroniclers wrote.

It is simply because no one else could be found to stand in the gap, that I venture to appear before you at this time, inasmuch as I must appear to the same disadvantage with our historians. I have, indeed, had access to sources of knowledge which were hid from their eyes; but I have enjoyed this privilege only a few days, and under the double pressure of ministerial and professional labors, as well as with one foot on the cradle, in the judgment of many a much greater impediment.

The subject which I would invite you to consider, is certain deficiencies in our State histories.

The controversy of Vermont with New York has never been described as its merits, and the richness of materials regarding it, demand. I have drawn up a list—which, pardon me, I do not mean to read—of fifty questions concerning it which demand elucidation. No historian hints—what every historian should have clearly shown—that that struggle was not merely about the price of land, but a conflict between New England and New York principles—those of the Puritan and of the Patroon—between our township system, with local elections and taxes, and New York centralization.

I am constrained to pass in utter silence, however, the manifold short-comings of our writers in respect to our relations to all our sister States.

The part Vermont took in the Revolution is rather shadowed forth than distinctly traced by our historians.

They claim for us indeed a share in the taking of Ticonderoga, as well as in the siege of St. Johns; in the battle near Bennington, and perhaps in the taking of Burgoyne.

But, though much is said of battles as far off as Braddock's defeat, instead of a distinctive account of Vermont's military career, her exploits are so blended with those of the continentals, or so imperfectly detailed, as to lose all individuality. . . .

In all our Histories there is a lack of characteristic minutiae. We ask for face-to-face details, we receive far off generalities "where every something blent together turns to a wild of nothing."

Seemingly trifling particulars catch our eyes as we gaze at a landscape; they affect the eye-witnesses of events—they bring the light of other days around us as we listen to the narrative of old age—they are the sparkling fountains—abstractions are the vapid stream.

Some writers may have neglected such fragments, deeming it beneath the dignity of history to stoop and gather them, as if history like the Pope was never to be seen except gorgeous with trailing robes, or were to represent nations, as some picture books represent kings wearing crowns and holding sceptres—even in bed. So far as the suppression of picture-like details has been a sin of ignorance, it is to be winked at, but not if it has proceeded from scorning them as nothing worth. Which of our historians might not profitably copy the following account of the evacuation of Ticonderoga . . . "About 11 o'clock on Saturday night, orders were given by our Colonel to parade. We immediately obeyed. He then ordered our tents struck and carried to the battery. On doing this, the orders were to take up our packs and march, which we also did, passed the General's house on fire, marched 20 miles without a halt, and then had a brush with the enemy."

How shall history hold the mirror up to nature if not by giving us the very words of the actors in bye gone times? Things cannot indeed be all described, then the world would not contain the books which would be written, but those parts, the least as well as the greatest, should be sought out, which most nearly produce the effect of the whole.

If the ballad writer be as influential as the legislator, why should our historians with one consent, refuse us, even in their notes and appendixes, a single specimen of popular songs, the Marsailles hymns—indicated by Rowley and others—sung at the crisis of our destiny.

Can we learn as much in regard to common schools at an early day from any of our histories, as from a single remark made to me by a woman, who had no thought of telling any great thing, that in the winter of 1780, her brother kept a school in one of the two rooms in his father's log house in Sharon, there being then twenty-eight families in town and that there was no school for five winters afterwards! Only two of the sixty-eight settlers in Bennington made their mark; all of the 1006 petitioners to King George wrote their names, and Elkins, a boy from Peacham, when a prisoner in England, receiving a shilling a week from Dr. Franklin, paid out four coppers of it for tuition.

Do not facts like these throw light upon the popular intelligence and desire of knowledge?

What incident in our histories shows the inspiriting effect of the Bennington battle so strikingly as a trifle they all omit—a rumor which straight way ran through New Hampshire, that Burgoyne himself was taken at Stillwater—coming events cast their shadows before.

I would not willingly be ignorant that in 1761 there were only about 100 families between the mountains and the river—that a post-boat from Canada was taken soon after the seizure of Ticonderoga—that an express could be sent from Newbury to Boston in three days, cannon from Lake George to the same place in seventeen days—that the Vermont uniform was green with red facings—that rum even when it rose to $96, continental money, a gallon, was dealt out in the rations—that Allen gave Warner 400 acres of land for cutting off the ear of a Yorker—that each Vermonter after the Bennington battle received $5 plunder money. Each of these trifles is a little window through which we can look into the distant past.

The little said in our histories in relation to religion, tends to disprove the assertion of Dr. Dwight, that "our first settlers were chiefly universalists and infidels." There is much to disprove it in the following details. Orthodox ministers were early settled in most towns; sermons longer than we can bear, and as searching were preached at the opening of every State Convention and Assembly;—requests for prayers abound in letters—pamphlets then printed have beyond all comparison more allusions to the bible than to all other books together. When one would put General Bailey on his guard against Tory liers-in-wait, he dropped in his path a paper with these words on it, "The Philistines be upon thee Samson."

The word of God was the law-book for all cases falling under no statute, and sentences were given according to its enactments. Where there was no church or preacher, meetings were held under trees and in private houses; such an assemblage delayed one day the burning of Royalton. My grandmother used to tell me that during the battle of Bennington, she and many others were met for prayer within the sound of cannon.

Our writers have not enough availed themselves of vivid particulars by way of indirect description.

What can give us a better idea what a long struggle was expected when hostilities began, or how our people rushed to the war, than these words, written one week after the bloodshed at Lexington from that quarter to this. "For heaven's sake, pay the closest attention to sowing and planting; do as much of it as possible, not for your own families merely. Do not think of coming down country to fight." What can draw and color more to the life the want of all things useful in war, during Burgoyne's invasion than these words of Stark, written at his quarters on the Connecticut:

"I am informed that the enemy have left Castleton and have an intent to march to Bennington. We are detained here a good deal for bullet moulds, as there is but one pair in town, and the few balls sent on by the State go but a little way in supplying the whole."

One pair of bullet moulds! [A] light visible result significant of how many things not so visible.

Such incidents, like the rude strokes in charcoal-sketches, produce more effect than many elaborate line engravings.

The impressiveness of our history is weakened because a thousand petty circumstances are scattered here and there through a Gazatteer or through voluminous documents—sometimes in widely sundered archives, like the elementary constituents of Mosaic work instead of being fitly framed together into a life-like picture, as those of the French Revolution have been by Carlyle.

The heroic deeds of our forefathers seem not to have been appreciated; sometimes they are mentioned as things of course, or unmentioned by our writers, though they are not a whit behind the chiefest deeds man can boast.

Luther when the Pope burned his books, burned the Pope's bull. In what did he surpass Allen's retorting the setting a price on his head by New York, with setting the price on the head of a New York dignitary?

At Bennington, a Green Mountain Boy struck a Hessian officer's sword from his hand with a stick, and forced him to make his file of men lay down their arms. How few know that hero's name!

We shall always remember two men that swam the Hellespont—the one from vanity, the other for personal gratification of another sort. We are in danger of forgetting a citizen of our own who swam as broad a strait at Ticonderoga, at midnight, threading his way through a hostile fleet, not for himself but for his country—Richard Wallace—worthy to bear the name of him of Scotland, and to be equalled with him in renown.

I have sometimes thought our writers particularly oblivious of female heroism as displayed in our history.

A French maid of honor who lost her arm by foolishly thrusting it in place of a door-bar to protect her queen, is eulogized. A woman of Vermont suffered the same loss, defending her husband, with the first weapon that offered against midnight kidnappers, and is passed over in silence.

French women are praised for digging and trundling barrows to rear a monument of national fickleness. The similar labors of Vermont women striving to take the places of their husbands who were dying in battle are more than half forgotten.

It is recorded in Scottish history that Knox's daughter would rather see him beheaded and catch [the] head in her apron, than have him turn papist. It is not recorded in our history what Vermont mother used her apron to staunch the blood of her wounded son, when both of them still every moment were exposed to be scalped.

None of our histories mention the name of Hannah Handy, whose entreaties rescued not only her own children but seven of her neighbor's children from going into captivity, after they had been already taken over White River, and who dared to cross that river on the back of an Indian, that she might bring back her jewels. Yet was she a heroine before finding a parallel for whom we shall search long.

But as anecdotes of Allen were eagerly coveted in his life time by distinguished Frenchmen, as we are learning that our curled maple and walnut may compare with mahogany, and that our marbles may vie with those of Carrara, which some have crossed an ocean to visit, so let us believe that heroes and heroines may not always be without honor in their own country, and in ours. Such seem specimens of the cardinal deficiencies in our histories as to our part in our histories of the Revolution, including our conflicts and our negotiations with the British, as to minute details, and as to our heroes and heroines.

These deficiencies, and countless others in relation to topics on which I have no time to touch, have not only been clearly detected by our President, but his labors have accumulated materials for supplying very many of them. He has gathered together fragments from lake to river, from Massachusetts to Canada—he has spent three months together in the collections of sister states, or of the general government; he has secured correspondents in Canada, and in the person of his son, he has broken through the Chinese wall of English exclusiveness—he has found laws and journals of the Legislature that had been given up for lost—he has doubled Thompson's list of Vermont books before its admission to the Union—he has saved letters by thousands that were ready to perish, and that cast each its ray on the dark past. He has recently added a third to the ponderous tomes obtained of him by the State two years ago—he has collected autographs, not to see which with more pleasure than Napoleon's would cast ominous conjecture on your patriotism, written in such a hand as was to be expected from pioneers, but who would look on letters of gold with half the pleasure?

Are all desiderata then supplied by the collections of our President? By no means. Properly speaking he has to do with only one department—military operations—and that during the Revolution. We ought to be thankful that he has magnified his office, yet not forgetful that he has exhausted none of the mines of investigation. A barrel full of papers left by the most interesting military character in our annals lies headed up and unexamined to this day.

The collections of other societies and public offices, whether state, national, or foreign, remain to be examined or re-examined. The papers of every man mentioned in our history are to be sought for, and in this search the name of every such man may prove a guide useful as a clue in a labyrinth. We must seek for sermons, histories, and biographies, hoards of newspapers, or those thrown away like autumnal leaves, journals in manuscript, letters sent out of the State to those from whom the settlers came forth. A rich mine of these is doubtless still unopened, for, among hundreds I have examined, I have discovered only two addressed to women, and none—no not one—written by a woman. But were not women in those days ready writers even as now? Proverbially the best letter-writers in all other countries, were they found wanting here? Did not their letters paint the lights and shades of life in this new State, as they have since portrayed western clearings, as those of busy men, less keen-eyed for the picturesque and trivial could not, or did not?

Other sources of historical facts will also be opened to us by lucky accident, too various to be described or too strange to be predicted. The gems of sister societies were sometimes found where least looked for. The original of the world-famed (English) Magna Charta was found in the hands of a tailor, who was just ready to cut it up for patterns. One of the most ancient and valuable maps of New Hampshire, when it extended to the lake, was discovered in a storehouse where a pedler had left it when he removed his rags, either through accident, or judging it not worth taking away.

What has been will be.

If such a list of questions as that prepared by the Massachusetts society were circulated throughout Vermont, township by township, beyond a doubt many early laws and journals of the Legislature, long ago given up as irrecoverably lost, as well as much equally valuable and more curious information concerning Town Committees and Committees of Safety, those cradles of our independence, lacking links of every sort in the chains of our annals, might be rescued from oblivion.

No doubt the drag-net of our research will gather of every kind. Criticism must therefore have its perfect work, in separating the precious from the vile. The mass of materials must also be classified according to their nature, the time to which they relate, the place where they are found, or the purposes for which they may be employed.

Many explanatory notes must be appended to the collections made by our President, or what is a plain path to him will appear to those who shall come after, "a mighty maze and all without a plan."

The fruits of our historical harvests and gleanings ought also to be garnered up in a chief place of concourse, instead of the corner where they are now secluded— even as the treasures of other states are honored with archives in Boston, Hartford, Concord, New York and Washington.

How beautiful thus to have a section of the past brought safe into the present and set down before our eyes!

Arrangements are making for publishing the earliest annals of our fathers. I trust such a publication will soon take away our reproach of being the only State which has had a Society for a series of years and yet published nothing, as if our investigations were labor lost, or were to be hidden in the chaos of a Museum.

The "Historical readings," published in the State Banner, were well received. Let us have more of them, a hundred fold. Let our printers whose types preserve knowledge, bring forth things old as well as new.

What is of more interest than a town history—to each man that of his own town? No where in Europe did I seek without finding one. How long shall we desire such histories in vain? What true patriot loves not his own village?

Who can doubt the capacity of our primitive period to furnish an anthology of incidents suited for a reading book in common schools! Such a book would have a greater charm for children than things far off and long ago. It might develop a spirit of research which must otherwise perish in embryo. Many an unique document which now appears to them as worthless as the jewel seemed to the barn-yard fowl, it might lead them to appreciate so that they would say, destroy it not, for a blessing is it.

The only incident relating to our history, I remember in my school books, is Howe's captivity, and that was in a book long since antiquated. Is there nothing, then, in our history such that we may fitly tell in the ears of our sons, and teach it diligently to our sons' sons!

As a means of securing the ends now suggested we may rejoice that we have a State Society, albeit as some think, it has but a name to live. Should we despise its low estate, knowing that all beginnings are small? Will it not be a rallying point, nay a magnet attracting to itself and binding in union all congenial spirits however scattered abroad? Is it not suited to be their organ of communication with those like minded elsewhere? Will it not increase their zeal, by kindling mutual emulation and by so dividing labors that each man shall have an office in keeping with his taste and opportunities. What better expedient can be devised to keep historical inquiries before the people, as well as to secure the cooperation and contributions of their thousand hands?

Is it not a nucleus, a reservoir into which rivulets without number, invaluable for its purposes though valueless as to all others, will naturally flow?

Is it not a company for mutual insurance—not against fire—but against a loss which can never, by any possibility be repared?

An association, of such a nature and of such aims, should commend itself to us all.

Statesmen! Among your motives to scorn delights and live laborious days is the hope to leave a name that men shall not willingly let die—can you be indifferent to what concerns the memory of your predecessors? Do to them as ye would that posterity should do to you.

Politicians! Will you not welcome our Society, as a little sanctuary where no war-whoop of party can be heard—where the interests of all parties are one. If you look to dollars and cents, are researchers to be sneered at, which by the papers of a single family have obtained nine pensions, and which may yet substantiate our claim to millions from the national treasury?

Scholars! Can you remember that Massachusetts has published scores of volumes to illustrate her history—that Connecticut, New Hampshire, New York, and even Georgia have followed in her footsteps, and blush not that we are behind them all?

Ye that have spoken of plants even unto the hyssop that springeth out of the wall —that have chronicled every creeping thing that creepeth upon the face of the earth—can you pass by on the other side any memorial of the leaves in our history, as if tithing cummin were the weightiest of matters?

Rich men! The British Museum has last year appropriated more than $20,000 to purchase books relating to America. Many of the rarest works on our local annals are led into captivity to London—materials, says one, for future Alison's to forge lies from. Will you only tighten your purse strings while men in deep poverty are struggling to secure for ourselves the documents which may be indispensible for refuting the half-truths, equivalent to whole falsehoods, which will be propounded, regarding our annals, by the party, or prejudiced writers of England?

Let us leave our history to be written by foreigners and it will be the play of Hamlet with the part of Hamlet omitted. The New York account of the taking of Ticonderoga is that "it was surprised by a detachment of provincials from Connecticut and Massachusetts Bay," as if there had no Vermonter raised a finger. The truth is, as we have seen, that the first measures for that capture originated in Vermont, and that all but one sixth of those engaged in it were Vermonters.

Our ancestors made themselves of no reputation for you who had done nothing for them. No debt can be more binding on you than to see to it that justice is done their memory.

Is there no hope of any further aid from the State? Shall not this State, like so many others, perfect its archives, or shall the only State that redeemed its revolutionary paper money at par neglect to finish securing even its own laws and journals, and the records of its courts?

It is not fitting for the State's money to be laid out to help a man travel in England; but it is a shame to us that we have not sooner secured the services of a gentleman who had gained access to the correspondence during the most critical period of our history—documents which others had in vain begged leave to examine—and who would have copied it cheaper and better than any other man. We have refused him hundreds though we might thus have procured a better reputation than we can now make of an aspersion which has been cast on the fame of our fathers. England is now lavishing thousands upon the same man for his assistance in obtaining documents in which she can feel comparatively but little interest.

Even Georgia has procured the copying of twenty folios regarding her history in British public offices.

The genius of our history says to us, all and each, that thou doest do quickly, like the sybil to the ancient king, she year by year brings with her fewer and fewer antique records, but unlike the sybil demands for them an eve[r] increasing price.

I trust our Geological scrutiny will meet with no interruption or delay, but were we to leave that scrutiny half unfinished, another generation may renew it, and suffer no evil from our neglect. Geological records are always with us, everlasting as the hills—they are graven in the rock forever, we may read them when we will.

The records of our fathers have in part perished with them,—some of them live in the memories of patriarchs who still stand among us with eyes undimmed and natural force not abated, as if on purpose that such as hold the pen of the ready writer may still embalm their sayings. For this end let each of us build over against his own house and rely on himself as though he were the only laborer. Let us redeem the time, since if our old men pass away unquestioned, no buried Pompeii can be raised from the grave to enlighten our wilful ignorance. How we lack what we have lost irretrievably! Many of you have stood in the Massachusetts Senate Chamber and seen suspended over the entrance, a gun, drum, sword and cap, trophies, not of Lexington, Concord, or Bunker Hill, but of Bennington. What would we not give to regain the similar relic—"those bruised arms hung up for monuments," which we threw away as nothing worthy. It is too late.

But let us be up and doing, each in his own order. Every fact hitherto undetected, we can glean and garner up by means of the art preservative of all arts, may be a monument more lasting than those trophies in Boston, or than any corruptible things, and what is more, vocal with speech that may be heard through all space and through all time.

<u>Chapter Six</u>

The Literature of American Local History:
A Bibliographical Essay

Introduction

Hermann Ernst Ludewig was born in Saxony, Germany, in 1809 and educated in the law at Leipsig and Gottingen. His interest, however, was in the preparation of bibliographies. In 1844, Ludewig came to the United States; two years later, he issued a bibliography of American local history in which he included state and local histories and travel literature. Ludewig's first American bibliography was followed by an expanded version several years later. Ludewig became a naturalized citizen. He died in Brooklyn in 1856.

Ludewig's essay on "The Literature of American Local History" is as much a political lesson as it is a historical treatise. Ludewig answers that democracy imparts a local independence that should be recorded and notes that that is one of the differences between this country and the Old World. But he also cautions that to know the historical literature of the United States, one has to "look sharp, help yourself, and go ahead." By that, Ludewig means that America's lack of a central repository for historical literature provides no easy access to published history.

The first half of Ludewig's essay expands upon his ideas of American exceptionalism and the unique features to be found in American democracy. In the second half, Ludewig defends the work and the significance of producing bibliographies and touches on the qualities one hopes to find in history.

The article is reprinted from *The Literature of American Local History: A Bibliographical Essay*, by Hermann E. Ludewig (New York: Privately printed by R. Craighead, 112 Fulton Street, 1846).

Hermann E. Ludewig, *The Literature of American Local History: A Bibliographical Essay* (New York, privately printed by R. Craighead, 112 Fulton Street, 1846).

* * * *

No people in the world can have an interest in the history of their country, as that of the U.S. of North America: for there are none who enjoy an equally great share in their country's historical acts. And who would not love his offspring, who remain indifferent even to the smallest incidents affecting them? There is also no country in the world whose history ought to be of higher interest to its citizens, than the United States, as their history contains treasures of experience in politics, as novel in the old as in the new world. It contains the annals of a new era in the political and moral history of mankind, and points out the way to that height of perfection, which a free nation ought continually to strive to attain, and which must be, therefore, pre-eminently desirable to the citizens of the United States. For they have entirely excluded from their system of government the antiquated principle of prescriptive rights, and have adopted in its stead the people's right to govern themselves; in politics they can therefore claim no longer the privilege and benefit of minors, having by an act of their own declared themselves of full age, to act independently and to follow their own course, spurning all foreign interference in matters of their own cognizance as intolerable to men who feel their worth. In whatever wrong they do, therefore, they have themselves to blame, not being allowed the privilege of laying it at the door of any hereditary rulers, who might occasionally be made to expiate with their lives the imbicility of the past and the consequently necessary degradation of the present generation. Allowing at the same time the fullest share of human rights to every one of their white fellow citizens, and realizing self-government on the most extensive scale known, it is quite natural that in the United States more than anywhere else, citizens should only be willing to yield to necessity, whether it be a material or a moral one; and, as necessity is not acknowledged as such until after experience, very often dearly bought, history, as the treasury of experience, should bear a far higher value with the sovereign citizens of a free State than with the subjects of a monarchy, who, having conceded to hereditary rulers the monopoly of those acts which constitute history, must pay a rather high price for the idle position of humble spectators to those acts, without even retaining the consoling liberty of demonstrating their displeasure.

But, though the history of the United States must be of the greatest interest to their own citizens, that which Europeans may attach to it from another point of view, cannot be much inferior to their own.

It has of late been shown most clearly, by De Tocqueville and other French political writers, that Democracy is the great end to which all enlightened nations aim, and to which they are led even unconsciously by every incident of historical importance. The best evidence of this assertion is the very form of government, by the adoption of which the subjects of monarchies have striven to attain, so far as this may be compatible with good order, the highest degree of liberty, the so-called Constitutional Monarchy. This mixture of the two elements of Democracy and

Monarchy, which must for ever be diametrically opposed to each other, is upon the whole nothing but an attempt to render change from the one form to the other easier and more decent, confining a mortal conflict within such limits as to make it harmless to the material interests of the people, and annihilating the one of these elements under proper form and by a legal proceeding, instead of using violence, which even in the case of self-defence might prove troublesome or afford a bad political precedent.

I will not decide upon the question, whether in a conflict between an evident and undeniable right, and a mere legal presumption, the strength of the former would finally destroy the latter or not; but the victory of democracy, which becomes from day to day more probable and unavoidable, must certainly turn the attention of every foreigner to the rise and progress of the United States; to the history of a country where, in a magic mirror, as it were, one may behold the future state of different European nations, and learn equally to avoid precipitation and sluggishness in adopting a form of government which, so far, seems best to answer the intentions of our Creator in making men moral, and consequently self-governing beings. . . .

Leaving now this subject, with our best hopes and wishes for a healthy and continued growth, we will turn our attention to the studies of those foreigners who may wish to gain, by researches into the Historical Literature of this country, a knowledge of its past, and a better understanding of its present state. Few, if any, will have given a clearer idea of the difference between the historical conceptions of this, and those of other countries, than Mr. Salma Hale has done, in an address he delivered, June 11th, 1828, before the Historical Society of New Hampshire. [See Chapter 4 in this volume, pp. 61–65.—ED.]

We see [in Mr. Hale's words] the adaption of the principles of democracy to the art of the historian; and whoever becomes acquainted with American historical literature, will admit that its prominent features are no less democratical than is the way of becoming acquainted with it. This may probably have been the reason why the historical literature of the United States has so often proved inaccessible to many, who gave it up, whenever ignorance, dislike, or envy would answer to their pertinent, but certainly misdirected questions, that there was no such literature at all in existence; an assertion, the falsity of which the following repertory will show.

The United States have a Historical literature; but in order to become thoroughly acquainted with it, the inquirer must not confine his researches to what information chance may offer, but trace it back to its sources. In doing this, however, he must strictly adhere to the observation of that triad of fundamental rules, which, not unlike the "tria praecepta juris" of the institutions of Roman law, democracy has adopted as the device of its unparalleled successes, viz.: "*Look sharp, help yourself and go ahead.*"—The inquirer has first of all to look sharp, in order to find the extent of American literature in general; next he has to know how to help himself in taking a survey of the different parts of this dominion, and in scanning and sifting whatever may be of use to him in his pursuits. In this he ought not to rely upon others, as he will find therein neither servants nor even helps, but must act and look out for everything himself, and if he wishes to succeed, he must go ahead with the same unshaken resolution, as a settler would in the backwoods, never to be discouraged by difficulties or impediments, which to the true scholar, as to every true-hearted laborer in any vocation whatever, will rather prove an incentive than a check upon him. And what are difficulties to true Americans? There was a time when one could speak of inaccessible rocks, of rapids and torrents, which the historian had to surmount and to cross, where he might run the risk of finding himself unexpectedly stopped in his advance, like the bold Emperor Maximilian in his adventurous hunting, by an insurmountable Martinswand of daring and mysterious interest, and to use afterwards the reader's charitable faith as the grateful ropes and ladders upon which he climbs again to the safer highway of every-day possibility. The times, however, are gone by, when the monopoly of becoming known and admired was granted only to imperial and lordly adventurers; and instead of the said Maximilian, calling by the sounds of his hunting horn not only his companions to the rescue, and exciting the humble astonishments of his faithful subjects, the gallant American sailor, the undaunted backwoodsman, if equally puzzled, whistles Yankee Doodle, and knows how to help himself, unnoticed indeed, but certainly not less courageous. Democracy knows no lasting impediments; her progress is not stopped by precipices or breakers, but only moderated by a lusty undergrowth, so moderated, as never to become exclusive, and kept in such a spirit that even the advancing pioneer cannot leave behind him the common interest of humanity. To show and explain this movement, the incessant advancing of mankind, guided by its pioneers to a daily more intimate consonance with natural laws and natural truth, is the peaceful task of the historians of Democracy. . . .

The few bibliographical works existing concerning America are almost exclusively devoted to historical literature, in which of course foreigners had always a very great share; but even those are generally devoted to the historical literature of the whole American Continent, or if, like the works of Mr. O. Rich, they pay particular attention to the history and description of the United States, yet they are too incomplete as to the single States of the Union. Still there is no lack of local histories, especially in New England, whose sons may justly be called a "documentary people." [See the *North American Review* 46: 475–599.—ED.] There is hardly a town of some extent in New England, the historical events of which have not been recorded in some work, particularly written for that purpose, or in centennial sermons, lectures or notices garnered up in the collections of their historical societies. Nor will it appear less surprising that no State of the Union, not even the youngest, is without some American literary production, partially or totally devoted to its geography or history. Little, however, is known abroad of this part of literature, and often not much more is known of it at home, a fact which may be easily accounted for. For, when we consider that American activity has found full employment in developing and regulating the wealth of such extensive territories; when we see how gloriously that mission has been fulfilled, and look at the flourishing towns and cities, and at the constant growth of agriculture, trade and commerce; when we perceive, how regions, which twenty years ago were only trodden by some Indian trader, or some hardy pioneer of science, are now already encompassed within the limits of well regulated States; when our admiration is awakened by all what has been done in so short a time for education, and for divine worship, for a speedy and easy intercourse between the different States by a vast set of canals and railroads; when we see everywhere libraries and literary societies multiplying, and the never sleeping public press untired in bringing every kind of ready information to the humble cottage of the poorest laborer; when we take all this together, we can only be astonished, that men, who did so much for their bodily and intellectual welfare, could find sufficient leisure for laying such an ample foundation of national literature, by far the smallest part of which the following repertory will exhibit. . . .

Public libraries, when not restricted to particular sciences, can nowhere be expected to be very complete in the historical part. Still, a highly commendable tendency to pay particular attention to the historical literature of the Union, has in several of the larger libraries led to the happiest results. The libraries of the existing Historical Societies, and especially the rich collections of those at Worcester, Mass., at Boston, and at New York, were more confined to American history. With regard to private libraries exclusively devoted to this branch of literature, particular mention is due to the very extensive collection of the gentleman in Washington City, to whom this repertory has been gratefully dedicated, and to whose kind and liberal promotion of all historical or literary researches more praise is due than words could well express. [The individual referred to here is Peter Force.—ED.]

It is more than probable that an accurate comparison would lead to the result, that from the time of the origin of this republic, more money has been spent in the United States for the formation and supply of libraries, than in any other country in the world; a branch of American activity and generous patriotism but little known abroad, perhaps because even native Americans will, in looking at these libraries in the spirit of impatient emulation, take as a scale the more voluminous but also far older libraries of Europe. If the ever active American liberality has not yet been directed to that really patriotic design of forming as complete a library as possible of writings concerning the history of the whole American continent, it may be hoped that the daily increasing and widely spreading feeling of the high importance of this object may soon lead to the conception of such a plan.

The American Continent, certainly not destined to foster the prejudices and the torpidity which generally press down, or paralyze any further elevation of the nations of the old world, has in the history of the abortive endeavors of Europe to impart to it her political and social miseries, the most effective preservative against enslaving compliance and degrading want of self-respect.

The colonial history of the settlements in America must appear to Americans like the early reminiscences of an independent, self-made man who, having once been an unloved step-child, was in his youth thrown back on his own resources, by the contempt and the privations he experienced, and finds now, upon a retrospect of his past struggles, the best encouragement for the maintenance of his independence, and the surest guarantee against backslidings. The history of their own country, which was the first to throw off the yoke of Europe, must fill Americans with a just pride and high sense of the real vocation of the western hemisphere; a vocation which only can be fulfilled by following strictly the policy so clearly pointed out by the best and greatest of the Sons of America, both by precept and example—the policy of keeping entirely independent of European politics, neither interfering with their affairs, nor allowing them to interfere in any way with those of the United States.

The United States, being the first of the republics of America, must have an incontestible interest in the fate of a continent, over which they are to spread the blessings of liberty; and to them it would prove, therefore, a highly creditable and patriotic undertaking, to collect in a particular library all the notices and facts recorded in the historical literature of this continent. They should not allow foreigners to anticipate them in such an undertaking, which will prove in future times of still higher importance as well as interest, than at present. The old objections, that there was no taste for literary pursuits of that kind in the United States, that hands would prove a better support of true democracy than papers, and that facts are wanted, not books, are now antiquated, and can no longer be taken as the true principle of a nation which has done already so much for its intellectual interests.

The spirit of genuine national and political economy, assisted by the blessings of a free constitution, has long shown to the citizens of the United States what position is due to material as well as to intellectual productions and interests; and a nation, which soon became convinced that it is given to intellectual power alone to reconcile the differences which in Europe have become so threatening under a state of pauperism, and which can no longer be peaceably endured by the side of the monopolies of the higher classes, will certainly be disposed to extend protection to every scientific undertaking which tends to throw a greater light upon the history of their happy country, and to renew the memory of the noble deeds of their forefathers.

May the following repertory, as far as possible, facilitate the foundation of such an American Historical Library; and may it prove useful to further researches into the history of a country, which every one must love, who knows how to understand it!

PART III

The Nature of Local History

Here the vigorous local interest that is sometimes channeled into antiquarian backwaters can join deep historical currents.

—Theodore C. Blegan, *Grass Roots History*

Chapter Seven

The Value of Local History

Introduction

Lewis Mumford was born in 1895 in Flushing, New York. He died in 1990 at the age of ninety-four. He is the author of a long list of books, including *The Culture of Cities*, which was published in 1938 when he was forty-three. From that time on, Mumford wrote about city planning, city growth, and the importance of cities. In 1982, the first volume of his autobiography, *Sketches from Life*, appeared.

In "The Value of Local History," delivered at Troutbeck, New York, on September 15, 1926, Mumford discusses the appeal of local history and its impor-tance in contributing to a knowledge of American life in general. He states that "local history implies the history of larger communities to a much greater extent than national history implies the local community." Yet, local history does not exist only to inform national history, or to provide the national story with interesting anecdotes to prove a larger point. Local history, Mumford insists, is the way to make real, to make important, the teaching of general history to schoolchildren. "The facts of local history," Mumford writes, "become parts of a person's own life," and local history, he reminds us, is everywhere.

This essay is reprinted from pages 22–26 of the Dutchess County [N.Y.] Historical Society *Year Book* 12, published in 1927.

* * * *

All of us feel, at bottom, with Walt Whitman, that there is no sweeter meat than that which clings to our own bones. It is this conviction that gives value to local history: we feel that our own lives, the lives of our ancestors and neighbors, the events that have taken place in the particular locality where we have settled, are

---

Lewis Mumford, "The Value of Local History," *Year Book* 12 (Poughkeepsie, NY: Dutchess County Historical Society, 1927), 22–26.

every bit as important as the lives of people who are more remote from us, no matter how numerous these others may be; or how insignificant we may seem alongside of them.

People who live in great cities are accustomed to identify themselves with the whole nation; for the Londoner, London is the British Empire; and for the New Yorker, New York is the United States. A great deal of our national history is written upon the assumption that nothing interesting or important has taken place in the country which did not, as it were, pass through Washington, by coming under public debate, or by being enacted into a law. If wars, political elections, and laws were all that history consisted of there would be some truth, perhaps, in these habits and beliefs; but ever since Green wrote his history of the English people, we have come, slowly, to see that the main subject of history is the drama of a community's life—that is, in what manner and to what purpose people have lived: what did they eat, how did they dress, at what did they work, what kind of houses had they to shelter their heads, what ideas and beliefs had they to fill their heads?

At present, it is almost impossible to write national history along these lines; for people's lives and habits differ from region to region; and we must know a great deal more than we do about each separate region, with all its intimate characteristics and peculiarities, before we can even begin to work this up into a single picture. In providing the materials for this new kind of history, the older parts of the country are in a more fortunate position than the newer ones: in New England, for example, the local historian has been busy since the early part of the nineteenth century, and as a result of the great mass of materials local historical societies and local archaeologists have dug up, New England can boast such classic regional histories as Weeden's *Economic and Social History of New England* or S. E. Morrison's *Maritime History of Massachusetts*, or Messrs. Cousins and Riley's complete description of Salem architecture. The first two of these books are models for regional histories in the grand style; and they have the great merit of showing immense interest and significance of local life in all its various details—details which the national historian is compelled to gloss over or neglect entirely when he is trying to treat as a single unit all the regional communities between the Atlantic and the Pacific Ocean.

Dutchess County has a past that is in some ways little poorer than New England's. In Dutchess County two different streams of civilization, the landholding and trading civilization of the Dutch, and the more firmly knit and communal civilization of the Puritans came together and mingled. Dutchess County is historically what the geographer would call an area of transition: in a small way it has been in the position of the Paris Basin, let us say, where two different traditions, the North and the South, came together. The gain and the loss that took place in this mingling and exchange show themselves very plainly in the architecture of the surviving houses, and in the layout of the villages. The patient Dutchman, used to building in solid brick in the old country, took every opportunity to build with stone or brick in his new home: the old Church at Fishkill or the Winegar House on the road to Amenia Union from Leedsville, are examples of his sturdy architecture. When the New Englander came as a separate individual into these new parts of the country, instead of coming as a member of a municipal corporation, he neglected to bring along the Common: and the absence of the common, or its reduction to a mere strip, as at Pawling, was a serious loss to the life of the Dutchess County villages. One who knows the early history of this region does not need the frontier marker to tell him that Sharon is in Connecticut and Amenia is in New York: the layout of the villages tells the whole story.

To come a little closer home, the mingling of the Dutch, English, and Huguenot strains is witnessed in almost every stone and every bit of history connected with Troutbeck. The Delamater Cottage reminds us of the numerous French Protestant names that were scattered about the early colony: the Century Lodge is an excellent example of the Dutch tradition in American country architecture, while down the Leedsville Road are a pair of houses, one of them bearing the repainted date 1837, which shows the penetration of the English influence, with the formality of a Palladian window, looking down upon the tight little Dutch stoop, built with the Dutchman's steady eye to comfort and convenience, let fashion be what it may. Just as the naturalist can reconstruct a whole animal from the few bones he may find in an old gravel pit, so the historian could reconstruct a large part of the history of the whole country, with no more to guide him than the existing names, places, houses, legends, and histories that have to do with so small a part of Dutchess County as the Amenia township. Local history implies the history of larger communities to a much greater extent than national history implies the local community. Every great event sweeps over the country like a wave; but it leaves its deposit behind in the life of the locality; and meanwhile that life goes on, with its own special history, its own special interests.

To follow even the life of a single family, like the Bentons, who worked over the land and the landscape of Troutbeck, is to see in a fresh and more intimate light events which are merely names and dates, not living experiences, when they are focussed at a long distance in an ordinary history book. Local history shows us the Bentons tilling the land around Troutbeck for upward of a century; it shows them helping to establish a woolen mill during the years when the Napoleonic Wars and the Embargo Act cut off the English supply of woolens; it shows them helping to project the Sharon to New York Canal, as men throughout the state were projecting imaginary canals when the success of the Erie was demonstrated; the minutes of an Amenia Literary Society show a young Benton suggesting names for the streets of the future metropolis of Amenia; it shows Myron Benton listening to the distant voice of Whitman, and corresponding with Thoreau, whose last letter was addressed to him; it shows another Benton going into the Civil War, and living to write about it in a vivid and veracious book. I am merely using Troutbeck and the Benton family as examples of a hundred other equally interesting histories: to preserve these histories and to understand them is an important and indispensable step to understanding what was going on in the country at large.

Because local history is relatively accessible and immediate; because it deals with the concrete and the commonplace, it is what is necessary to vitalize the teaching of general history to the child at school, to say nothing of more mature students. The things that we can see and touch are those that awaken our imagination. Gibbon suddenly felt the Decline and Fall of Rome as he sat amid the ruined stones of the Forum; and nothing has ever made me, for one, feel the might of the Roman empire more keenly than stumbling across the tiles and foundation of a Roman villa in the midst of a quiet English field. Local history touches off these things that have happened on the spot; and the facts of local become parts of a person's own life to an extent which is rare with scenes and incidents one has taken solely out of books and secondhand accounts. To learn about the Indians who once lived in America, and not to pick out the Indian place-names on the map or to dig up the arrowheads that still remain here; to learn about the Dutch and the Puritan settlers and not follow the place-names and the family names creeping up and down the Dutchess County countryside; to learn about the Revolutionary War and not be able to recognize at sight the houses that survive from that period, or to be able to locate the mines and forges which supplied the soldiers with muskets and swords and ammunition; to learn about the commercial growth of the United States after the Civil War and not to know that the first school of business was started upon in Poughkeepsie just before the conflict broke out, and was overrun with pupils by the end of it—in short, to learn the abstractions of history and never to observe the concrete reality is to throw away local bread under the impression that imported stones are more nourishing.

Every old part of the country is filled with the memorials of our past; tombstones and cottages and churches, names and legends, old roads and trails and abandoned mines, as well as the things we built and used yesterday. All these memorials bring us closer to the past; and, so doing, they bring us closer to our own present; for we are living history as well as recording it; and our memories are as necessary as our anticipations. Communities seem to differ from individuals in this respect, that their expectation of life grows, the older they become: the more history lies in back of them, the more confident we are that more will lie in front. A good past is a guarantee of a good future; and to preserve the records of what came before us promotes that sense of continuity which gives us the faith to continue our own work, with the expectation that our descendants will find it equally interesting.

Local history is a sort of benchmark to which all more generalized and specialized kinds of history must come back to, for verification, as a point of reference. The value of local history for stimulating the imagination and giving the student something concrete and accessible to work upon has been recognized in the best English school; and it is beginning to take root in America, as well. At King's

Langley and at Saffron Walden in England one group of children after another has contributed material to a little museum of local history. If nothing of this sort exists in Dutchess County, the local historical society members might well look into the possibilities of using their local material, and it remains for enterprising teachers of history to turn it to their special advantage. The point is that history begins at home, inevitably; but it does not end there. With local history as a starting point the student is drawn into a whole host of relationships that lead him into the world at large: the whaling ships that used to cast anchor at Poughkeepsie and other river towns will carry him to the South Seas; the discovery of the Hudson will take him back to the Crusades; once one begins to follow the threads of local history, local manners, local industry, local peoples, one finds that they lead in every direction. And that is the proper method. Local history is not a means of exciting false pride in little things or exaggerated pretensions to local virtues that do not exist: on the contrary, it promotes to a decent self-respect: it is that form of self-knowledge which is the beginning of sound knowledge about anyone else. Just as the story of every one's life would make at least one novel, so the story of any community's life would make at least one history. To know that history and to take pleasure in it is the beginning of that sympathy with remote times and foreign peoples which tends to make one truly a man of the world.

Chapter Eight

The Value of Local History

Introduction

Born in 1897, Constance McLaughlin Green grew up in an academic family. She was writing urban history before that field was clearly identified, and she was a historian at a time when there were few other women professionals. She is known for her history of Holyoke, Massachusetts, her study of Naugatuck, Connecticut, and especially for her Pulitzer Prize-winning history of Washington D.C., which included a volume called *The Secret City* about the capital's African American population.

Constance McLaughlin Green promotes the writing of American history from the bottom up. Local history should be of value not only to the locality, for the examination of local materials, Green claims, is needed for a more complete understanding of American cultural history. Green calls for local studies that explore a number of topics, many not previously associated with local history. She would like to see investigation of the conditions of labor, the culture of working people, the accumulation of capital, business leadership, mobility, nondominant groups, the influence of environment, and the differences and similarities found in a geographic area. She also proposes studies that plot regional differences.

This important essay is as timely today as when it was originally published. It is reprinted from *The Cultural Approach to History*, edited by Caroline F. Ware (New York: Columbia University Press, 1940), 275–86.

* * * *

For any true understanding of American cultural development, the writing and study of American local history is of primary importance. There lie the grass roots

Constance McLaughlin Green, "The Value of Local History," in Caroline F. Ware, *The Cultural Approach to History* (New York: Columbia University Press, 1940), 275–86.

of American civilization. Because of our varied population stocks and their sharply differentiated cultural inheritances, the widely differing environments which the United States includes, and the rapidity of changes in our economic life, the problems confronting the social historian assume mighty proportions. American history in the past has been written from the top down, an approach feasible enough as long as scholars were content to write only political and diplomatic history. But the necessity of studying American life from the bottom up becomes obvious for the cultural historian. The story of how American people have lived as individuals and as communities must be told by details.

It is evident that detailed material may be assembled in various categories by various schemes. Data extracted from a specific locality are clearly local materials, but they may be used for a topical study which includes a number of separate communities. For example, a compilation of school laws and their educational effects in many widely scattered towns and cities may be multiplied until the historian has at hand the basic materials for generalization upon American education of a given era. Again, a study of one aspect of life in a particular community must employ local sources, as in the examination of the race relationships of a southern town, past and present. Still there remains the use of local materials for the study of a specific community in its entirety.

Such a study—local history simon pure—becomes the life history of a community. The student, using the local materials, sets himself the task of following out all the significant factors in the community's history and evaluating their relative importance. Confined within a frame imposed by geographic or jurisdictional limits, his study may be a complete social and economic history in miniature. In the focusing upon one locality, local historical research may make a peculiar contribution to American cultural history.

Obviously "locality" may be interpreted with considerable elasticity. Any community having clear geographic or cultural unity, however extensive in area, may come within the terms of any reasonable definition. Demarcation by political jurisdiction can be regarded as an accident growing out of a fundamental geographic and economic unity, although it is true that political administrative unity, once established, tends to exert an enduring cohesive influence which affects cultural evolution. The unit may be a scattered agrarian community—a county in Georgia, even the Great Plains of Webb's illuminating book—or a concentrated urban group, a region or a colony within a city. Not only a history of Chicago but a history of Greenwich Village within New York City comprises local history.

More thorough examination of local materials, whether directed at separate community life histories or at wider topical studies, is needed for adequate American cultural history. Our social history, as written to date, has been inaccurate in detail and lacking in pattern because generalizations have been based upon insufficient evidence and criteria. For example, it has been assumed that the West has been peopled by the push from the East. Immigrants, even peasants eager to take up farms in the Middle West and the Great Plains, have been supposed to have landed at Ellis Island and to have moved thence westward. Local studies indicate that numbers entered the port of New Orleans and headed north and west from there. Similarly, much of western New England was invaded direct from the Connecticut River and Connecticut ports, sometimes via Boston, sometimes not. Again, careful local studies in Kansas demolish the whole frontier population-movement thesis. A study of Cincinnati, in course of preparation by Daniel Aarons, suggests that the universal religious piety of America of one hundred years ago, as described by historians, is a myth.

In the field of American economic history there are many topics upon which specific information is badly needed to supply data for generalization. Since ours has become largely an industrial civilization, problems of the relations of capital and labor are manifestly important in their bearing upon American culture. We need local studies of conditions of labor and changes in the social status and attitudes of work people; exact histories of capital accumulation in various communities; the emergence of varying types of business leadership; careful analyses of the growth of that vague entity we call the American middle class; detailed examination of population movements from one community to another, whereby might be found surer clues to the whys and hows of labor migration. Without a number of thoroughgoing studies of individual localities, generalization upon these subjects must remain mostly guesswork. The inadequacy of business history has been recognized by scholars of late. Recently this situation has been partly corrected by detailed attention to individual business firms, but local histories of business communities must prove invaluable in meeting this want more fully.

Still more striking is the gap in our knowledge of the cultural role of the "statistically numerous, nondominant groups." The cultural historian early becomes aware of the difficulty of gauging the attitudes and influence, even the behavior, of the great mass of the inarticulate in America. Even the best local studies to date have contributed little there. Students of American life have sensed the weight of these groups, but an evaluation of their importance and effect upon cultural development has scarcely been attempted. Anthropological studies such as Hortense Powdermaker's *After Freedom*[1] may indicate the way and offer useful material for interpreting the present. But the problem of reconstructing and understanding the vanished past, of which few specific written records exist, is even harder. Class antagonisms, religious rivalries, emergence of a sense of social responsibility are admittedly essential elements in cultural evolution. Yet about these questions the most rigorously selected Gallup poll of the nation could elicit little valid information, since responses inevitably would derive from the articulate groups only. Hence the wisdom of localizing studies, seeking to cope with such tenuous and fragmentary data as must suffice for the interpretation of the way of life and modes of thought of persons who rarely wrote letters and whose opinions have found scant expression in the press. Cultural history may not ignore these people. Careful collecting of scraps of evidence about them by the local historian would appear to be the surest means of viewing the character and significance of their part in the American scene.

Many of the topics listed in early paragraphs can be dealt with by the use of local materials without any special community focus. But for the effective interpretation of data dealing with the fugitive, evanescent stuff of the nondominant, inarticulate groups, the historian must consider the local setting with attention. Certainly by marking out a particular community for study, the probability of his achieving accuracy in depicting behavior and in gauging influence is greatly increased. Furthermore, I suspect that it is upon the mass of the inarticulate in American society that effects of environment are likely to be most marked. And to trace the influence of environment, natural and cultural, it is virtually essential to have a definite locality under the historian's microscope.

What are the peculiarities of environment which appear to impose a behavior pattern upon the people of one community differing from that of another? Why or wherein does a lumbering town in Maine differ from lumbering town in the state of Washington? What makes a farming district in Iowa a contrast to one in Mississippi, a Waterbury, Connecticut, distinct from a Detroit and a Flint? Is the principal differentiating factor the difference in nationality stock, or the diversity or homogeneity of the population, the age or youth of the settlement, the accessibility to or remoteness from other communities? What are the effects of disparities of soil and weather conditions? The social historian must seek more than true pictures of American life as it has been; he must endeavor to explain the process, why it took those forms, what the directing forces were. Analysis of the natural and cultural environments of many communities, examined locality by locality, can best answer these questions with any certainty.

But emphasis upon local differences can induce confusion rather than clarity of any view of the whole of American cultural history. Multiply the number of studies in which differences are stressed, and the result might well be merely greater difficulty in finding any broad pattern for the whole. We must also seek similarities. We need to establish categories of communities, classified probably by general region and then by type within each. Perhaps the Turner sectional thesis may be usefully applied. May we not assume some fundamental geographical unity for each section of the United States? A tentative plotting of regions should be helpful, with a number of studies projected in each. As such studies progress, it might happen that some of the regions would be shown to have been falsely plotted. A shift would then have to be made. For example, one might project a local study in Maine as part of the industrial New England section, only to find that it belonged more nearly in the category of agrarian Michigan. The analysis of why that situation obtained might be illuminating.

In each region the various types of community should be studied, the agrarian areas, the agricultural market towns, the transshipping depots and commercial communities, the manufacturing cities, the lesser financial centers and the true metropolis of each section, mining towns, college towns as centers of intellectual life, perhaps artists' colonies, suburban communities, summer resorts. Possibly even trailer camps, as manifestations of the nonlocalized elements of American society, should be included. The fact that one locality could be characterized as belonging in several of these categories at one and the same time might prove provocative of valuable investigation. Certainly the rise of semi-industrial, semiagricultural communities, whether of the type of Henry Ford's vision or other, suggests a trend demanding study. Series of such local studies, compiled region by region, should furnish means of estimating the validity of the sectional thesis. And meanwhile such tentative classification should be a useful guide to the student of any individual locality.

For some vision of the relation of the local fragment to the whole, regional, national, or world-wide, is essential, if the local historian is to make his chronicle significant. American local history as written in the past has been so exclusively localized as to appear to have no meaning for any community but one. American town and county histories are legion. Scarcely a village founded over seventy years ago but has its own local chronicle. But self-glorification or antiquarianism, or both, have dominated their pages. The lack of perspective, the inability to see his own town as part of a larger community, has often made the local biographer's labors nearly sterile. Determination to paint his home town as a Garden of Eden, to enlarge upon the virtues of its leading citizens, and to portray its achievements as unparalleled, has rendered his work unsound and generally dull. The antiquarian's history, on the other hand, may be exhaustingly accurate in its detail, but the conclusions he derives from his lengthy factual compilation, if indeed he attempt any, seem lacking in any importance. Still, to the antiquarian's industry and enthusiasm the scholar with wider vision may be deeply indebted. While the genealogical tables and minutiae of property transfers as listed by the antiquarian, or his accounts of minor local episodes may in themselves be meaningless, from that detailed factual array the historian, gifted with perspective, may evolve a significant story. For example, genealogical tables, linked to data relating to occupation, activity, wealth, and participation of persons listed, should prove invaluable in following out the concentration or dispersion of capital in a community and in tracing the development of prestige groups. Detailed accounts of real-estate transfers might give clues to the emergence of special vested interests and serve to show that the venturesome, risk-taking pioneer business man, dear to American tradition, was rather a cautious soul whose shrewdness consisted only of gambling on a sure thing, a rise in land values. The antiquarian's findings supply the raw materials which, digested and presented in connection with other data as part of a pattern, can tell a story of deep social import.

The historian who aspires to write local history from the broader point of view must supplement the antiquarian sources with a great variety of other materials. He may well employ field-study techniques, as worked out by the sociologists. Inasmuch as the historian, in contrast to the cultural anthropologist, must be concerned less with the immediate present than with the developments of the past out of which the present grew, one particularly useful borrowed device may be the questionnaire, or interview, directed at some three different age levels. The social historian then has spread before him the reflection of the changes of attitudes of nearly one hundred years. Derived from one locality, where natural environment can be assumed to be identical for all, such information may reveal the effects of the time factor. Unlike political history, cultural history is less a chronicle of deeds and misdeeds than a survey of human feelings and attitudes of mind and inter-relationships. Personalities are of its very essence. The interpretation of these demands personal contacts. And, let me repeat, a definite setting for persons as part of the community in which they live makes that interpretation easier and surer.

For locating documentary evidence, the quantities of records being listed and described by Works Projects Administration workers on the Historical Records Survey will be of enormous assistance to the local historian. Specific methods of finding and evaluating additional local materials must be evolved by the ingenuity and common sense of the research worker. Careful map-making of the locality may reveal graphically startling truths. Assisted by the town directory—particularly if occupational data are included—and aided by lists of assessors' valuations and lists of directorates of local enterprises, the student can readily plot out a map of his community which will be thought-provoking. The juxtaposition of facts not before observed in any close connection, geographic or otherwise, should indicate further lines of inquiry. This method of finding and using material, possible to employ in a study of only one specific community at a time, emphasizes again the value for social history of a local focus. Other kinds of information are sometimes turned up in unexpected places. Travel books may offer interesting comparisons between one city and another and point the way to significant relationships. Not only news items and comment in the local press but changing types of advertisement over a span of years may bring to light facts and tendencies not easily observable elsewhere. Even the kinds of patent-medicine advertisement and the matrimonial-bureau notices might give clues to the habits of thought of a bygone generation. Collections of sermons, showing changes of theme over a period of years, the lists of acquisitions for the public library year by year for several decades, if such lists have been preserved, lists of membership of social clubs and fraternal organizations—these are merely a few of the sources which the alert local historian may tap.

The obstacles in the path of the student of local history in his search for material are, however, frequently disheartening. They may be those of the historian in any field: lack of evidence upon particular subjects, inaccessibility of material, opportunity to secure only data obviously unreliable, not representative, or irrelevant. But the special difficulties which the local historian encounters are born of the local character of his inquiry.

The first of these peculiar problems grows out of public indifference to his undertaking. Much of his material is likely to be in private hands. But who cares about the sources of the familiar local scene? Everyone knows about that. We threw out Grandfather's papers twenty years ago; they were a nuisance. Homely things are too close to be of interest. It seems unnecessary to give the research worker either full or especially accurate information. A little free advertising certainly, only let it be calculated to portray the family and the community in the most favorable light! There is likely to be a certain unconscious condescension on the part of local residents in dealing with the seeker for local historical light. He is marked as a person of little importance in the scholarly world. Else why should he concern himself with such trivia as this local story? Scholars write about the fall of the Roman Empire or the history of slavery or the theater in Shakespeare's time. Ergo, let's turn off this inquirer with the suggestion that he look in the public library.

Paradoxically, the local historian next confronts the antipodal difficulty of being at the mercy of the town wiseacres, who are convinced that Podunk is vitally important and that all that is significant in its history is at their tongues' tips or to be found among their family papers. And the result may be distortion for the historian, in spite of his best efforts not to be deceived. By way of illustration: when the Federal writers were collecting data for one of the state guide books, in one town the research man was frostily received by local leaders; only one small industrialist was at pains to be informing to the WPA writer. When the guide book appeared, the rest of the town's business men discovered with a shock of annoyance that their own town was described as having only one important industrial enterprise, the establishment of the genial host who had talked so graciously to the writer.

Along with obstacles arising from public indifference and misconceptions are perhaps even greater ones growing out of fear. Dead men tell no tales, and locked records reveal no unsavory secrets, no facts open to misinterpretation. Particularly does this point of view prevail among prestige groups, notably among business leaders. The business man has felt himself the special quarry of the academic and of reformers. In an endeavor to trace the growth of capital in a community, the student perhaps seeks access to corporation books which show the capital setups over a period of years. Not infrequently his request will be refused. The heads of the companies may explain: "Doubtless you as a scholar would be fair. If you found that for years we had paid stockholders 10 percent in dividends and that yearly we put back 25 percent of earnings into upkeep and expansion, you might not accuse us of greed. But how do we know that someone else wouldn't pounce on such facts in your book and cry, 'Bloodsuckers! Those profits should have been paid out in wages'? It is too risky." Evidence which might be used in derogation of business men as a class, even of the business pioneer of three or four generations ago, must be suppressed, lest it prove subversive of the social order. To combat that attitude is as necessary as it is difficult. Again, fear may close the mouths of the individuals best qualified to give information. Their jobs or their standing in the community they may feel to be jeopardized by revelations. No promise of anonymity will induce them to speak. The smaller the community the more likely are such personal apprehensions to exist.

Yet in spite of the probable closing of some avenues of inquiry, the local historian is only too likely to be overwhelmed by the mass of material available to him. We have the advantage over the European local historian in that rarely, if ever, are the origins of an American community so remote that patience will not suffice to produce fairly clear evidence of its beginnings. Gaps in the sources for the earlier periods there often are, and in later periods data may be so hidden as to prove difficult of access. More often, however, the problem of sources becomes one of choosing the significant. For the American local historian the chief problems consist of weaving together into meaningful pattern the numberless strands that go to make up an American community. How is the student to sift out the essential? Familiarity with the characteristics of the category into which his locality may be expected to fit gives him at once some basis of selection. A series of questions of why and how, as well as whence, must be perpetually before him. In using the answers he may work out, he must constantly ask himself: "So what?" It is wise to stress this point to the novice in local historical research—and here most of us are still novices —since more than in most fields the multiplicity of petty detail may easily obscure any larger vision. Why did Mechanicsville specialize in tool manufacture when a village ten miles downstream remained a dairy center—geographic factors, personality forces, accident?

In examining materials and presenting findings, recourse to the sampling method should be useful. The futility of trying to study in detail all the institutions, movements, and trends in a community seems self-evident. Which appear to conform to the pattern of the general classification the investigator experimentally assumes? Which run counter to the type? Judicious selection from the mass may be determined by the existence of comparable material in another community, although unhappily the paucity of competent local histories makes the employment of the comparative method today enormously difficult. Only by comparison are the uniquenesses born of environment or of heredity to be seen. What are the features that are peculiar to any one community? What are shared by its neighbors? How significant is the unique, and what special circumstances created that uniqueness? If so, why? What is the unifying core? Sampling, however, may well be used without comparisons with another locality. The student will find it reasonable to restrict his analysis to the three or four churches that have obviously determined the religious atmosphere of his town, as he may then infer why other groups withered away. He may confine his investigation to the most vigorous of the local industries instead of attempting to study all, and within the principal industries he may trace the course not of all the companies but of the strongest, the weakest, those nearest the middle. Let him also, however, heed the failures, the ventures which proved ill-adapted to his town. For him as a historian, study of the nonsuccesses may be as important as examination of the successful dominant. In part, his intuition must guide him in his selection of materials and in his relative emphasis in presentation. He must be sufficiently part of the community he is scrutinizing to be able to understand what has importance and meaning for its citizens and why. Perception of the values that obtain in his community should serve as a guide.

Indeed some feeling of oneness with the community of which he writes, some sympathetic comprehension of its attitudes, is probably an essential factor in writing sound local history. Many an unjustly hostile twist can be given to facts viewed by an alien observer. Local historians should write not only for the initiate and for the compiler of general history, they should also write for the local public. For "a knowledge of its own past is essential for any community to achieve cultural adulthood." History for the historian alone would be like law for the lawyers or the church for churchmen. If historians are to continue to pose as teachers, they must consider who is worthy of teaching. As citizens of a democracy, can they afford to disregard their neighbors in order to speak only to Lowells and Cabots?

Grant that the historian should give local citizens opportunity to gauge the part their community has played in the national drama; grant that justified local pride, coupled with critical judgment of a community by its own citizens, is a socially constructive force; nevertheless, since the local public will not read drearily written, dry history even of its own past, must the scholar lower himself to the level of the public mind? In answering this query, we may well quote the late Ulrich B. Phillips, "There is no law against having history interesting." The popular and the scholarly are not necessarily incompatible, although for wide popularity the writer must doubtless stress the colorful. And it is only when the community is aware of the interest and value of its local history that it will cooperate intelligently in making accessible the sources of that history. Such cooperation is frequently all-important. The public may find much of the truth about its past unpalatable, but it must also find such rough fare more nourishing than the sweet adulteration often dished up by the untrained enthusiast, to whom American local historical writing has been largely relegated.

The professional historian's disdain of the nonprofessional has not been conducive to the writing of better local history. Today the outstanding achievements of Works Projects Administration writers and workers on the Historical Records Survey should show the feasibility of enlisting the aid of the professionally untrained. But wider professional recognition of the importance of the field of local history is also needed. In writing cultural history, local historical research must take rank as a basic discipline.

NOTES

1. Hortense Powdermaker, *After Freedom: A Cultural Study in the Deep South* (New York, 1939).

DAVID E. KYVIG ■
MYRON A. MARTY

Chapter Nine

Nearby History:
Connecting Particulars and Universals

Introduction

David Kyvig and Myron Marty are the authors of *Nearby History: Exploring the Past around You* (1982) and coeditors of "The Nearby History Series," published by AltaMira Press. David Kyvig is professor of history at the University of Akron in Ohio; Myron Marty is dean of Arts and Sciences at Drake University in Des Moines, Iowa.

Written for teachers of history, this essay insists on connecting events, causes, people, and places when teaching or writing history. Whereas current students might find history irrelevant, community members disagree—and in great numbers explore family, organizational, and community history.

The authors use the term "nearby history" to avoid what they consider are negative connotations connected to the expression local history; yet it is local history that has been revitalized in the United States during the past few years. In this essay the authors offer a list of books, some of which are local history, as well as academic monographs that have somewhat greater scope than what is usually found in local history. Although the word "student" is used throughout the essay, the authors are speaking, as well, to local historians and to others interested in local history.

The essay, "Nearby History: Connecting Particulars and Universals," is reprinted from *Teaching History: A Journal of Methods* 8(1) (Spring 1983): 3–10, by permission.

David E. Kyvig and Myron A. Marty, "Nearby History: Connecting Particulars and Universals," *Teaching History: A Journal of Methods* 8(1) (Spring 1983): 3–10.

* * * *

To look for meaning in history is to look for connections. We find meaning when we see connections between one occurrence and another; between people and places; between causes and consequences; between past, present, and future. As we begin to perceive connections becoming more abundant and weaving together, we discern patterns, trends, or movements. To understand history, then, is to have a feel for the connectedness of things.

Novelist Wright Morris uses the idea of connections in recalling his childhood:

> There's a story in the family, on my mother's side, that my Grandmother Osborn started west with her man, her Bible, and her cane-seated rocking chair. As things got bad she had to give up both her man and her Bible, and to keep from freezing to death she had to burn the chair. But first she unraveled the cane-bottom seat. She wrapped it around her waist, and when she got to where she was going she unwrapped it, put it in a new chair. Her kids grew up with their bottoms on it. The cane seat was the connection with all of the things, for one reason or another, she had to leave behind. Which is what these women were doing with me now. They were putting a cane seat, an approved one, in my bottomless chair. Making the connection. The rest would follow, naturally.[1]

As historians and teachers of history, we are in the business of making connections. It comes naturally to us. Wherever we go, we sit on chairs with cane-bottom seats. Indeed, it is our inclination to take a connected, all-encompassing view of human existence which distinguishes us from those who focus on one or another of its social, economic, political, psychological, cultural, physical, or other dimensions. We often employ their specific techniques; but while they concentrate on single elements, we seek the connections to others.

Not so with students. Connection-making of the sort practiced in most classrooms neither occurs nor appeals to them. It may well be, as Ronald Butchart argued in a 1979 article in *Teaching History*, that students are not simply bored with history as conventionally taught, but that they are fundamentally alienated from it.[2] In our consumer-oriented, materialistic culture, the past has no apparent importance. They see no material benefits to be gained from its study. Consequently, they feel no pain in being cut off from it.

Contrast this alienation with the out-of-school population's apparent fascination with the past. Widespread interest in family history, which preceded as well as followed the appearance of [Alex] Haley's Comet, has taxed the energies and patience of archivists. The history of buildings, neighborhoods, organizations, and communities attracts growing attention. The whole nearby world appears to be of interest. Part of the concern for history shared by older persons is no doubt attributable to the fact that having lived a little helps them know how to make connections, to perceive relationships, to sort out the relevant and significant from the irrelevant and insignificant. But do younger persons have an inherent curiosity about the past—expressed in questions like: "Where did I come from?" and "What was it like when you were little?"—that is being stifled? Do those who teach the young neglect laying the groundwork for connection-making because they fail to start with people and places that are at hand, close-by? Possibly they lack interest, or perhaps they do not understand how to proceed?

Consider this: at the 1981 meeting of the Organization of American Historians in Detroit, three neighborhood history projects were described by those involved in them. They were all excellent projects, helpful in understanding small communities—their celebrations, their activities in preservation and rehabilitation, and the relationships between the economic, cultural, and political benefits of these activities. None of the three speakers [had been] trained as a historian. Rather, they were trained in romance languages, librarianship, and fine arts; they were learning research methods in history on their own because they were interested. Fewer than a dozen professional historians attended the session.

The nearby world is not the only world to be studied in history courses in schools and colleges, nor does studying what is close at hand offer a magic formula for helping students make connections. But the nearby world offers fertile fields for study, which to ignore deprives students of an opportunity to make connections in ways that build historical senses. The term "nearby history" is used here to avoid the negative connotations and limited reach that has attached to other terms. "Local history" has long been a term of academic disparagement used interchangeably with "provincial," "nostalgic," and (worst of all) "antiquarian" in scornful reference to what were perceived as narrow and trivial interests pursued in unsophisticated fashion. Those who investigated this world from within a historical or genealogical society or as an independent venture responded by regarding academics as pedantic, aloof, and out of touch with reality. As well as being unnecessarily divisive, the term "local" or "community history" limits itself to a concept of place. Similarly, "family history" is confined to consideration of relationship, and "material culture" restricts the discussion to objects. "Nearby history" seems to encompass the entire range of possibilities for investigation in a person's immediate environment and to encourage thinking about the connections among the various elements. A course in history that pays no heed to the nearby past is one-sided and incomplete. A comprehensive course is one that finds ways to draw connections between the nearby past and the conventional core of political, economic, and social issues essential to the study of history. To state this position so forthrightly is to raise important issues of legitimacy, practicality, pedagogical soundness, and purpose. They should be considered one at a time.

Is the study of the nearby past a legitimate undertaking? Consider how it encompasses a wide range of interests and trends, within the field of history and beyond it. It focuses on the grassroots, on ordinary folks in ordinary walks of life. It looks at the past from the bottom up and the inside out. It offers opportunities, specifically, to pay proper heed to the historical roles of ethnic groups, families, women, and minorities. It goes hand in hand with enthusiasm for studying regional characteristics and examining qualities of distinctiveness. It provides necessary underpinnings to preservation efforts, and it capitalizes on interests in folk arts and crafts. Exploration of the nearby past complements enthusiasm for photography —taking pictures, studying them, and preserving them. Likewise, it offers an outlet for the desire to capture recollections from the past on tape. Studying the nearby past provides opportunities to approach history as stories to be found and retold, on the one hand, and as quantifiable data for analysis and interpretation on the other. It capitalizes on an interest in things, whether they be family antiques or artifacts preserved under glass in museums. It fits nicely with the desire of nonschool, nonacademic historians, museum curators, for example, to play a role in academic instruction in history. And it seizes upon the apparently growing interest in local history among academics. In a sense, it revives the concern for nearby history shown by early generations of academic historians. Surely there is some legitimacy in all this.

Is the study of the nearby past a respectable undertaking? The ways in which historians of good repute have drawn connections between the particulars of the nearby world with the universals of the world out there will be discussed later. It is, perhaps, sufficient to note here that their endeavors have done much to affirm its respectability by enhancing our understanding of both the nearby and the distant, the particular and the universal. But consider something else. The June 1980 *Journal of American History* listed 175 recent doctoral dissertations; among them were at least 26 that seemed clearly to fall into the category of nearby history. When you note that biographies were not counted in this category, this appears to be a substantial number. The June 1981 issue listed 160 dissertations, 33 of them dealing with the nearby past.

Is the study of the nearby past a practical undertaking? What could be more so? It is the past around us. It is there. It contains people and traces of the past that, in most instances, have not been studied to death. If students are puzzled by lectures on revisions of revisionism, think of what it means to them to be the first to study something of specific historical interest to them.

Is the study of the nearby past pedagogically sound? A fundamental pedagogical principle calls upon teachers to take students from the concrete to the conceptual, from the nearby to the more distant, from the particular to the general (and maybe back again). Studying the nearby past offers the first steps to larger and more general undertakings—something historians have known for a century.

Is the study of the nearby past purposeful? Done right, it is indeed. Recall that "history" derives from the same Greek root as "inquiry." Investigating the past of the nearby world trains students in inquiry. They can hardly engage in such inquiry without being clear on why they are doing it. Is it mere curiosity? Why are they curious? To what will their curiosity lead? Do they have a practical purpose in mind? Will their inquiry lead to an end product—a paper, a film, a tape, an illustrated lecture, a collection of papers for an archives or of artifacts for a museum?

As they seek to clarify their purpose, their subject will come into sharper focus. And as this happens students will learn where to turn for information and how to organize their quest for it. Continuing their inquiry, they learn how to use the information they gather. To use it properly, they need to know how to address questions to it. What can they draw out of their sources that will enable them to offer clear, accurate descriptions of their subjects, whether their subjects be people or places or events? Other questions will be aimed at finding ways of measuring change or sameness over time. Still others will seek to analyze causes and consequences. Out of it all, students will begin to discern patterns and peculiarities. They will develop a feel for both the ordinary and the unusual. To do this, of course, they must learn how to treat traces of the past properly; to sort them out, evaluate them, test their credibility and applicability; to compare the message of one trace with another; to reconcile apparently contradictory traces; and so on.

Our responses to the questions raised so far have shown an enthusiasm for nearby history that may be misleading. We are mindful of the warning given by David Gerber in *The History Teacher*: the very temptations and enthusiasms offered by the study of local and community history, he says, "require that we look closely into the nature and consequences of this new trend." An unexamined plunge, he continues, "into the current modes of popular local and community history may have classroom consequences which are, because of their tendency to present students with a false view of themselves and an incomplete view of the past, unproductive and even negative."[3]

In light of Gerber's worry that excessive enthusiasm for doing the history of the nearby world may carry high costs, it must be emphasized that such history, particularly if it is done under the sponsorship of professional historians and teachers of history, should be done well. If it is to have the sanction of schools and colleges, careful and explicit attention ought to be paid to drawing connections between the particulars of history in the world nearest to lives of students and the universals represented in the collective memory of humankind.

Ample evidence exists that such a standard can be attained. Connections between the particulars of the local scene and the universals of collective history have been drawn in some of the most innovative and impressive works of historical scholarship of recent years. They demonstrate the potential for locally focused history to give clarity and elaboration to abstractions. At the same time, they demonstrate that precise and detailed examination of social, economic, and political processes at the local level can spawn new or revised generalizations. In sum, they affirm the assertion of British historian H. P. R. Finberg that family, community, national, and international history are a series of concentric circles, the study of each of which benefits from constant reference to the others.[4]

The broadest themes of concern to historians have been illuminated through the careful examination of local circumstances. The impact of currents of thought on social structure and personal behavior, for instance, received attention in such works as Darrett B. Rutman, *Winthrop's Boston: A Portrait of a Puritan Town, 1630–1649* (Chapel Hill: University of North Carolina Press, 1965) and Paul E. Johnson, *A Shopkeeper's Millennium: Society and Revivals in Rochester, New York, 1815–1837*, (New York: Hill and Wang, 1978). Another transcendent issue, the pattern of mobility—social and economic, geographic and generational—was clarified for the colonial era in Philip J. Greven, Jr., *Four Generations: Population, Land, and Family in Colonial Andover, Massachusetts* (Ithaca: Cornell University Press, 1970). Mobility in a later period received equally enlightening consideration in Stephen Thernstrom's pioneering work, *Poverty and Progress: Social Mobility in a Nineteenth-Century City* (Cambridge: Harvard University Press, 1964) and a host of similar studies, outstanding among which were Peter R. Knights, *The Plain People of Boston, 1830–1860: A Study of City Growth* (New York: Oxford, 1971); Clyde Griffen and Sally Griffen, *Natives and Newcomers: The Ordering of Opportunity in Mid-Nineteenth-Century Poughkeepsie* (Cambridge: Harvard University Press, 1978); and Howard P. Chudacoff, *Mobile Americans: Residential and Social Mobility in Omaha, 1880–1920* (New York: Oxford, 1972).

The study of political leadership, too, has benefitted from close attention to local circumstances. Edward M. Cook, Jr., *The Fathers of the Towns: Leadership and Community Structure in Eighteenth-Century New England* (Baltimore: Johns Hopkins University Press, 1976) and John M. Allswang, *A House for all Peoples: Ethnic Politics in Chicago, 1890–1936* (Lexington: University of Kentucky Press, 1971) reflect the range of possibilities. The effect of international strife on a society is another universal theme that can be dealt with profitably by the investigation of local particulars, as ably demonstrated in Robert A. Gross, *The Minutemen and Their World* (New York: Hill and Wang, 1976).

Themes of universal importance—modernization, industrialization, and urbanization—have been most successfully explained in terms of the evolution of particular communities. The shift from traditional, repetitive, preindustrial society to a modern society with a faith in progress through technology, efficiency, and bureaucracy has been illuminated in such works as Michael H. Frisch, *Town into City: Springfield, Massachusetts, and the Meaning of Community, 1840–1880* (Cambridge: Harvard University Press, 1972). Industrialization and its social effects have become better understood through such works as Thomas Dublin, *Women at Work: The Transformation of Work and Community in Lowell, Massachusetts, 1826–1869* (New York: Columbia University Press, 1979) and Tamara Hareven and Rudolph Langenbach, *Amoskeag: Life and Work in an American Factory City* (New York:

Pantheon, 1978). The complex process of urbanization has been better appreciated as a result of studies like Sam Bass Warner, Jr., *Streetcar Suburbs: The Process of Growth in Boston, 1870–1900* (Cambridge: Harvard University Press, 1962) and Howard L. Preston, *Automobile Age Atlanta: The Making of a Southern Metropolis, 1900–1935* (Athens: University of Georgia Press, 1979).

Ethnicity, the varied experience of different cultural groups, and the clashes between them offer yet another historical universal that benefits from the examination of particulars. Individual ethnic experiences have been revealed in, among others, Kathleen Neils Conzen, *Immigrant Milwaukee, 1836–1860: Accommodation and Community in a Frontier City* (Cambridge: Harvard University Press, 1976); Humbert S. Nelli, *Italians in Chicago, 1880–1930: A Study in Ethnic Mobility* (New York: Oxford, 1970); and John Modell, *The Economics and Politics of Racial Accommodation: The Japanese of Los Angeles, 1900–1942* (Urbana: University of Illinois Press, 1977). Relations among ethnic groups have been illuminated in Ronald H. Bayor, *Neighbors in Conflict: The Irish, Germans, Jews, and Italians of New York City, 1929–41* (Baltimore: John Hopkins University Press, 1978).

The topics of universal applicability and the historical works that use particular localities to explore and clarify them that have been mentioned here represent only a minor fraction of the successful efforts by scholars to enhance general historical understanding through contemplation of the nearby world. Similar connections between particular and universal can be drawn by students. If the product is less grand, perhaps, the intellectual process of linking a tangible reality to a distant abstraction is equally attainable and worthwhile.

To use nearby history effectively in the classroom one must have a clear understanding of one's objectives and appropriate techniques to achieve them. We offer here a set of suggestions, based on our experiences, observations, and conversations with others who have learned by doing, whether to good avail or for naught.

First, we find it helps to begin with the premise that you don't take history to students, you bring it out of them. For us, a good way to arouse student interest has been to use a single piece of evidence, something specific, that relates to the student's past—a document, an artifact, a picture, or possibly a document that he or she constructs out of a recorded interview with a knowledgeable person. We have had success with putting students to work finding out everything they possibly can relating to this single, specific piece of evidence. One student, for example, found a copy of the job application form filled out for his grandmother after the death of her husband when she was a young woman. A recent immigrant from Poland who spoke no English, she faced many obstacles in providing for her family and raising small children. Fascination with her plight drew her grandson into a study of labor conditions, immigration and citizenship laws, and schooling in the 1920s and inspired him to urge his relatives to contribute copies of other interesting documents to a family archive.

Second, we aim at investing students with a sense of context—and that at the very outset, with the single piece of evidence they start with. We think it helps our students to establish the understanding that the "content" of history exists simultaneously with other such content and that one cannot understand one piece of the content apart from the others. Two ideas are critical. First, many things happen at once, involving many people in many places. Simultaneity alone is a relationship, but cause-and-effect relationships are also discernible in simultaneity. And things happen consecutively, there is a continuity to history, events have consequences. To have students grapple with simultaneity and continuity in analyzing a given piece of evidence is a valuable exercise. An assignment we have used for such an exercise has called for students to write the history of a notable but not especially dramatic day in the history of their community, something like the cornerstone-laying for a school or church building, for example. The day draws its significance, students often discover, from the context in which it occurs.

Third, as we move beyond the beginnings, we find it aids students if we insist that they work with different kinds of evidence: the printed word, the spoken word, artifacts, pictures, and so on. We discourage undertakings that rely only, let us say, on tape-recorded interviews. This helps to demonstrate that historical knowledge is shaped from many types of evidence, each with its own values and limitations. A newspaper account of a significant occasion, accompanied by a photograph, can be used to encourage interview responses and to demonstrate the interplay between kinds of historical evidence.

Fourth, we encourage students to seek to tell a story as they carry their research further. This seems to help them find a conceptual framework for their investigation. Such frameworks do not need to be elaborate. Consider the possibilities, we tell them, of this single conceptual scheme for telling the story of a family, an organization, or a community: (1) origins; (2) dynamics; (3) milestones; and (4) character. It is natural to pay attention to origins; doing so compels one to think about people who were in on them, their time, their place, and so on. In examining dynamics, look at what moved the people, how power was held and used, and how decisions were made. Again, people are at the center of the examination. Contemplating milestones means that one considers such things as times of marked change, great occasions, measuring points on the continuum of routine, and turning points. In looking at character one seeks to put a finger on distinctive features that set one's subject apart from others of the same general type. A story told against such a framework will very likely survive critical measurement against a number of important questions: does the story deal with people, both as individuals and in groups? Is it clear on time and space? Are events clearly delineated? Does the story have some ideas packed into it?

Analysis, particularly with concern for change over time, is part, too, of historians' work. We have found it worthwhile to urge students in telling a story, to keep in mind that the past is filled with subtle developments as well as obvious ones. Some matters that are conspicuous at the moment when they occur have sometimes been labeled manifest events. The really significant manifest events are sometimes called epic events. At the same time, there are slight alterations occurring in unspectacular aspects of life, many of which go largely unnoticed by contemporaries but which over a long term represent significant change—shifts in family size or structure, economic patterns, or assimilation of minorities into the dominant culture, for example. Some historians call these latent events. The relationship between manifest and latent events is a central consideration for historians. As Bernard Bailyn has pointed out, "the essence and drama of history lie precisely in the relationship between latent conditions, which set the boundaries of human existence, and the manifest problems with which people consciously struggle."[5] Involving students in the use of composite census data, on the one hand, and the information the census provides about individual families, on the other—perhaps showing them on the move from one state to another and yet another—can give them a sense of these relationships.

Fifth, we find it pays to stress the proper use of traces from the past, the documents, artifacts, memories, and other survivals that can be put to use in forming a historical understanding. Be clear, we tell students, on relationships between the traces and the events or ideas to which they are related. Do not make a trace do more than it is capable of doing, we insist. It seems to help if we explain that traces always need to relate to events in positive and identifiable ways, and that it is unsafe to assume much from the absence of a trace. (Suppose, for example, that a family has a tradition of recording its holiday gatherings with family portraits. A gap in a series of such portraits would not necessarily indicate that no gathering had occurred at the time of the missing portrait.) We try to show students how they can enhance their understanding of one trace by relating it to others. Above all, we strive to teach students that traces do not exist in isolation. A most important question to be faced in the study of history is: how do we know that we know? Careful work with traces, first-hand, helps students raise that question at the proper moments, whether they are reading, researching, or writing history.

Sixth, we consider it important to avoid the negative aspects of what might be called the "science fair syndrome." We believe in involving everyone. We try not to put too much stress on winners or on attractiveness of projects or exhibits they might make. We don't set up the assignments so that only the most able students have the opportunity to engage in the pursuit of the history of the nearby world. Average and below-average students have as great a need as the brightest student to understand the influence of the past on their circumstances.

Done properly, nearby history can reawaken interest in the academic pursuit of history, persuade students of the value of historical study, and inform the search for universals by increasing awareness of particulars. It offers a means, in other words, for making vital connections. That well-known social philosopher Henry Ford acknowledged the value of nearby history, once he outgrew his "history is more or less bunk" phase. He began concentrating his earnest, if not always well-directed, efforts upon preserving and presenting nearby history through his vast collections of artifacts relating to the lives of ordinary folks. At the entrance to Ford's Greenfield Village museum stands a sign with his conclusion, to which we heartily subscribe: "The farther you look back, the farther you can see ahead."

NOTES

1. Wright Morris, *The Home Place* (1948: reprint, Lincoln: University of Nebraska Press, 1968), 59.

2. Ronald E. Butchart, "Pedagogy of the (Less) Oppressed: Second Thoughts on the Crisis in History Teaching," *Teaching History* 4 (Spring 1979): 3–9.

3. David A. Gerber, "Local and Community History: Some Cautionary Remarks on an Idea Whose Time Has Returned," *The History Teacher* 13 (November 1979): 8. Gerber's article, incidentally, includes a valuable review of three waves of interest in local and community history. The first of these he sees as centered in pre-Civil War New England, initiated by native white Protestants to extol the supposed virtues of the world their ancestors had created and to credit that world with giving rise to the Revolution. The second, prompted by the centennial celebrations, responded to dislocations resulting from industrialization, urbanization, and the beginning of an influx of immigrants from southern and eastern Europe. In this second wave, he says, appeared the first generation of academic historians, "Heavily comprised of Anglo- and Germanophiles influenced by germ theories of civilization. It set as its goal the discovery of the distant Anglo-Saxon origins of idealized American institutions." The third wave came with the depression. It celebrated folk themes and folk peoples, quite in contrast to the elitist character of the earlier waves.

4. H. P. R. Finberg, "Local History," in *Local History: Object and Pursuit*, by H. P. R. Finberg and V. H. T. Skipp (Newton Abbott, England: David R. Charles, 1967), 39.

5. Quoted in Michael Kammen, ed., *The Past Before Us: Contemporary Historical Writing in the United States* (Ithaca: Cornell University Press, 1980), 38.

JOHN ALEXANDER WILLIAMS ■

Chapter Ten

State, Local, and Regional Studies

Introduction

John Alexander Williams was born in Texas in 1938 and received his Ph.D. in American history from Yale University. He has taught at the University of West Virginia and is the author of *West Virginia: A Bicentennial History*, in The States and the Nation series published by the American Association for State and Local History. Williams created a course in West Virginia history and served as a program consultant for state and local history at the National Endowment for the Humanities. For a time, he was director of the Christopher Columbus Quincentenary Jubilee Commission in Washington, D.C.; at present Williams is director of the Center for Appalachian Studies at Appalachian State University in Boone, North Carolina.

Williams' essay "State, Local, and Regional Studies" is reprinted from *Humanities*, the magazine of the National Endowment for the Humanities (*Humanities* 1, no. 3 [June 1980]). It contains many references to works of state, local, and regional history. Williams' inclusion of regionality is most important, for local historians often fail to look beyond their immediate home place to the region surrounding it—however "region" is defined. For some local historians, "region" might mean an area within a state where architectural styles are similar, or where foodways are shared; for others, "region" will mean a larger area within which locality and state fit, where people share similarities of thought or expectation. The commonality of life shared with other places is certainly a part of local history.

* * * *

"The American State is a peculiar organism," Lord Bryce wrote; "[it is] unlike anything in modern Europe, or in the ancient world." One peculiarity that Bryce

John Alexander Williams, "State, Local, and Regional Studies," *Humanities* 1(3) (June 1980).

noted in 1888 has continued to shape the perception of the states among both scholarly and popular audiences: the states are older than the federal union, yet they are subordinate to it.

In Bryce's day, it already was apparent that the states were "diminishing quantities" in national affairs, and so it is not surprising that modern scholars have studied the states primarily for what they could tell us about national matters. Political scientists study states as political systems and tend to approach them comparatively (as in Daniel Elazar's *American Federalism*) and empirically (as in Ira Sharkansky's *Regionalism in American Politics*).

Historians tend to take states one at a time, although political historians almost always relegate the name of their state to the subtitle of their book and present findings as case studies that use state data to sample national or regional trends. Lee Benson's *The Concept of Jacksonian Democracy: New York as a Test Case* (1961) is an influential study of this type.

State history also provides a convenient mode of testing the merits of fledgling historians and of new fields of research. Such luminaries as Frederick Jackson Turner, U. B. Phillips, Carl Becker, and Herbert E. Bolton began their careers with state history monographs. Two recent state studies that advance a developing field of research in American history are Rudolph M. Lapp, *Blacks in Gold Rush California* and John Dittmer, *Black Georgia in the Progressive Era, 1900–1920.*

Yet Americans have never been content to regard the states simply as background. Tradition holds that the states are something more than territorial and political subdivisions. They have official or quasi-official identities symbolically linked to heroic ages of colonization, conquest, and the achievement of independence or, in the cases of new states, statehood.

Thus history, as Bryce wrote, provides each state with "a sense of historic growth and indwelling corporate life which they could not have possessed had they been the mere creatures of the federal government." It is a commonplace that the American commonwealths are not only states, but states of mind.

This same sense of identity also provides the basis of public support for an array of institutions dedicated to preserving or interpreting the history of a particular state: libraries, archives, museums, and state and private historical organizations, the oldest of which, it might be added, antedate professional academic training in history by several decades.

These same institutions perpetuate the colonial habit of enclosing a wide array of cultural, historical, and geographic inquiries within the boundaries of a single state. This habit may make little sense to academics who are absorbed in the analysis of national life, but it obviously appeals to a wide public. And it can produce some good books. Case in point: Kenneth and Mary Clarke's *The Harvest and the Reapers: Oral Traditions of Kentucky*, a volume in the University Press of Kentucky's Bicentennial Bookshelf. Writing with remarkable economy, the Clarkes manage to teach us something about Kentucky traditions, about the nature of folklife in general, and about the development of folklife studies as an academic discipline. Other volumes in the series deal with topics as wide-ranging as biography, medicine, moonshine, county government, art, literature, Civil War battles, and mountain feuds.

The States and the Nation series of one-volume short state histories falls within still another tradition—one that attempts to study the whole nation by examining the states individually, *seriatim*. This is a habit that goes back at least to the American Commonwealths series of the 1880s and is represented among journalists by the state-by-state surveys of John Gunther and Neil Pierce. Often compared to the state guidebooks of the Depression-era Federal Writers' Project, The States and the Nation series offers the diversity expected in such undertakings. In the fashion of academic historians, Richard Jensen treats Illinois as a microcosm of national society and politics, as Thomas C. Cochran's *Pennsylvania* does of national economic growth. Joe Frantz's *Texas* is an engaging collection of anecdotes by a master storyteller. Norman Clark's *Washington* deftly interweaves the best and worst traditions in state historiography, using the boosterism and racism of an 1876 centennial oration to counterpoint a thoughtful essay on issues and personalities that have shaped the state as it is today.

* * * *

If there's a book in every person, there's also a book in every place. How good a book depends on the writer. Muncie is famous beyond most cities of its size because the Lynds found "Middletown" there; Montaillou, because Ladurie was able to use the details of existence in this one French village to frame universal questions about medieval life.

Most places are not so lucky. Many writers who are drawn to local history are so overwhelmed by the particulars of their place that they cannot see—or at least cannot communicate—the larger lessons to be learned there. Such writers often create compendia—collections of facts, dates, pictures, and lists of every description —that are useful as a sort of community album. But while this type of local history flatters, it does not teach. It distinguishes no meaningful pattern of existence to help explain a place to its residents, much less to anyone else.

Manchester, New Hampshire, is perhaps the luckiest place of all in terms of recent local historical writing. It is the setting of *Amoskeag: Life and Work in an American Factory City*, by Tamara K. Hareven and Randolph Langenbach. The form of this book is oral history, but its interviews rest upon meticulous archival research in the records of the textile company that, in 1900, employed 14,000 of Manchester's 55,000 people. Hareven has interpreted these same data in a number of technical articles (such as "The Dynamics of Kin in an Industrial Community"), which remind us that, in its sociological quantitative form, local history is one of the frontiers of modern historical scholarship. But few practitioners of "the new social history" have been as sensitive to community concerns as Hareven or as able to communicate research findings to a nonscholarly audience. Similarly, few architectural historians have shown themselves to be as sensitive as Langenbach to architecture's social setting. It is gratifying to note that reviewers have already hailed *Amoskeag* as a classic and that the authors' research has also served as the basis for a museum exhibit in Manchester and for a television film.

More representative of the luck that most places can hope for is Eric Johanessen's *Cleveland Architecture, 1876–1976*, published by the Western Reserve Historical Society. Johanessen's chief contribution is the rediscovery of a local tradition in urban design. Cleveland's architectural practice, he concludes, was respectable, though conservative. The city's outstanding achievements were in planning, particularly in the innovative use of public space. Examples include the city's famous Public Square (1796), a delightful glass-roofed shopping arcade (1890), the nation's first civic center (1903), its first industrial research park (1911), one of the first planned suburban developments (1911) and shopping centers (1927), and the Terminal Tower complex (1922–1930). Many of these innovations involved an imaginative linkage of public space and public transportation. The automobile eclipsed this tradition, but Johanessen has rediscovered it at an obviously opportune time. If Cleveland's civic activists seize on this book as they should, local history will become a basis for community planning: a tool through which citizens can use their community's past to assess its present needs and future options. Local history of this type has obvious relevance not only for older cities like Cleveland, but for burgeoning newer places whose inhabitants are trying to put down roots.

* * * *

In their 1936 classic *American Regionalism*, Howard Odum and Harry Estill Moore listed some forty definitions of the term "region." Later a special community of geographers spent years trying to frame a standard definition of the term, but without success. At issue is whether a region is a thing or a concept.

Social scientists see "region" as a concept. To call an area a region is to state a hypothesis that can be tested through observation of political, economic, or cultural behavior to see if the hypothesized region is more meaningful than some other set of spatial or nonspatial relationships. Regional analysis of this type is an old field within geography, a new frontier of anthropology, and the core of the discipline known as regional science. While this approach is empirical, it is not necessarily quantitative. A case in point is D. W. Meinig's *Imperial Texas*, a geographic analysis that argues persuasively that Texas is not only a state, but a region whose cultural and economic influence extends irregularly north and west of its political boundaries.

For most humanities scholars, a region is a thing. Students of American history and literature tend to accept the South, the West, Appalachia, the Great Plains, New England, the Midwest—plus assorted subregions—as real entities, about whose dimensions there is little reason to fret. Instead, they concentrate their energies on analyzing the human activities that take place within given boundaries.

Thus Richard Beale Davis's prize-winning three-volume study *Intellectual Life in the Colonial South, 1585–1763* devotes no attention whatever to the question of whether the categories of South/non-South are superior for cultural analysis to other sets of categories (such as seaboard/backcountry or proprietary/nonproprietary), which also applied to the British North American colonies. For Davis, as for generations of regional historians before him, the South simply is—and was (and ever more will be?).

The popular dimension of regional studies used to be called regional writing. This genre flourished from the 1930s through the 1950s, notably in the Rivers of America series, which had many imitators (Lakes of America, Regions of America, American Trails, American Forts, American Folkways). Carl Carmer's *Stars Fell on Alabama* (1934) and Paul Horgan's Pulitzer Prize–winner, *Great River: The Rio Grande in North American History* (1954) provided other models for the genre.

Whatever their topic, regional writers served up regional, state, and local history and culture in an informal literary style, sometimes folksy and anecdotal, sometimes brooding and romantic, as befitted the sense of destiny-haunted landscapes they liked to convey.

Regional writing still flourishes, though it no longer travels under that name. A good example is Wilma Dykeman's *Tennessee*, a volume in The States and the Nation series and a best seller in the author's native state. The following passage from pages 7–8 of this book conveys the flavor of regional writing. It takes its point of departure from the regionalist poet Allen Tate's identification of knowledge of one's home as "knowledge carried to the heart." Such knowledge, says Dykeman,

> is won through the senses: sight of blue, hickory-wood smoke rising from a mud-daubed chimney up an isolated Appalachian cove, or a winter sun disappearing westward, trailing scarlet sashes across the sky above a Memphis skyscraper; sounds of Saturday night in gaudy back-alley honky-tonks replaced by the timeless call of Sunday morning church chimes flowing like honey over drowsy courthouse towns and clustered city blocks; smell of black river-bottom earth submerged by flood, a redolence acrid and fetid with primeval fertility, and odors of cedar fence rows and pine woods in the stillness of high noon, of tobacco curing to golden brown in autumn barns, of spring honeysuckle and newly cut summer grass; taste of wild blackberries and winesap apples from the hills and sun-ripened strawberries from the lowlands, of crisply crusted catfish and hush-puppies, succulent ham and red-eye gravy, the common pungency of collard greens, sweet potatoes, white "soup" beans, cornbread

baked in ironware from freshly ground meal, plus the subtle savor of mountain trout in butter, syllabub and Sally Lunn and great-grandmother's special ambrosia; touch of fresh wind ushering rain-clouds after a long drought over scalded strips of interstate highways and parched hay fields, feel of emerald woods-moss velvety against the hand, and summer Spanish needles, snow slashing against the face atop Mt. LeConte or Clingman's Dome in January, and heat burning arms and neck in a July cotton field.

Knowledge so won, Dykeman adds, "is distilled by memory." And it is refined by a skillful writer attuned to the need among a mobile and distracted people for a sense of wholeness anchored in a sense of place.

PART IV

Thinking Anew
about Local History

A local history explored without noting its wider manifestations is like a plant deprived of access to the light.

—Richard M. Sutton, *Local History Today*

Chapter Eleven

Changes in the Community

Introduction

Constance McLaughlin Green attended the University of Chicago and received her Ph.D. from Yale University. Thereafter, she taught at Mt. Holyoke and Smith. Before the term public historian came into use, Green was the historian at the Navy Ordinance Department and then chief historian at the Army Historical Division in Washington, D.C. She was the director of the Washington History Project based at American University and received the Pulitzer Prize for History in 1963 for her book, *Washington, Capital City*.

In this essay, delivered as an informal address before an audience of New York State municipal and county historians, Green calls for local historians to be aware of the setting in which their communities exist, to look for comparative materials, and to seek change over time. She expands the topics that the local historian might consider to include culture and attitudes and she points to the use of census information in the locality. Her essay is sprightly, and she outlines a mode of operation that a local historian might want to consider if he or she plans to write a community history.

The work is reprinted, by permission, from *The Challenge of Local History* (Albany: New York State Education Department Publication, 1968), 16–26.

* * * *

The historian, whether he's writing about a small village or a nation, has responsibilities, and I believe passionately that he must not only explain what happened, and when, and where, and how much, and how, but also *why*. Of course,

Constance McLaughlin Green, " Changes in the Community," *The Challenge of Local History* (Albany, NY: The State Education Department, Office of State History, 1968), 16–26.

it is the "why" that becomes the overwhelming problem for most of us, in fact, I think even for Lord, God on high.

I think you have an unusual opportunity here in the State of New York because you have what every urban historian in the past has coveted—a ready access to comparative material. You work on the history of your own town or city or village; but you know that your neighbor is also preparing a record and an analysis of what is at his doorstep. You know that the historian on the far side of the State is similarly at work, and a letter of inquiry will supply you with comparative material that saves you the quandary that the urban historian in the past has had to face. Either he has to guess at what the analogies would be with another place, or he has to dig it out for himself. So, I feel distinctly envious of you in having your comparative materials virtually spread out before you and available at the expense of a postage stamp and a letter of inquiry. And it can be an enormously illuminating thing to have the comparative material at hand. Almost every local historian comes to feel (if he didn't to begin with) that his particular locality is really unique. Every place does have very distinctive features and qualities that do differ from those of every neighbor. But, on the other hand, practically every place has similarities so pronounced with other places that the similarities, or even the identical kind of historical past in given lines, are likely to be as pronounced (and rather more so) than the uniquenesses. In any case, you do have the advantage of having, presumably within relatively easy reach, a certain amount of material for comparisons.

In talking about changes in the community, I equate them virtually with talking about history. What is history? It is the twofold, and seemingly paradoxical strands of perpetual change and never-ending continuity. If I say never-ending, I realize that ghost towns *do* occur which may be said to be the end of the continuity of a community. But, by and large, there are still the two elements to consider—and in focusing attention upon change—let me remind you to keep your eyes open for the continuity that does go on even if it is slightly changed in form.

Perhaps I might interrupt my own planned progression of discussion to illustrate that particular point here and now. Only last spring an extremely interesting discussion took place at the meeting of the Organization of American Historians in Chicago, in which a young man, who has concentrated his adult historical research on the emergence of big cities, was tracing the steps by which a city emerges. He began by talking about what first sounded like the alarming theme of Social Geography.

Perhaps I am a timid soul, but my blood slightly congealed at that impressive sounding phrase until I got it into my cranium what it really meant. It simply meant: where what kind of people lived and with what kind of neighbors; what their occupations were; what were the national origins of the mélange or the homogeneous group within the community; or a segment of the community, what their religious differences or similarities were; and, how a geographic pattern developed. This discussion centered upon Philadelphia, under the engaging title, "If all the world were Philadelphia." At first the center of settlement was in the core of the city. It was more or less a mélange of all kinds of people with the poorer living on the fringes and the well-to-do and the powerful at the heart of the city. Then, as time went on, the inner core became the poorer section; the well-to-do moved out, and there was a series of concentric rings with the shifts from 1775 to 1930, with the rich and well-born in the heart of town and the poor at the fringe; then, by 1860, a shifting hodgepodge and mingling and by 1930, with the rich and well-born at the outer edge or actually in the suburbs with the slums, the ghetto, and the down-and-outers in the heart of the city. A series of statistical tables showed the situation at the three dates that Mr. Warner, the speaker, had chosen to illustrate some of the changes that had occurred over 155 years. The first was 1775, when the city of Philadelphia was a great colonial trading center, with some manufacturing, and was about to become the political capital of the new United States. Considered next was 1860, as the point at which an industrial city of some half-million people had come into being; and finally 1930, when it was the mature center of a metropolitan area of great importance and diversity. Extremely interesting and elaborate statistical tables compared one period with the next. They showed where people's occupations were, and what the racial and nationality distributions were, and what the location and income were (in so far as that was possible), so that you could get an idea of the kind of groupings within the city and how intensive they were.

Again, a phrase that was new to me, and which I found very frightening at first, was the "index of dissimilarity," which I thought sounded so obscure and esoteric that I decided: well, this was not for me and I would just hope that I never had to use the term. What this phrase really added up to was a way of approximating a measurement of how intense was the congregation, say of Negroes, in any part of the city at any one of these three dates: where Irish people lived, where the Dutch, where the English, where the well-to-do, where the poor lived. Also taken into account were their occupations: whether they were engaged in wagon making, in locomotive building, in weaving and textiles, in domestic or laundry work. The transportation methods at each period of time were shown, so you could see what the interrelationships were at any given period in any given section of the city. You could see all sorts of provocative possibilities and then you would have to do a lot of thinking about it.

What I'm getting at with this matter of change in continuity is expressed in an extremely penetrating comment from a sociologist who was one of the commentators on this paper. As Professor Warner had made his point about these extraordinary changes over this long span of time, and explained how these measurements helped one understand the changes, everyone gasped a little bit with astonishment and interest when the sociologist arose to make his comment and said, "I have found this an extremely interesting paper. But what is most surprising to me is not the character of change, but the exceptional continuity when you look at the statistical percentages that these tables present. You find that in 1775 something like 3 1/2 percent of all Philadelphians were engaged in the professions. In 1860 you find that it is 4 percent, and in 1930 you find it is 6 percent. Now that seems to me to represent a continuity rather than a staggering change that I think bears ruminating about." And in that fashion, he took the statistical evidence that Mr. Warner had very carefully and effectively compiled, and showed that change occurred in numbers; but in percentages of the overall, the change was astonishingly little.

Well, you may very well say, "So what!" My comment at this moment is, "So what to watch," in doing your own study of your own community. What is the degree of change? How penetrating is it? Is it more dramatic at first glance than it is in actuality? Is it effective when the newspaper or a sudden discovery makes it evident that some great change is about to take place, and in 1960 you make assiduous note of this, and are tempted to point to it as a great dramatic moment in the history of the community, only to find maybe by 1980 that, after all, it was incident rather than a turning point?

I've now wandered a little bit from the order in which I was intending to proceed. But I do think it is important to remember that you must watch not only for change but for the continuity.

What are the materials that are the major subjects with which you have to work in dealing with the history of a community? Well, obviously, first and foremost are the people; and second, the physical environment both natural and manmade, and all the changes that that may involve. Third, I think, to state it simply are the institutions that arise in a community, some the result of environment, but more of them a result of the attitudes and the pressures of the people living there, their neighbors, the State, and the nation at large. Institutions, I think, can be treated as the outgrowth of people's wishes and efforts, modified at best by the natural circumstances, forces of nature under which they have to live.

What do I mean by institutions? They are the forms of government, whereby people can live together, the religion, schools, business organizations, methods of carrying on trade, satisfaction of human needs, institutions of learning, institutions of public welfare, institutions of health, etc.—institutions in the widest possible sense.

Now, if you are willing to grant that these are the main problems, how are you going to decide what to look for and what to watch for? Might I as well say, "Just go out in the street and look at everything you can see and you will know"? I think the quality of what you collect in the way of information, and what you put together, depends upon the questions you ask yourself; or questions that other people may put to you and then you ask yourself and look for the answers. But at every turn if you ask: "Why, why did this take place, why didn't the community follow a different course (how and why)?" you will keep your antennae out in a way that will make you able to collect and to analyze with much more penetrating quality than you do if you simply take what comes to hand and jot it down. But in the process of looking for definitions of areas that you must watch for, it seems to me, that you can just name a number of things that you're going to follow. Sometimes, in trying to tackle a study of local community, I called at six, sometimes seven, sometimes eight areas to determine how people earn their bread and butter; what kind of people came; what the age distribution was; what their national origins were (that's likely to be a question of major interest in the United States); what race (another question in and of itself); the religious affiliations; and the age distribution, young, old. Other questions were: "Did the young people move out and leave the old behind, and was it then the newcomers that kept the city going at all?" And then, of course, there was the character of the attitudes that emerge from this conglomeration of personalities and physical setting.

What about the amenities? How much attention does the community or individuals give to painting, sculpture, literature, and the creative and the performing arts? What about recreation in the more casual sense? Is it football, skiing, poker, bridge, TV, hockey, horse racing, or a little bit of everything? The diversions as well as the serious preoccupations are a factor that one must explore. The whole series of public services which one could say comes into the category of political history or maybe social history. What kind of services are performed by the tax-paying public: care of streets, garbage disposal, and schools.

Now, if you have a whole series of questions to ask yourself, and inevitably you do have, how are you going to find the materials that will give the answers, and then how are you going to organize your findings? How are you going to put them into literary form, assuming that your responsibility does not end with collecting the data but in putting it into written form for the next person to see and make use of readily? Almost all materials that you will have to consider fall either, I believe, into the category of the exactly measurable numbers or into the nonstatistically measurable that involve questions of judgement and opinion. The measurable aren't always as easy to get as one might think, but, on the whole, they are easier than measuring the degree of religious toleration within a community. How do you measure that? And how do you measure the quality of education that the public schools provide? You don't find a tabulation of that in a statistical table that will satisfy most historians or most citizens. There you have to turn to other sources. But I want to call attention to the assembling of the numerically measurable, the statistical information that you can get in various ways. I'm thinking of the astonishment that I myself felt when I discovered how much a careful scrutiny of the Federal and the State census tabulations would provide.

Some years ago, I had asked a group of students to write term papers, each of about 5,000 words on the history of his own community. If the situation were such that a student couldn't get the necessary information in Washington, I told him to take some aspect of any place that he wished upon which he could get the necessary information. To my intense gratification, one young man who lived in Oregon chose to take Washington in 1860 and 1870. He simply put together every scrap of information that he could find in the United States census for those years, comparing 1860 with 1870 in every category that the Federal census had any information about. I happened, at that time, to have known that particular period very intimately, and I was impressed at the skill with which, by using that source alone, he was able to portray, quite accurately, many significant phases of the city's life at those two periods. It was an eye-opener to him and to the rest of the class when I read some of his paper to them. It showed what you can do even with the limitation of statistics; even statistics that in the earlier census materials are likely to be a little lacking in detail, or not to have anything like the kind of analysis that later and more sophisticated censuses could take.

The census can be extremely hard to use when you look at the 15 and 20 volumes of the last two censuses. Where, down to 1860, there was one volume for the entire United States—I can't even remember how many it runs to now—but just for the decennial census, itself, I think, it's well over 22 volumes. In addition, there are the special in-between censuses. And insofar as it is feasible to lay hands on them, I strongly recommend looking carefully at every table in the Federal Census that could possibly have any relevance for your particular study. You are also the beneficiaries of the New York State censuses. I had never looked at the New York State census until the other day, when I decided I'd better do my homework and really find out what some of the early volumes contained. So, at random, I chose the volume for 1855. I was fascinated, because the Massachusetts census, which began in 1845, was a skinny little book with two or three pages allotted to each county but with some very useful and illuminating material in it nevertheless. The 1855 census, as no doubt many of you know, is quite thick and practically a quarto volume. It has a very illuminating introduction, which, to be sure, is mourning because a new State law had made it impossible for the local community to appoint its own marshal to do the collecting of the material. These were State employees, and therefore not necessarily very much interested in the local community and rather prone to be careless. Be that as it may, out of a perusal of the census, even in the most general way, you will find that you get all sorts of ideas that wouldn't have occurred to you; at least that is my experience. As a sampling I'd turn to Albany to see what I could learn about Albany in 1855. Then I discovered that some of the tables that I had hoped would be there in much more detail, city-by-city, or communities over 20,000 people, were given county-by-county. Nevertheless, to my fascinated eye, I discovered that Albany County in 1790 (this by carrying things from 1855 back) had the largest number of slaves of any county in the entire State (over 3,000 slaves) and I found that absolutely staggering. The next nearest was not New York County, or whatever Brooklyn falls into, but Tompkins County.

Well, I don't know exactly what you do with that oddment of fact, but it is at least thought provoking. Why? Why would they be in Albany? Can you in any way trace it to the Dutch Patroons? Were some of those slaves Indians that had been captured sometime earlier, and had been kept on as slaves? I have no idea of what the answer is, but it is the kind of brain-pricking fact that you will turn up that may lead you into some extremely interesting questions to yourself and, in turn, to finding at least a semblance of answers that would be of great interest and usefulness to other people.

Another stray oddment, again about the Albany statistics and this time—in 1855, there were 11 stone houses, of which 9 were all in one ward. The value of those 9 in Ward Nine was set at $351,000. In other words, if my arithmetic is any good, about $39,000 apiece. In 1855, $39,000, as you know, was a very large sum of money, and these were dwellings not public buildings. Well, what does that suggest? Well, it certainly suggests a city with segments of very great wealth. The fact that they were clustered in one ward certainly indicates that there was a very distinct differentiation between the areas in which the influential and well-to-do lived as opposed to the "hoi polloi"—and simply as a point of departure—it seems to me to suggest other inquiries that may derive therefrom.

Out of a city that had some 6,000 odd dwellings, there were 11 stone houses, about 3,200 brick, 3,100 frame, and then the maddening category that's always on census materials, "other." Well, those "other" were conceivably stucco, or I suspect tar paper and tin. Be that as it may, if you were patient enough, you will really find that from the census you got a good headstart on the numerical basis of analyzing town and city. The fact that census tables change the basis of their computations is maddening, and you'll find that the early censuses, of course, pay very little attention to all sorts of things that later become of great importance and are recognized as such. The 1855 census did not bother to record marriages or marital status by community, but by county, you could find just how old every person was at the time of marriage. So you can count up the number of couples that were married at 13 and the number that were married at 70. What you do with it I don't know, but it may come in handy, and you may find that it will have relevance in connections that you don't see at first.

There are, of course, dozens of other sources besides the census for the numerical material. And if the exact number again doesn't always matter, it may matter very much to be able to know that the town doubled in population within 20 years and tripled in its geographic expanse. There are the taxes, if the town or city records were carefully kept and haven't been destroyed by fire. There are, of course, such things as health records in most places; there are certainly probate records so you can really find out who was the richest man in town at the time of his death, and get some notion of the distribution of wealth. Then there are that source of enormous interests to the antiquarian and to the historian, namely the land records and the registry of deeds. I have never found the deeds or probate records or tax lists of sufficient usefulness to do more than take a quick look at them and then abandon the search, because it meant narrowing down a field of inquiry to such small lateral dimensions in order to permit you to dig all the way down.

If you are going to treat a whole city that is one thing. If you are going to treat one ward of a city, or one small suburban area, or one ghost town, then you can dig in depth and see if it, in turn, doesn't contribute a very considerable amount to understanding of the State of New York. In this instance, to see how one place, one small segment of it, developed in every particular, you have, of course, to pick and choose how far you can go and with what sources.

But what do you do about the things that you can't gauge by numbers or by percentages? How do you find clues to what people's attitudes of minds were? How do you figure out the quality, if any, of racial tolerance? New York State, I would imagine, up until the 20th century had few places with any sizable Negro minority. Certainly that is not the situation today. But prejudice or antagonisms of majority toward minority are a necessary part of a penetrating and analytical history of any place. How are you going to determine the character of the social and intellectual attitudes toward any minority? Inappropriately, I attempted to include in the minority, "What is the attitude toward women?" Well, in a large part of the United States, of course, women are now a majority. Nevertheless, in a good many places long after they became a majority, they were also occupying the status of a minority. But, be it the attitude of Protestant toward Catholic, or vice versa, or white versus Negro, or white versus oriental, or male versus female, or older generation versus younger, the attitudes of mind (insofar as you can determine them) are an essential part of the recording and interpreting of the history of the community and of its present.

Where it comes to interpreting, of course, you are bound to fall back upon judgment. What is more important than what? What sources do you draw upon? Of course, there is private correspondence, if you can get it, and if it is in the period that you are concerned with. Sometimes you find—at least my experience has been—that you thumb through mounds of personal papers preserved by the local historical society or in the neighboring library and find that it is mostly an exchange between relatives upon the state of everyone's health. You find account books that seem to record nothing but the latest price of hay and how many milk cows you could get in exchange for one bull. You find that account books, or day books, are frequently one long record of the weather. Nevertheless there are certainly letters, personal letters, that at least reveal the opinions, sometimes about matters of general interest to the entire community, that are expressed with an openness because it is a personal letter that you never will find equally well represented in the newspaper. But newspapers, as Dr. Graebner has pointed out, are a major source; again, that depends upon the newspaper.

In the last book that I worked on, *A History of Race Relations in Washington*, I found that one of my Negro readers said to me: "Why did you rely upon the press so heavily?" And I said, "Well for the obvious reason that the number of personal collections of family papers that were available to me were very limited and of relatively minor interest as far as the history of the community as a whole went, and because there just didn't seem to be much of anything else. What should I have looked at?" And he said, "Oh! you'd have gotten a much, I think, a much better balanced view of the Negro community by church records." Well, I had used some bits of the records of two churches, but I had not found them very satisfactory, and certainly my experience in using the records of white churches was that it may reflect attitudes of a particular congregation at a given moment, but even that isn't very certain. Take the vestry records of an Episcopal Church, and you'll find again that a large part of them are given over to a discussion of whether to put cushions on the pew seats, or whether to charge rental for the pews, or whether to pay the sexton a dollar more a week. That is likely to be the sum total over long spans of time. Not necessarily and not always, but I found it interesting, if nothing else, that the young Negro scholar believed that I would have found a more dispassionate and encompassing interpretation of the Negro community at any given moment by examining the records of 35 Negro churches, than I would by combing the local Negro press.

No doubt you have heard Lewis Mumford has said that technological change produces changes in urban community and urban community induces technological change. A relatively new group of American historians have been leaning very heavily upon the history of technological change to explain an enormous amount of change in any local community, big or small. Take the changes that you yourselves can remember in building materials and transportation, all the way from roads and canals not only to airplanes, but helicopters and rent-a-cars at airports. Think of the changes in the foods we eat—from home grown stuff or foods bought by barter or at the local store to commercial canned goods, to frozen foods, to Metrical, and to the method by which you purchase them. Time was, when the peddler came to your door selling apples and corn (well, that of course wasn't first; first you got it out of your own garden), then came the peddler, followed by the telephone and the delivery, and later the do-it-yourself supermarket. Consider the changes in purchasing methods from barter to cash, to checking accounts, to installment buying, to credit cards, and now even your bank checks which have to have a number on them so they can be automated through the Federal Banking System. There isn't an area of everyday life that has not been affected, for you and me and everyone younger and everyone older, by the succession of technological change. Whether technological change came because the city forced the change, or because the technology brought about the social and urban change may be unimportant.

If you are going to be able to get beyond the stage of collecting material at all—and until you do of course, you're only potential historians, not true historians—you are assemblers, archivists, but not historians until you begin to put it together. If you are going to put it together, two things seem to me all important.

Don't wait to begin writing until you have all your research done. All your research will never be done, not only because time is moving on, but because new things are always turning up. Divide your topic into periods. Do as much research as you can within that period, and then before moving on put it into writing. I know that it isn't generally accepted as a method to proceed, but in my own experience and that of a number of people I've known, it is an extremely useful way to go. In the first place you aren't so overwhelmed by the pile of shoe boxes full of notes as to make your heart sink when you think, "Mercy, how am I ever going to put all that down." More importantly, it is only as you begin to use it and to create the pattern that is part of the job of organizing and interpreting your material, only as you put it into sentences and paragraphs do you begin to see the holes, the things that you hadn't thought to look for or which perhaps you thought of, but still have no answer to, but now have more of an idea of how you can resolve the question. In the third place, it will serve as a toehold, or a large platform, from which to start upon the next period and it will call attention to themes that you must look for. That is, it seems to me, a very important thing to do. You are not overwhelmed by the mass of it. You are evolving your ideas as you go and, of course, when you have moved on to the next period and finished that you're probably going to have to rewrite what you've already done, or you may very well have to, because you'll find that the perspective of things have changed. What seemed all important at the end of one period, you'll find at the end of the next has rather dwindled or else has become more significant. But, in any event, don't wait too long, because I think it will take the freshness out of your findings. What you want to produce, if you're going to write at all, is something readable enough to catch the attention and imagination of your readers.

My last exhortation is, I'm afraid, deplorably pontifical or schoolmarmish— whichever you want to call it. For heaven's sake use the active voice. It's easy as pie to say: "A company was formed." All right, who formed it? And why? And, if you take the shortcut you are likely to fall into almost absentmindedly, of just saying "it was formed," you say the company was what was important, it doesn't matter very much who the organizers were. It also throws light on why, and the consequences of this also became clearer and sharper. However condescending it may sound to remind you of this, since you are dealing with people, people are the agents. Give them the subject place in the sentence and you'll find that your writing takes on a liveliness that the passive voice will kill quick as can be.

<u>Chapter Twelve</u>

Changes and Opportunities in Writing State and Local History

Introduction

In this essay, adapted from a speech delivered before a meeting of the Indiana Historical Society, Michael Kammen talks of the challenges before local historians, noting the significance of their work. The opening remarks of that address have been deleted here; what remains is a discussion of some of the reasons why local history has been written, some of the problems encountered in writing local history, and the challenges presented by new historical interests and methods in updating the models that local historians follow.

Important for local historians is Kammen's discussion of the classics of local history. Interesting, too, are the historical studies Kammen listed in his notes, as many of those works present new and different models for the writing of local history.

Michael Kammen won the Pulitzer Prize for History in 1973 for *People of Paradox*. He has also written a number of other important books that explore aspects of American culture. Two of his most recent books are *A Machine that Would Go of Itself: The Constitution in American Culture* (New York: A.A. Knopf, 1986) and *Mystic Chords of Memory: The Transformation of Tradition in American Culture* (New York: A.A. Knopf, 1991).

This essay is reprinted, by permission, from Michael Kammen, *Challenges and Opportunities in Writing State and Local History* (Indianapolis: Indiana Historical Society, 1983).

Michael Kammen, *Challenges and Opportunities in Writing State and Local History* (Indianapolis: Indiana Historical Society, 1983).

* * * *

The writing of local history has been (and will continue to be) significant for many different reasons. I shall offer you half a dozen reasons; but I know full well that you could multiply my list with many of your own.

The first and most obvious reason has to do with the very human need for a sense of place, and a natural curiosity about the particularities of one's own locale. Rudyard Kipling summed it up very well in a poem:

> God gives all men all earth to love,
> But since man's heart is small,
> Ordains for each one spot shall prove
> Beloved over all.[1]

Mark DeWolfe Howe, the Boston biographer and antiquarian, quoted those lines on the title page of a book (published in 1930) that he called a "Town Biography" of his birthplace: Bristol, Rhode Island. We tend to assume that New Englanders like Howe—many of them, at least—share that special sense of place. Perhaps; but New Englanders certainly possess no exclusive monopoly of it. Howe himself had been raised in Philadelphia, and therefore provides an instance of someone's becoming "more New England than the ordinary Yankee." C. Vann Woodward and David M. Potter, distinguished twentieth-century historians, have rightly insisted that "personalism and persistent local attachments" are "evidence of the survival of an authentic folk culture in the South long after it had disappeared in urban culture elsewhere."[2]

A sense of place has also been important to our newcomers, however, and consequently the term "local history" acquires yet another aspect when we apply it to the history of immigration and ethnicity in American life. Irving Howe has written, in his masterful work called *World of Our Fathers* (1976), that while the eastern European Jews who came to the United States "seldom felt much loyalty to Russia or Poland as nations, they brought with them fierce affections for the little places they had lived in, the muddy streets, battered synagogues, remembered fields from which they had fled. The *landsmanshaft*, a lodge made up of persons coming from the same town or district in the old country, was their ambiguous testimony to a past they knew to be wretched yet often felt to be sweet."[3]

Since World War II these American *landsmanshaften* have published hundreds of memorial volumes, histories of the tiny towns in eastern Europe from which their members came. Although this genre of local history is little known, it, too, is a significant part of the literature—as pertinent to understanding this "nation of immigrants" (to use Franklin Delano Roosevelt's phrase) as it is to the history of eastern Europe *per se*.

It is by now a truism that immigration and continental migration have been central factors in shaping American history. Thomas Jefferson was prophetic when he wrote from Paris in 1786 that "our confederacy must be viewed as the nest from which all America, North and South is to be peopled."[4] Nevertheless, we have not fully recognized the consequences those factors have had in complicating our sense of place.

Mobility has inevitably meant rootlessness for many. But those individuals, families, and communities that stayed put, on the other hand, have been responsible for a considerable amount of local and regional chauvinism. In many instances, unfortunately, local pride felt by one group is misunderstood by another—or worse, is bitterly resented. We have not sufficiently recognized that the efforts of local historians can be significant in creating and perpetuating social tensions in the United States.

The most dramatic example known to me involves the hegemony of New Englanders over the writing of American history—a phenomenon that persisted throughout the nineteenth century and well into the twentieth. This tendency has been resented by New Yorkers, by midwesterners, even by Californians; but nowhere has it been despised so much as in the South.

Perhaps I might illustrate this point with a couple of extracts from correspondence that passed more than half a century ago between two leading southern historians. Philip Alexander Bruce, a Virginian, had just read the claim that women played a more important role among the Pilgrims in early Plymouth than in early Virginia. That claim got his bile flowing, for as he explained to Lyon G. Tyler, the retired president of William and Mary:

> The Pilgrims have beaten the Jamestown settlers in history, because, from the start, they had a talent for the use of the pen; and that talent has only grown more active with the progress of the years, until, by this time, the New England points of view have become the dominant ones in our national shibboleths.

Two weeks later Bruce continued this theme, and the refrain began to sound like a diatribe.

> The only hope that I have that the superior claims of our prior settlement will be fully admitted lies in the certain expectation that the wealth and population, and, therefore, the importance of Virginia will grow enormously; and that with that growth, there will spring up a band of local historical scholars who will possess both the means and the literary culture to enforce on the attention of the world the superior part which Virginia played in the history of colonization.[5]

This story of regional and local rivalries for historical hegemony constitutes an important yet unwritten chapter in our cultural history. And the competition continues to this day, whether we wish to acknowledge it or not. In 1968, for example, a group based at Boston University conceived of a Committee for a New England Local History Bibliography. By 1972 the project had acquired many sponsors, a major federal grant, and a full-time staff. In 1976 the publication of huge, thorough bibliographical guides to local historical writing began to appear: Massachusetts, Maine, New Hampshire, and Vermont are already "out." Rhode Island will appear in 1983; Connecticut is scheduled for 1986; and a final volume on New England as a whole is planned for 1988. These books are the most useful works of their kind ever prepared. They make the available references for localities in other states look very inadequate by comparison.[6] So once again, whether we like it or not, New Englanders seem to lead the way in doing local history.

Rather than resent their leadership, however, we would do well to be grateful, and to note that for more than a decade now a major preoccupation among professional historians has been to test the conventional wisdom of American history through in-depth case histories—what Bernard DeVoto used to call "post-hole digging."

Most of the pioneering examples of this new genre were, predictably, studies of New England towns, especially during the colonial period; but by the later 1970s and early 1980s scholars had become interested in states, counties, and communities all over the United States and had begun asking different sorts of questions, using new methodologies, and producing works of great potential value to non-professional historians as well as to scholars.[7]

This body of work has helped us to appreciate several reasons why state and local history is significant. First, because we have begun to understand, as never before, just how pluralistic and decentralized American society has always been, with consequences that we scarcely envisioned a generation or two ago. As Oscar Handlin has written of the seventeenth century:

> Power tended to devolve to its local sources. Whether that involved the town, as in New England, or the local powers sitting in the vestry, as in Virginia, the characteristic political organization was decentralized. Whatever acknowledgment might be given to the authority of the Crown, political institutions were decisively shaped by the necessity of defining connections to local power.[8]

More often than not, the most critical decisions affecting the lives of ordinary people were made by local citizens and implemented through local institutions. That is one rather obvious reason why local history has very properly become so interesting to us in recent years. (Recall the observation made by T. S. Elliot in 1948 that "a local speech on a local issue is likely to be more intelligible than one addressed to a whole nation."[9])

Another reason for the rediscovery of local history by professional historians has to do with the inescapable fact that you see different things when you use the microscope rather than the telescope. To cite just one example, historians who have examined the colonial rebellions of 1689–1691 have long been impressed by the terrible instability, human conflict, and institutional disruption of those years. Detailed studies of particular counties and communities, however, have recently given us a very different perspective. Outside of the provincial capitals life continued and sources of authority functioned—not without anxiety and, in many instances, not without changes in personnel; but the ultimate point is that people carried on, the basic web of human relationships did not disintegrate, and therefore instability was not so pervasive as historians assumed fifteen or twenty years ago. We owe this more balanced perspective to what might be called a "new particularism" in American historical writing.[10]

Despite these achievements, the challenge of state and local history continues to be twofold. There is the challenge for us to continue these innovations rather than resting content with the achievements of the 1970s. And there is also the challenge to spread much more widely—among the general public as well as among historians—the good news that a revolution has occurred in writing local history. Back in 1873 Friedrich Nietzsche wrote an iconoclastic essay called "The Use and Abuse of History." One passage, in particular, still stands as a tough challenge to you, to me, and to anyone who cares about the past for its own sake and wishes to respect the "pastness of the past." Listen to Nietzsche:

> History is necessary to the man of conservative and reverent nature who looks back to the origins of his existence with love and trust; through it he gives thanks for life. He is careful to preserve what survives from ancient days, and will reproduce the conditions of his own upbringing for those who come after him; thus he does life a service. The possession of his ancestors' furniture changes its meaning in his soul, for his soul is rather possessed by it. All that is small and limited, moldy and obsolete, gains a worth and inviolability of its own from the conservative and reverent soul of the antiquary migrating into it and building a secret nest there. The history of his town becomes the history of himself; he looks on the walls, the turreted gate, the town council, the fair, as an illustrated diary of his youth, and sees himself in it all—his strength, industry, desire, reason, faults, and follies. "Here one could live," he says, "as one can live here now—and will go on living; for we are tough folk, and will not be uprooted in the night." And so, with his "we," he surveys the marvelous individual life of the past and identifies himself with the spirit of the house, the family, and the city.[11]

One of the greatest challenges that local historians face, therefore, is to answer this charge of conservative antiquarianism. Part of the solution, I believe, lies in overcoming the worst excesses of ethnocentrism. When the poet Dante wrote that "My country is the whole world!" he meant that universals of human existence could be found in the microcosm of Florence, Italy. Faulkner must have felt the same way about his imaginary county in Mississippi. For so many practitioners of local history, however, the words of a distinguished, contemporary French historian are pertinent and true: "the village all too often spent its time contemplating its own navel—that is for most members of the community the parish pump was the centre of their little universe."[12]

This has been a worldwide tendency throughout most of human history. Our parochialism is no more egregious than that of the Chinese, the English, the French, or the Southeast Asian societies.[13] But what can be done about it? What *must* be done if we are to have a good state and local history is for practitioners to read more widely than they do—to read important monographs on Newburyport, Massachusetts; Rochester, New York; Germantown, Pennsylvania; Lunenberg County, Virginia; as well as outstanding recent studies of, say, Montaillou, France, or Vienna, Austria.[14]

The local historian should be an unashamed but discriminating borrower of concepts, methods, and contexts. Let me illustrate my point by quoting at length from an obscure little essay published in England by the Middlesex Local History Council in 1963.

> The economic historian and the local historian have much to gain from keeping an eye on each other's work. We economic historians look to local history for much of our raw material, particularly in these days when increasing attention is being devoted to economic development in particular regions. As we scan the local history journals, however, we become very aware that few of the articles we find there make use of works of economic history which might be of help in interpreting local evidence. Economic historians are getting more out of local history than local historians are getting from economic history. This seems rather an unfair bargain.

> Perhaps this lack of communication in one direction is most evident in the local historian's frequent reluctance to explain the timing of the events which he describes. According to him, they just happened. Yet, it is clear from the history of our own times that the moment of decision is often dictated by changes in the economic climate—movements in bank rate, for instance, or a slight increase in the level of unemployment. The same is true of the past; even truer, in fact, because financial crises were then more severe, and swings in the level of unemployment more extensive. Much has been written lately by economic historians about these ups and downs in the economic life of the country and, as a consequence, it is often now possible, by looking up a few readily-obtainable books, to understand more about why local developments took place when they did.[15]

Yet another lesson to be learned from innovative recent work done by English historians is that understanding the relationships between centralized units of political authority and regional and local organizations is essential if we are to avoid the pitfalls of doing local history in a vacuum. My colleague, Clive Holmes, has expressed this point quite well in his introduction to *The Eastern Association in the English Civil War*, a book that treats the eastern counties around Cambridgeshire during the very critical years 1643–1645.

> The history of the Eastern Association can only be explained adequately, not by the invocation of the region's unique homogeneity however defined, but by the close analysis of the complex and tension-ridden dialogue of the three principals: the legislators at Westminster, the Association's authorities and administrators at Cambridge, and the county committees in the localities.[16]

It is my belief that state and local history, most especially, should not be regarded in isolation. We have had too much physical mobility, too much social diversity, and too many bonds between disparate places in a widespread market economy to justify isolated examinations of local history. Onondaga salt was sold all the way from New York City to upper Canada and Michigan during the antebellum period, for example, while the Oneida Indians, whose historic home was upstate New York, are to be found in diaspora near Green Bay, Wisconsin. It has become a platitude that to do local history well brings one inescapably into regionalism and regional history.[17] I do not disagree; but I would like to push the point one step farther by suggesting that local history, properly conducted, can lead one simultaneously into the histories of several different regions. In 1894, for example, a violent confrontation in Hammond, Indiana, occurred because of an American Railway Union strike in support of the Pullman walkout. It would be extremely instructive to compare what happened in Hammond with simultaneous episodes in Chicago, Los Angeles, and elsewhere.

I would like to make a special plea for a mode of investigation that may sound perfectly reasonable, yet has not been pursued by local historians in any systematic way. I have in mind the ubiquitous story of two communities—roughly equal in size and in resources when they were embryonic—which compete with each other to become the county seat, or to be the major commercial enterpôt, or to serve as the site for some special institution, such as a university, a hospital, or a jail. Whether it be Winchester vs. Stephensburg, Virginia, in the 1740s; or Elizabeth vs. Newark, New Jersey, in 1807; or Seneca Falls vs. Waterloo, New York, in the 1830s; or Santa Rosa vs. Sonoma, California, in the 1850s. I am talking about a competitive pattern that has recurred hundreds of times in United States history. Although we used to glorify the match race between sleek, powerful horses, and we love to read Mark Twain's account of the Mississippi River steamboat racing the fire-breathing locomotive, few historians have made it their business to tell the cutthroat saga of neighboring communities which struggled mightily for economic and political dominance.

There is an obscure essay which ought to be required reading for every local historian. (The essay was jointly authored because it originated as two separate papers.) It explores the cultural dynamic of a midwestern community which has had a "mainstream" history as well as a dissenting tradition. Although most communities are probably in a similar situation, the alternative or dissenting voice tends to get muted with the passage of time. Let the authors explain.

> ... in this country most of the history written during the nineteenth century must have taken the form of local and county histories, produced or sponsored by local residents rather than by trained scholars. These frequently shapeless and always self-gratulant community chronicles exhibit in the main only the haziest notions of historical method or philosophical consistency. They can nevertheless reveal the sense of particular local pasts in relation to given stages of local development.

After tracing the optimistic and boosteristic versions of historical writing about Kansas City, Missouri, the authors label them the dominant tradition, "drawing its force from conceptions of what the city was supposed to *be* and what it was supposed to become." The authors then identify certain local figures who, "whatever their reasons, have found themselves drawn toward different aspects of the city's history and have shown that much of what the written tradition takes for granted is in fact highly problematic. These divergent expressions . . . have taken the form of addresses to 'old settlers' associations, letters to editors, and unpublished reminiscences; they can be described, for contrast, as a sort of 'oral tradition.'"
The authors' conclusion is highly instructive.

> Obviously, there is more than one "past" in Kansas City. The written tradition—with its success story of prophecies redeemed, boldness vindicated, and the city itself a continuing testimony to a triumph over the wilderness—exercises an almost hypnotic influence not only over its historians but in the city's present-day publicity. . . . The conflicts between and within the traditions we have called "written" and "oral" mark a range of questions that remain open for new investigations and fresh judgement. It is quite clear that adequate local history can be written in terms of neither stereotype.[18]

That challenging assertion brings me to the third item on my agenda today: the opportunities that lie ahead for local historians. It is perhaps disappointing to learn that there is no neat and tidy formula for everyone to follow—no prepackaged method that would be appropriate to every community. We can console ourselves, however, by recognizing that there is also no consensus among historians of the United States in general, or among historians of women, or within the so-called American Studies movement, or within the *Annales* school in France, about the one best way of doing any kind of history. The most appropriate balance between theory and description, between cultural and economic emphasis, between narrative and analysis, involves issues that historians disagree about just as intensely as ever.

If I were asked to recommend the classic example—or even a classic model—of American local history writing, I would be hard pressed to do so. Classic works do exist, but none of them will serve very well as an all-purpose model. What about W. Lloyd Warner's work on Newburyport, Massachusetts, or Robert and Helen Lynd's work on Muncie, Indiana? Too sociological and insufficiently historical. What about Blake McKelvey's five-volume work on Rochester, New York? Invaluable, yet old-fashioned in methodology and lacking in comparative perspective. What about I. N. P. Stokes' six-volume iconography of Manhattan Island? It is a gorgeous work, yet narrow in focus and *sui generis* in content. Very few localities have the richness of visual materials that makes such an approach possible.

Well then, what about Merle Curti's *The Making of an American Community: Democracy in a Frontier County* (1959), on Trempeleau County, Wisconsin? Based upon collaborative work, and utilizing quantitative methods, it may come as close as any work that we can find to being a "classic model." Nevertheless, other communities will have types of data available that Curti lacked (and vice versa), and pose questions that Curti and his colleagues did not. Other communities will have existed for double the time span of Trempeleau County, thereby creating multi-generational opportunities as well as methodological problems. And for more urbanized localities a problem-focus quite different from the "Turner thesis" will be far more appropriate.[19]

It is essential to bear in mind the diversity of what local historians do. They tend to be "held responsible" for everything that happened in their communities: that is, they are expected to be knowledgeable about the entire story, from genesis to the present and from political history to architectural aspects. That's understandable; but it should not blind us to the fact that local historians have specialized and even should specialize. They may write the history of a local institution, such as a church, a factory, a hospital, a university, or a utopian community. They may write the history of an artifact, such as an unusual bridge, building, or market.[20] They may even write the *legendary* history or folklore of a locality. The story of Valley Forge, for example, as a symbolic phenomenon in American culture is almost as important as the actual encampment that occurred there during the winter of 1777–1778.[21]

Two recent developments within the historical profession may be particularly reassuring to local historians. The first is a revival of interest in, and respect for, narrative history. For several generations now prominent academic historians have been more interested in analyzing pieces of the past (to see how they worked) than in synthesizing what they have learned into a coherent "story." That is changing, just as abstract expressionism in art is giving way to new modes of representationalism. Most local historians, I believe, feel comfortable reading and writing narrative history. Well, these trends seem to run in a cyclical fashion, and new modes of narrative seem to be on the way "in" again.[22]

The second pertinent development is that historians have become increasingly interested in the history of failure: of losers, like the Loyalists in the American Revolution; or political movements that aborted, like socialism in Spain after World War I; or things that should have happened but didn't, such as treaties between the Hispanic colonists in the New World and Native Americans.[23] Many local historians feel awkward because, as they often put it, "nothing *important* ever happened in our community."[24] Does that refrain sound familiar? What if your town is not Concord, Massachusetts; or Nauvoo, Illinois; or New Harmony, Indiana; or Santa Fe, New Mexico; or Monterey, California? Take heart! Some of us have ceased to tell American history as an unbroken series of successes by famous folks. Therefore, in my own state, the towns that were not located along the Erie Canal, and the decline of certain Adirondack industries, and the collapse of the whaling industry from Long Island and New England ports, and even the fiscal decline of New York City are all stories with fascinating lessons for us, living as we do in an age of economic crisis and contraction.[25]

State and local history, in short, have moved beyond "boosterism." The town scandal is infinitely more interesting than complacent prosperity with a dénouement that "they all lived happily ever after." Students of the past are at least as concerned about ordinary chaps as they are about elites, about rates of social change and patterns of human fertility. The decline of fertility in the western world since the mid-nineteenth century has begun to captivate the interest of more and more historians. As the relationship between human population and food resources becomes ever more problematic, it is not even possible to say whether the decline of fertility is a story of success or of failure. It may simply be an adaptive aspect of human survival. In any case, it is a phenomenon which can be traced in most of our communities, and it should be.

My final point has to do with the question: who can or should write local history? My answer may be somewhat surprising, because I do not believe that one has to be a lifelong resident of Vincennes, or Crawfordsville, or Tell City in order to write its history. I do not believe that women necessarily write women's history better than men, or that blacks necessarily have an advantage in writing black history, or (for that matter) that only Americans can write about the history of the United States. Thomas S. Kuhn has told us that "almost always" the people who are responsible for dramatic innovations in the natural sciences "have been either very young or very new to the field whose paradigm they change."[26]

Let me cite just two examples in the field of local history. William Lambarde's *A Perambulation of Kent* (London, 1576) is one of the finest local histories in the entire Anglo-American tradition. In several key respects Lambarde is the progenitor of English county history-writing. Nevertheless, he settled in Kent the very year that he wrote this famous book, and his entrance into a particular community was the cause of his undertaking the *Perambulation*.[27] Similarly, in 1835 Ralph Waldo Emerson researched and wrote his well-known bicentennial discourse about Concord, Massachusetts, because he had just moved there and was about to be married. The history he wrote helped to legitimize his status in Concord. As for age, bear in mind that Emerson was thirty-two years old when he wrote it.[28]

Well then, what lessons do I wish to derive and drive home? We should welcome the talented outsider who would write a history of our community. An "oldtimer" is not the only person who can write local history. A native will not necessarily be more accurate than a newcomer, or a believer more sympathetic than a nonbeliever. A recent president of the Mormon History Association, Professor Jan Shipps of Indiana University-Purdue University here in Indianapolis, is not a Mormon. She has earned their admiration and trust, nonetheless.

I suspect that I may be preaching to the converted today. In 1979, when the Indiana Historical Society commissioned a sesquicentennial history of the organization, it sought an "outsider" rather than an "insider" because it did not wish to promulgate an official history. Lana Ruegamer had been associated with your organization for less than four years, and considered herself a "nonparticipant" as well as a newcomer.[29]

I have spoken of challenge, of opportunities, and finally of qualifications. My views are inevitably personal—perhaps even idiosyncratic. They are the product of what I read, of conversations that I have had with other historians, and of reactions to professional situations that I have observed. I don't know that I can offer a Local Historian's Creed, but I shall conclude with three declarations of faith.

1. Local historical writing in the years ahead must find a middle ground between the old-fashioned variety that was richly anecdotal and the type of "new social history" as local case study, which deals with people as impersonal aggregates. The serious and humanistic historian must identify trends, to be sure, but should exemplify them with flesh-and-blood individuals. It's not a matter of simple human interest, or of precision versus impressionism, but rather one of defining the historian's vocation as comprising narrative plus analysis. Narrative without analysis is a beast with a hollow head, but explanation without vivid illustration is stultifying and unsatisfying.

2. Local historical writing, for better or worse, endures longer than any other form of historical writing. A great amount of it was produced, for example, during the 1880s. Those books are still read by members of (and visitors to) the communities they describe. I cannot say the same about the "scientific" monographs written by professional historians a century ago. If I may quote Johan Huizinga once again, "there are wise historians among the amateurs of local history and dull gleaners of fact among the renowned professors of the universities." *Vanitas, Vanitas.* Write local history and you may achieve one variant of immortality.[30]

3. To do local history well, one must read broadly. A comparative perspective is essential. Nevertheless, each of our communities is a cosmos unto itself, and each one contains many, though not *all*, of the universals of human experience. Henry David Thoreau put it very well in 1849: "The characteristics and pursuits of various ages and races of men are always existing in epitome in every neighborhood. The pleasures of my earliest youth have become the inheritance of other men."[31]

I hope that the pleasures of your youth and neighborhood will appear in your histories—but also your scandals. I hope that insiders as well as outsiders, old-timers as well as newcomers, will appear in your histories. I trust that the unique as well as the universal will appear, and that you will make an effort to distinguish between the two. However you write your histories, the responsibility you bear is considerable, because good, bad, or indifferent, your histories will become, as Thoreau put it, "the inheritance of other men." And women.

I am quite fond of an admonition given to young Hoagy Carmichael during World War I by Reggie Duval, the black pianist from Indianapolis. "Never play anything that ain't *right*," Duval remarked. "You may not make any money, but

you'll never get hostile with yourself."[32] That sounds to me like very good advice—
as sensible for state and local historians as it is for musicians.

NOTES

1. Quotes in Helen Howe, *The Gentle Americans, 1864–1960: Biography of a Breed* (New York: Harper & Row, 1965), 18.

2. See David M. Potter, "The Enigma of the South," *The Yale Review* 51 (October 1961): 150–51 and C. Vann Woodward, *American Counterpoint: Slavery and Racism in the North-South Dialogue* (Boston: Little Brown, 1971), 19–20. See also Allen Tate, "A Southern Mode of Imagination," in *Studies in American Culture: Dominant Ideas and Images*, edited by Joseph J. Kwiat and Mary C. Turpie (Minneapolis: University of Minnesota Press, 1960), 99; Susan Elizabeth Lyman, *Lady Historian: Martha J. Lamb* (Northampton, MA: Smith College Library, 1969), 23; Karal A. Marling, *Wall-to-Wall America: A Cultural History of Post-Office Murals in the Great Depression* (Minneapolis: University of Minnesota Press, 1982), 95; Wallace H. Cathcart to Victor H. Paltsits, October 9, 1907, Paltsits Papers, Box 2, New York Historical Society; J. Franklin Jameson to Isaac J. Cox, December 4, 1909, Jameson Papers, Box 117, Library of Congress (Manuscript Division); Rev. A. W. H. Eaton to J. Franklin Jameson, December 6, 1911, Jameson Papers, Box 94, Library of Congress, (Manuscript Division).

3. Irving Howe, *World of Our Fathers* (New York: Simon and Schuster, 1976), 183–84. See also pp. 189–90.

4. Jefferson to Archibald Stuart, January 25, 1786, in *The Papers of Thomas Jefferson*, vol. 9, edited by Julian P. Boyd (Princeton: Princeton University Press, 1950–), 218.

5. Bruce to Tyler, July 26 and August 10, 1925, Tyler Papers, Group V, Box 4, Swem Library, College of William and Mary. By the mid-1920s, there were even historians in New England who were critical of "the absurd worship of everything that is of New England. . . ." See Worthington C. Ford to Lyon G. Tyler, July 7, 1924, ibid.

6. Compare John D. Haskell, Jr. (ed.), *Massachusetts, A Bibliography of Its History* (Boston: G. K. Hall, 1976) with Harold Nestler, *A Bibliography of New York State Communities: Counties, Towns, Villages* (Port Washington, NY: Ira J. Friedman, Inc., 1968).

7. See Thomas H. Smith, "The Renascence of Local History," *The Historian* 35 (November 1972): 1–17; Kathleen Neils Conzen, "Community Studies, Urban History, and American Local History," in *The Past Before Us: Contemporary Historical Writing in the United States*, edited by Michael Kammen (Ithaca, NY: Cornell University Press, 1980), 270–91; Robert C. Twombly, "A Tale of Two Towns," *Reviews in American History* 8 (June 1980): 161–66; Alan Dawley, *Class and Community: The Industrial Revolution in Lynn, Massachusetts* (Cambridge, MA: Harvard University Press, 1970); Anthony F. C. Wallace, *Rockdale: The Growth of an American Village in the Early Industrial Revolution* (New York: Knopf, 1978); Edward Countryman, *A People in Revolution: The American Revolution and Political Society in New York, 1760–1790* (Baltimore: Johns Hopkins University Press, 1981); and Mary P. Ryan, *Cradle of the Middle Class: The Family in*

Oneida County, New York, 1790–1865 (Cambridge, England, and New York: Cambridge University Press, 1980).

8. See Oscar Handlin, "The Significance of the Seventeenth Century," in *Seventeenth-Century America: Essays in Colonial History*, edited by James Morton Smith (Chapel Hill: University of North Carolina Press, 1959), 5, and Edward Countryman, "'Out of Bounds of the Law': Northern Land Rioters in the Eighteenth Century," in *The American Revolution: Explorations in the History of American Radicalism*, edited by Alfred F. Young (De Kalb, IL: Northern Illinois Press, 1976), 57. Norman K. Risjord, *Chesapeake Politics, 1781–1800* (New York: Columbia University Press, 1978), looks closely at politics in the Maryland House of Delegates in 1788. He finds twelve roll calls devoted to two issues of province-wide importance; the other sixty-two roll calls concerned what Risjord calls "local interests or nonpartisan social issues."

9. T. S. Eliot, *Notes Towards the Definition of Culture* (London: Faber and Faber, 1948), 87.

10. See Lois Green Carr and David W. Jordan, *Maryland's Revolution of Government, 1689-1692* (Ithaca, NY: Cornell University Press, 1974): Langdon G. Wright, "Local Government in Colonial New York, 1640–1710" (Ph.D. dissertation, Cornell University, 1974). See also Richard Cobb, *Reactions to the French Revolution* (London and New York: Oxford University Press, 1972), 13, 16.

11. Friedrich W. Nietzsche, *The Use and Abuse of History*, with an introduction by Julius Kraft (Indianapolis: Bobbs-Merrill, 1957), 17–18.

12. Emmanuel Le Roy Ladurie, *The Territory of the Historian* (Chicago: University of Chicago Press, 1979), 99. See also Stanley Hoffman and others, *In Search of France: The Economy, Society, and Political System in the Twentieth Century* (Cambridge, MA: Harvard University Press, 1963), 230–31; and Conrad M. Arensberg and Solon T. Kimball, *Culture and Community* (New York: Harcourt, Brace and World, 1965), ix–x.

13. See O. W. Wolters, *The Fall of Srivijaya in Malay History* (Ithaca, NY: Cornell University Press, 1970), ix; John Clive, *Macaulay: The Shaping of the Historian* (New York: Knopf, 1973), 494; and Barbara W. Tuchman, *Stilwell and the American Experience in China, 1911–1945* (New York: Macmillan, 1970), 31. Among the papers of Victor Hugo Paltsits, in the New York Historical Society, there is a letter from Dr. W. Inglis Morse, whose address in 1937 was Pansy Patch, Paradise, Nova Scotia.

14. See Stephen Thernstrom, *Poverty and Progress: Social Mobility in a Nineteenth-Century City* (Cambridge, MA: Harvard University Press, 1964); Paul E. Johnson, *A Shopkeeper's Millennium: Society and Revivals in Rochester, New York, 1815–1837* (New York: Hill and Wang, 1978); Stephanie G. Wolf, *Urban Village: Population, Community, and Family Structure in Germantown, Pennsylvania, 1683-1800* (Princeton: Princeton University Press, 1976); Richard R. Beeman, "Social Change and Cultural Conflict in Virginia: Lunenberg County, 1746 to 1774," *William and Mary Quarterly* 35 (July 1978): 455–76; Emmanuel Le Roy Ladurie, *Montaillou: The Promised Land of Error* (New York: G. Braziller, 1978); and Carl E. Schorske, *Fin-de-Siecle Vienna: Politics and Culture* (New York: Knopf, 1980).

15. T. C. Barker, "Modern Economic History and the Local Historian," *Middlesex Local History Council Bulletin*, 16 (November 1963): 1–3. For two important examples of what

can be achieved, see Michael P. Weber and Anthony E. Boardman, "Economic Growth and Occupational Mobility in 19th-Century Urban America: A Reappraisal," *Journal of Social History* 11 (Fall 1977): 52–74, a case study of Warren, Pennsylvania, 1870–1910; and Daniel Walkowitz, *Worker City, Company Town: Iron and Cotton-worker Protest in Troy and Cohoes, New York, 1855–1884* (Urbana: University of Illinois Press, 1978).

16. Clive Holmes, *The Eastern Association in the Civil War* (London: Cambridge University Press, 1974), 3–4.

17. See Joseph L. Love, "An Approach to Regionalism," in *New Approaches to Latin-American History*, edited by Richard Graham and Peter H. Smith (Austin: University of Texas Press, 1974), 137–55; *The Chesapeake in the Seventh Century: Essays on Anglo-American Society*, edited by Thad W. Tate and David L. Ammerman (Chapel Hill: University of North Carolina Press, 1979); Roberta Balstad Miller, *City of Hinterland: A Case Study of Urban Growth and Regional Development* (Westport, CT: Greenwood Press, 1979), which treats Syracuse and Onondaga County, 1790–1860.

18. R. Richard Wohl and A. Theodore Brown, "The Usable Past: A Study of Historical Traditions in Kansas City," *Huntington Library Quarterly* 23 (May 1960): 237–59, quotations from pp. 237, 258–59.

19. Cf. Clyde and Sally Griffen, *Natives and Newcomers: The Ordering of Opportunity in Mid-Nineteenth-Century Poughkeepsie* (Cambridge, MA: Harvard University Press, 1978); Ronald H. Bayor, *Neighbors in Conflict: The Irish, Germans, Jews, and Italians of New York City, 1929–1941* (Baltimore: Johns Hopkins University Press, 1978); and Bruce C. Daniels, ed., *Town and County: Essays on the Structure of Local Government in the American Colonies* (Middletown, CT: Wesleyan University Press, 1978).

20. See, for example, James J. Divita, *Slaves to No One: A History of the Holy Trinity Catholic Community in Indianapolis on the Diamond Jubilee of the Founding of Holy Trinity Parish* (Indianapolis: Holy Trinity Parish, 1981); J. M. Bumsted, "Revivalism and Separatism in New England: The First Society of Norwich, Connecticut, as a Case Study," *William and Mary Quarterly* 24 (October 1967): 588–612; Tamara K. Hareven and Randolph Langenbach, *Amoskeag: Life and Work in an American Factory-City* (New York: Pantheon Books, 1978); Walter Muir Whitehill, *Museum of Fine Arts, Boston: A Centennial History*, 2 vols. (Cambridge, MA: Harvard University Press, 1970); Margaret A. Erskine, *Mechanics Hall* (Worcester, MA: Worcester Bicentennial Commission, 1977); Emily Williams, *Canal Country: Utica to Binghamton* (Utica, NY: [H.M. Cardamone], 1982), on the Chenango Canal.

21. See Barbara MacDonald Powell, "'The Most Celebrated Encampment': The Valley Forge Experience in American Culture, 1777–1983" (Ph.D. diss., Cornell University, 1983).

22. See Lawrence Stone, "The Revival of Narrative: Reflections on a New Old History," *Past and Present* 85 (November 1979): 3–24 and Bernard Bailyn, "The Challenge of Modern Historiography," *American Historical Review* 87 (February 1982), especially pp. 7–9, 23–24.

23. See Bernard Bailyn, *The Ordeal of Thomas Hutchinson* (Cambridge, MA: Harvard University Press, 1974); Gerald H. Meaker, *The Revolution Left in Spain, 1914–1923* (Stanford: Stanford University Press, 1974); Charles Gibson, "Conquest, Capitulation, and Indian Treaties," *American Historical Review* 83 (February 1978): 8–9; and Alfred D.

Chandler, Jr., "Industrial Revolutions and Institutional Arrangements," American Academy of Arts and Sciences *Bulletin* 33 (May 1980): 50.

24. See Charles Warren's letter to Mark A. DeWolfe Howe, May 31, 1938, in which Warren thanked his friend for sending a copy of *Old Bristol* and indicated that he had read the book with great interest. "You were singularly fortunate in having a town to write about which had a good deal of tradition hanging around it and which contained many rather unique individuals with marked characteristics. My old Town of Dedham was a much more prosaic place and when I was preparing my Tercentenary Address, I was astonished to find how few stories regarding individuals were extant in the Town, either in writing or by word of mouth." (Houghton Library, Harvard University.) But cf. Kenneth A. Lockridge, *A New England Town: The First Hundred Years, Dedham, Massachusetts. 1636–1736* (New York: W. W. Norton & Company, 1970).

25. See, for example, Philip L. White, *Beekmantown, N.Y.: Forest Frontier to Farm Community* (Austin: University of Texas Press, 1979); Peter D. McClelland and Alan L. Magdovitz, *Crisis in the Making: The Political Economy of New York State since 1945* (Cambridge, England, and New York: Cambridge University Press, 1981).

26. Thomas S. Kuhn, *The Structure of Scientific Revolutions*, 2d ed. (Chicago: University of Chicago Press, 1970), 90.

27. See Peter Laslett, "The Gentry of Kent in 1640," in *Shaping Southern Society: The Colonial Experience*, edited by T. H. Breen (New York: Oxford University Press, 1976), 42.

28. "Historical Discourse at Concord, on the Second Centennial Anniversary of the Incorporation of the Town, September 12, 1835," in volume 11 of *The Complete Works of Ralph Waldo Emerson*, edited by Edward W. Emerson (Boston and New York: Houghton Mifflin Company, 1932), 27–86; Ralph L. Rusk, *The Life of Ralph Waldo Emerson* (New York: C. Scribner's Sons, 1949), 221–23. For additional examples of important local historians with roots elsewhere, see the works of Joel Munsell and Frederic F. Van De Water, historians of Albany, New York, and Vermont, respectively, who grew up in Massachusetts and New Jersey.

29. Lana Ruegamer, *A History of the Indiana Historical Society, 1830–1980* (Indianapolis: Indiana Historical Society, 1980), v.

30. Huizinga, "The Task of Cultural History," in Huizinga, *Men and Ideas: History, the Middle Ages, the Renaissance*, translated by James S. Holmes and Hans van Marle (New York: Meridian Books, 1959), 21; and J. Frank Dobie, *Some Part of Myself* (Boston: Little, Brown, 1967), 198–99.

31. Henry David Thoreau, *A Week on the Concord and Merrimack Rivers* (New York: Crowell, 1961), 21–22.

32. Quoted in Hoagy Carmichael, *The Stardust Road* (New York: Rinehart and Company, 1946), 16–17.

RICHARD WOHL ■
A. THEODORE BROWN

Chapter Thirteen

The Usable Past:
A Study of Historical Traditions in Kansas City

Introduction

In this important essay, the authors discuss the many pasts to be found in Kansas City—an exercise in expanding the subject of local history from the usual players to a more rounded cast. Wohl and Brown look at the traditional history of the city and what it purports to tell us and then at the other pasts that are there to be found: the oral, the deviant, the inarticulate traditions. Their discussion of the way local history has been used to promote the business of the community is also interesting and has lessons for local historians.

This paper is based on two earlier papers: the first was coauthored and read to the Urban History Group lunch of the American Historical Association, in St. Louis, in December 1956; the second paper, by A. Theodore Brown, was read at a session of the Mississippi Valley Historical Association meeting in Lincoln, Nebraska, in April 1957. The leading ideas and much of the phraseology here are Dr. Wohl's; due to Dr. Wohl's death in 1957, Brown, the junior author, assumed responsibility for the entire article.

The work is reprinted, by permission, from *The Huntington Library Quarterly* 23 (May 1960): 237–59.

* * * *

Essays on historiography generally deal with the careers of important historians and the changing practices of professional scholarship. Quantitatively, however, in

---

Richard Wohl and A. Theodore Brown, "The Usable Past: A Study of Historical Traditions in Kansas City," *The Huntington Library Quarterly* 23 (May 1960): 237–59.

this country most of the history written during the nineteenth century must have taken the form of local and county histories, produced or sponsored by local residents rather than by trained scholars. These frequently shapeless and always self-gratulant community chronicles exhibit in the main only the haziest notions of historical method or philosophical consistency. They can nevertheless reveal the sense of particular local pasts in relation to given stages of local development. They illustrate the conception of "usable past," and hence provide us with one meaningful index to cultural history in general.[1]

By way of example, investigation of the origin and content of Kansas City's historical traditions, which are embodied in ten published books and many reminiscent articles, may suggest lines for comparative study. A history of this community's historiography shows that most of the writing has been closely related not only to attitudes toward the respective historians' "presents," but also to current prophecies about the future. The primary concern, at first, was with economic history. As the city grew, the scope of inquiry widened and came to include a tentative kind of social and even cultural history. Extending over all of the written histories, there has been a dominant tradition, drawing its force from conceptions of what the city was supposed to *be* and what it was supposed to become.

This dominant tradition more or less monopolizes the local history that has found its way into books, leaving to competing interpretations only the evanescent hospitality of occasional newspaper columns and the near oblivion of unpublished reminiscences. The written histories of Kansas City that have appeared since 1880 yield the picture of a community blessed by geography, made up of remarkably acute businessmen, more or less immune to the partialities of political argument, and engaged for a century or so in prophecy fulfillment. The tradition traces back not to the founding of the original town, but rather to a later stage: the middle 1850s, when the Kansas-Nebraska Act first stirred urban ambition and visions of unlimited development among the community's power elite. This means, of course, that the tradition arose in the competitive town-boosting that was universal over the expanding Middle West. Early boosting literature puts forth exuberant claims as to the bright destiny that awaits a particular spot among all others and suggests that great rewards await the men who will keep faith with the prophecy. So far as they concern Kansas City, the nineteenth-century prophecies were associated with a changing idea of what the West was good for. One line of thinking held that it was "the Great American Desert"; a counterpropaganda, some of it launched from Kansas City, asserted that the West was instead a veritable Garden of Eden. In the 1840s and 1850s William Gilpin achieved a measure of lasting fame by enunciating the geopolitical theory that the site of Kansas City—significantly called "Centropolis" in his writings—was certain to support a commanding metropolis as continental development progressed. It was in this historical setting, a bantling town striving for growth while the potentialities of its hinterland were debated, that something like a philosophy of local history crystallized in Kansas City.[2]

The crystallizing agent, and the leading source figure for later local historians, was Robert Thompson Van Horn. Born in Pennsylvania in 1824, he became early in life a kind of typical American journeyman intellectual. Schoolteaching, legal training, river-boating, and experience as printer, then editor, of Ohio and Pennsylvania newspapers made up his education. Van Horn always assumed the editorial burden of town-boosting: "standing around scratching heads," he wrote in Ohio in 1850, "will never make Pomeroy the city nature intended it to be." Even before he is likely to have heard of Gilpin, he was a good western nationalist, maintaining in one editorial that "in this valley is to concentrate the population, wealth, and civilization of America."[3] One of his ventures was an ill-fated daily paper in Cincinnati; its plants burned to the ground. "It has failed," he wrote to his parents, "and I am again loser." Referring to his own optimistic disposition, he mentioned that he had a temporary job clerking on a river boat and concluded: "if I can financier so as to be able to raise a few hundred dollars, I am going out West, probably to Nebraska, where I hope in a few years to retrieve my fortunes and kick up a dust generally among the natives."[4]

In St. Louis in July 1855 Van Horn met a lawyer from the young and ambitious settlement known as Kansas City. The lawyer was acting for a committee of Kansas City businessmen who wanted someone to take over an enterprise at which they had so far been unsuccessful: the operation of a local newspaper. After a quick trip to the place with the lawyer, Van Horn took the job. He paid the businessmen $250 as the first installment on the plant they had set up and was to pay them a second $250 to complete the contract one year after starting operation. By that time, however, Van Horn had succeeded so well in giving the Kansas City men the kind of newspaper they needed that the second installment was waived. From, in his own words, "a loser" in the summer of 1854, Van Horn had changed his base and become a spectacular local success.

He had done this by transforming business ambitions into community ideology. In doing so, he developed a Kansas City orthodoxy through the columns of his paper (the *Kansas City Enterprise*, later called the *Western Journal of Commerce*) and in other public deliverances, every premise of which was later taken up organically into written Kansas City history. The premises seem to be four, as follows: (1) Kansas City's natural advantages; (2) the need for imaginative, unflagging enterprise to cooperate intelligently with nature; (3) the pitfalls of partisan politics; (4) the existence of historical continuity whereby the rise of Kansas City fulfills a process long under way even before business development came along.

Van Horn's first premise rested on a geographic determinism similar to Gilpin's and stated simply that Kansas City's growth was predestined by natural advantages. "God," he said on one occasion, has marked out by topography the lines of commerce . . . and it is by studying these great tracings of the Almighty's finger that the pioneer of trade and the herald of civilization has selected the site of those gigantic cities of the Republic, and which has fixed upon the rock-bound bay of the Missouri and Kansas as the last great seat of wealth, trade, and population in the westward march of commerce. . . . If men will only study topography the problem is solved.[5]

This theme was frequently elaborated and even entered the editor's private correspondence. Inviting an Ohio friend to visit Kansas City, Van Horn predicted that "you will be led to wonder why God in his mysterious Providence first offered the continent to men at its eastern portals, and so long kept the great and glorious West a *terra incognita* to humanity. This is the masterpiece of creation and the perfection of topography."[6]

Portrayals of natural advantage lent themselves especially well to outside consumption, but they raised obvious difficulties at home. Van Horn was aware of the danger, and it led him to his second premise: the need for constant entrepreneurial aggressiveness. "Most of our people," he wrote, "were too inclined to trust to our 'natural advantages' and too slow to recognize the fact that the money and enterprise of rivals could overcome and filch away that which is but the fruits of natural advantages properly improved." Without vigorous action, he warned, the advantages given by nature would be "just so many monumental mockeries of [our] folly."[7]

Held together in a healthy tension, these forces—nature and enterprise—need fear only one obstacle: the catastrophic stupidities of politicians. Van Horn saw partisan politics as a vast and treacherous bog in which the brightest prospects of wealth and progress might be at any moment sacrificed to demagogy. Kansas City needed certain things that, unfortunately, involved government action: mail and army contracts, railroad grants, arrangements of Indian land titles, etc. These interests might be damaged in the political arena if they were not protected. Hence, Kansas Citians would be forced into political activity but only to defend requirements that would otherwise be neglected. The importance of politics was always that of its negative threat. "Congress may wrangle," Van Horn wrote, "this man or that man may succeed, and yet neither the success of the one nor the failure of the other will build our railroads, regulate our banks, maintain our public institutions, or protect our growing internal interests."[8]

Events seemed to confirm this attitude; referring to the Kansas troubles of 1855, he wrote that everything had been going along very nicely with Kansas City until "*political* influences in the Eastern portion of the Republic" interfered. The Civil War itself, arising from expressed issues in which Kansas Citians were largely uninterested, seemed only to prove that an undue concern with political matters spelled disaster for a hopeful western town.[9]

Van Horn's own political career reveals so many party changes that it can be interpreted as reflecting only the rankest opportunism unless this philosophy of politics is kept in mind. Albert D. Richardson, who had worked with Van Horn in Cincinnati, was surprised to find him proslavery in 1857; four years earlier, issue after issue of their Ohio paper had condemned the Kansas-Nebraska bill as "the Nebraska infamy."[10] In a laudatory biographical sketch published in 1888, the writer approvingly noted Van Horn's political migrations. Before the Civil War he had been (in Kansas City) a Democrat, "and, as Jackson county was largely of that faith, he was respected and influential at home, and able to accomplish more than if he had been of any other politics." By 1865 events had made him a Republican, "and again he was on the side where he could do the most good for the town."[11] An essentially negative attitude toward party politics was part of the larger opportunism of town-building.

The guarantees for Van Horn's metropolis were not in politics; instead, they were in nature and enterprise, to which might be added a kind of historical guarantee. The fourth of his premises holds that the growth of Kansas City is but the culmination of a long series of historical processes that have taken place on the same ground. Urban greatness will arise in time on the spot where earlier enterprises had flourished. Canoes yield to flatboats, which yield to steamboats, which in turn give way to railroads. This point, less explicit than the other three, means simply that history is but a fulfillment that might have been predicted far back in time. The proof offered was that such prophecies had indeed been made. Late in his own life, in a memorial address on one of his fellow town-builders, Van Horn emphasized the farsightedness of the vigorous little group that had pushed Kansas City forward. Fifty years ago, the scene had not been prepossessing, but today, he said, the prosperity of Kansas City and the surrounding region "vindicates the prophetic ken of these early settlers. . . . To be the commercial metropolis of this empire was the ambition of Kansas City, and its fulfillment, then a dream, a prophecy, has become an actual realization."[12]

On the basis of this four-part theory, Van Horn produced hundreds of editorials, addresses, and memorials. When writers approached the subject of Kansas City history, they found the conveniently arranged data waiting for them. They would in any case have had to consult the files of the *Western Journal of Commerce*, but the point is that in taking the paper and its editor as sources, they took also the extant presuppositions they found there. The felt needs of time and place had given rise to a theoretical structure of beneficent determinism, which continued to be of vital importance to the city builders as long as growth was a radical problem.

This theory was worked into one of the first books printed in Kansas City, Charles C. Spalding's *Annals of the City of Kansas*, which carried a brief account of the town's beginnings and was designed to attract favorable attention to the place. Spalding had come west with a university degree and a background in civil engineering; during the struggle to organize Kansas, he published a proslavery newspaper there—despite his Vermont birth and upbringing. In 1855 he came to

Westport, Missouri, where he functioned both as city engineer and newspaper editor. The following year he moved up to the river settlement and joined the small staff of Van Horn's Kansas City paper.[13] Van Horn encouraged him in putting together the materials for his book, much of which came straight out of the columns of the paper. Spalding says his inspiration came from "almost invariably" hearing steamboat passengers at the Kansas City levee saying to one another, "come, let us go ashore and examine the business resources of this place." The local Chamber of Commerce officially approved the work, and the city council helped circulate it.[14]

Spalding's main point, of course, was that Kansas City had a golden future. What he lacked in history—the city was, after all, but a fledgling community—he pieced out with prophecy. The past, indeed, was nothing but prologue for this enthusiast, as for many who followed him. He began with a direct quotation of four pages from Gilpin's *Central Gold Region*, in which it was argued that "these plains are not DESERTS, but the opposite, and are the cardinal basis of the future empire of commerce and industry, now erecting itself upon the North American continent." Coming closer to home, Spalding refers to prophecies Senator Thomas Hart Benton was supposed to have made concerning a future great city where the Kansas and Missouri rivers come together. The force of the prophecies and the basis of Spalding's conviction was in the theory that underpinned them: nature herself had prescribed an urban future for the site, and history had only to report first the realization of this fact by prophetic men and then the unfolding of destiny. Highly confident, Spalding refers to "these great natural advantages that we enjoy, such as soil, climate, and rivers, which come to us stamped with the patent of the creator."[15]

If Spalding's *Annals* can be called history only by courtesy, the same is not true of William H. Miller's *History of Kansas City*, which appeared in 1881. A native Missourian, Miller was born in 1843; he was another wandering journalist and had edited or written for a number of western newspapers in the 1860s and 1870s. Among them was Van Horn's, for which Miller specialized in what would today be called business news. In 1877 he forsook journalism to become full-time secretary for the Kansas City Board of Trade, an organization in which Van Horn had been and still was active.[16] Miller's history, indeed, appeared in its first form as part of the *Kansas City Daily Journal*'s "Annual Review" in 1877.

Miller's book, the matrix of nearly all later written Kansas City history, reflects a consistent stress on economic matters. The emphasis was realistic, since by far the greatest energy had been devoted to economic growth in the city of his day. It led Miller, however, to ignore a great deal of local history. He sketches only briefly the colorful life of the early French fur trading community; this, to him, was not the real stuff of history. The French community had been stagnant; it had made no effort to build a city. Again, the inhabitants of nearby Westport who were southerners and who developed a characteristic social life of their own, get short shrift from Miller.[17] The South, and the southerner's outlook, both lost out in the competition of events. These people were not aggressive or expansive enough and hence were left behind by the times; Miller probably thought they deserved no better from the historian of the city's affairs.

Reluctantly, he gave a few pages to political matters; the events of the border warfare leading up to the Civil War of course bore directly on Kansas City's economic fortunes. But Miller hurries on; politics, in his eyes, constituted an unfortunate obstacle in the path of his main concern. Political conflict was, from his point of view as from Van Horn's, wasteful because divisive. It comprised an order of things more or less "bad" for the city. In 1858 Spalding had remarked of Kansas City's hinterland that "The adjustment . . . of her political affairs will be seed-time and harvest for her sovereign farmers," and had cherished a hope that perhaps the politicians would not have their war, since, after all, "the great idea of progress and money making, so peculiarly characteristic of the American mind, is rapidly over-stepping and losing sight of the operations and negotiations of politicians,"[18] Miller, to whom this seemed a just and sensible view, regretfully notes, with the memory of the war fresh in his mind, that "During the excited political contest of 1860 public attention was so much absorbed with politics that there appears to have been but little effort to inaugurate new enterprises."[19]

Investment and trade are more relevant than wars and elections to the story Miller tells. He asks, in effect, this question of the past: how did it happen that between 1838 and 1881 a group of small, rather unimpressive settlements at the junction of two rivers became transformed into the booming confusion of an urban establishment? Everything else is marginal to this, the real issue.[20] As has been suggested, this was also the real issue so far as the people who were riding or guiding Kansas City's future were concerned. The main point in 1881 was still to make the city grow, and following this logic to its end, if history was useful at all it was because it might offer pertinent instruction. Miller employs all the usual paraphernalia of the economic historian: trade figures, population growth, the course of investment, the diversification of commerce—showing us all the arts and devices that made Kansas City a great market place. His account, however, is given rational coherence and intellectual dignity by a careful working out of the theory of urban development pioneered locally by Van Horn.

In his introductory chapter Miller describes ancient cities as having been founded by the fiat of monarchs, with some consideration of military advantage and soil fertility. There follows a hiatus until after the American Revolution, when the requirements changed. (This contrast may not be so arbitrary as it appears, since Miller is distinguishing, substantially, between town-building before and after the Industrial Revolution.) In the later dispensation the crucial determinant was access to transportation facilities, and nowhere was this more true than in the American West. Kansas City was peculiarly fortunate in this vital respect, since—Miller says—"there are but few, besides our own city, that from the first have held the advantage over all rivals in all phases of transportational development, or that stand to-day more pre-eminent in this regard." In its most general form, the theory is stated as follows: "the long since observed physical law that 'motion follows the line of least resistance'. . . . All effort employs the methods, and follows the lines that most facilitate the attainment of its object."[21]

Such is the theme of Miller's book, stated, restated, and illustrated. The river junction first drew the fur traders, then the more comprehensive Indian trade, then the Santa Fe, Oregon, and related trades. So unshakable was the influence of this determinant, that, in Miller's eyes, it carried the city through crisis after crisis with perfect safety. Early land-title uncertainties, the menace of cholera epidemics, negative interpretations of Kansas City's hinterland, even the Civil War, which was an unqualified catastrophe—all these proved unavailing against the geographic talisman. By 1865, Miller remarks,

> This city seemed to be well nigh out of the race for commercial supremacy, and would have been so regarded had it not been for her well demonstrated natural advantages, and the fact that the main line of the Union Pacific Railway started at this city . . . and the fact that the Missouri Pacific was nearly completed. These gave heart to her citizens to renew the struggle, and an era of unprecedented activity followed.[22]

This bland and apparently lucid statement introduces again the ambiguity in natural advantages that had bemused Van Horn. The railroads, after all, came to Kansas City because campaigns were waged by groups that wanted them, because financial contributions were raised to attract them, because deliberate and ultimately successful entrepreneurial tactics were adopted. By the time railroads appeared on the scene, the logic of geographical advantage was no longer decisive; the lines could have gone to Leavenworth or St. Joseph. Miller, unconsciously paradoxical, makes this apparent when he enthusiastically quotes one of Van Horn's postwar editorials, according to which "There is a tide in the affairs of men—and the same is true of cities. . . . If we do not act at the tide of our opportunities, our future history will be a record of failure. . . . Providence never assisted a lazy man— fortune never smiled on an indolent community."[23] With the opening of the railroad era, Miller's "line of least resistance" wavers, and will no longer support his interpretation. Still, he does not abandon it but adroitly restates it so as now to include a qualifying implication. Kansas Citians must at least cooperate intelligently with nature. This seemed to involve mostly the avoidance of factional passion: "Kansas City has but to preserve . . . unity of action to acquire the trade of the whole trans-Missouri country west to Arizona and south to Mexico."[24]

Van Horn's booster theory of urban growth had been plastic enough to allow for both natural determinism and enterprise. One of the lasting effects his protégé, Miller, had on the historiography of Kansas City stemmed from his overlooking the tension between them and passing on to his successors his own patchwork explanation. His subsequent role as an authoritative historian effectively quelled further exploration of the problem, since Miller's text rather than the contemporary sources became the wellspring from which most later historians drew their material. After the fashion of medieval chronicles, following a safe and respected authority, writers down to the 1940s paid Miller the high compliment of amiably plagiarizing his text. We are not stressing the equivocal ethics of unacknowledged borrowing. Instead, we wish to note what seem to be the reasons for such wholesale use of Miller's material. Miller himself had made up fully 10 percent of his book by quoting Van Horn directly. It appears certain from the context of later borrowings that the authors assumed Miller's work to be the canonical version of what had happened in the past, which it would be idle to check or try to improve on. It was only worth while to embellish the text with added comment and a few confirming glosses. Secondly, and even more important, this consistent plagiarism gave a unity to much of the history that has since been written about Kansas City by providing a classic framework in which the city's past could be contained. The systematic transmission of what was originally a booster's conception of city history has ruled out, since Miller's formulation of it, any substantial consideration of the early French community or of the environing cultures in Westport and Independence and, most of all, any realistic and accurate account of the personal and community enterprise that helped win Kansas City's battles with her urban rivals.

Miller's immense influence is clearly prefigured in the work of the next local historian, Theodore Spencer Case, whose *History of Kansas City* appeared in 1888. Originally a physician, Case was in his long life by turns an army officer, a lawyer, politician, and member of the directorates of an extraordinary variety of public and private organizations in Kansas City. He arrived there in 1857 and lived through the heroic years when the city was securing its foundations and winning out over nearby communities. He was an old-timer, so to speak, by the time Miller arrived in the city in 1871.

In writing his own history, Case was dealing with a period of change and growth that he had himself experienced.[25] We might, on this score, expect vivid and original personal testimony. There is, in fact, little in Case that is not in Miller, aside from compilations of business statistics for the years after 1881 and up to 1888. It is probably a tribute to Case's celebrated geniality and talent for sociability that much appears in his work about the city's voluntary organizations and clubs. Again, however, the focus is on the wonderful transformation of a wilderness camp into a burgeoning city. "It has been impossible," Case writes, "to do it full justice. Older citizens are so bewildered by it as to have lost track of old landmarks, and their memories are at fault, while the newer ones have been so completely engrossed by current progress as not to have taken the past into consideration at all. Even the present is more than they can keep up with."[26] At the outset he states the familiar deterministic doctrine: "as if nature had designed the place for a great city,"[27] but his comment on the text diverges significantly, if almost imperceptibly, from Miller's. The supporting evidence for the doctrine is strongest, of course, in the earliest years of the city's history. Case runs quickly over this phase of the story and turns rather abruptly to more recent experiences. And in so doing, he obliquely makes a different point: enterprise, not natural bounty, accounts for the fulfillment of the prophecies. Railroads provided the city's leaders with an opportunity that, if missed, would have resulted in fatal loss. Case remarks quite casually on a set of facts Miller never paused to notice. He asserts directly that there was local opposition to railroad projects in Kansas City;[28] unfortunately, he does not develop this topic, but it does suggest the influence of artificial advantages in shaping the city's course.

In diverging from Miller in this respect, Case does not abandon his model so far as to avoid the problem. He simply adds "the energy and enterprise of its citizens" to Kansas City's natural advantages and then drops the question, only recollecting himself a few pages later with a lame addition: "many persons, in viewing the wonderful growth of Kansas City . . . imagine it was forced into prosperity by reason of its geographical position . . . but . . . it was only by great vigilance and a hard struggle on the part of her citizens that she obtained the advantages above mentioned."[29] Still, as given, the explanation in Case's history diverts attention away from economic decisions in favor of an immanent geographical mystique.

William Griffith, who followed Case as a city historian, seems to have earned the almost total obscurity that now shrouds his name.[30] For the most part, he simply transcribes Miller and could be dismissed but for two remarks that indicate a new stress entering into the city's history around 1900. In the first place, while sedulously underscoring the site's locational advantages, Griffith was properly impressed with the coming of the railroads and pointed to the successful bridging of the Missouri River as the circumstance that brought them. This coup, he concludes (quite incorrectly), was "due to the decisive, intelligent action of a few well-known business men, aided and abetted by the united assistance of the entire populace."[31] Wherever, in fact, Griffith makes interpolations into Miller's text, the stress is on enterprise and strategic risk-taking, despite the oft-repeated bow to natural advantages.

More important, in the light of what was to come, were Griffith's reflections on the changing appearance and style of life in Kansas City. Already in 1900 he could remark with shocked surprise on what the place had looked like twenty years earlier. The prospect in 1880 had been dismal indeed:

> The old-fashioned Missouri hog, fitter for the race-track than for the pork-barrel . . . patrolled the streets and disputed the king's highway with the king and all his subjects. At night, when the hogs were off duty, a billion frogs . . . told their troubles to the stars and saluted the rising sun with croaks of despair. In wet weather the town-site was sea of mud and in dry weather a desert of dust. There was no paving. . . . The water supply made whiskey-drinking a virtue and the gas was not much better use than to be blown out. The population of the city included as fine a collection of the ruffian brotherhood and sisterhood of the wild West as could well be imagined. Renegade

Indians, demoralized soldiers, unreformed bushwhackers, and border ruffians, thieves, and thugs imported from anywhere, professional train-robbers of home growth, and all kinds of wrecks of the Civil War, gave the town something picturesquely harder to overcome than the hills and gulches of its topography.

All this, he says, was "a sight to make granite eyes shed tears." Indeed, Kansas City in the full bloom of its economic growth offered "not a single pleasing prospect except the towering ambition, indomitable determination, and volcanic energy of the good people of the place." [32] Here is the new theme: celebration of the city's increasing urbanity, which is studied by tracing the evolution of an increasingly organized social life in Kansas City.

The earlier theme—accounting for the city's growth—is still prescient; in Griffith and his successors it becomes a set formula, phrased in classic terms of such apparently unimpeachable validity that it hardly seems to call for extended comment. Carrie Whitney in 1908, Charles Deatherage in 1928, and Roy Ellis in 1930 all repeat it with ritual emphasis. And the same stress, although modified by these new emphases, continues in the work of the city's latest historians. [33] Spoken of in this vein, the histories carry on the great tradition of seeing Kansas City's past as the fulfillment of prophecy, a conception that was central with Van Horn and Spalding. As the most recent writers justly remark, "Kansas City was a connoisseur of prophets." [34]

But when the prophets are gone, what of the prophecy? Already, late in the 1890s, young William Allen White saw in Robert T. Van Horn, Kansas City's prophet par excellence, the sad picture of a man who has survived his era: subdued, living in the past, largely ineffectual. "Perhaps," White wrote many years later, "I was too preoccupied . . . to sense very clearly what a mauve tragedy in the background, set in old age's shabby pastels, was passing across the stage before my very eyes." [35] The city's history had left Van Horn behind, and its historiography, too, veered into different channels than those by which the editor had steered his course. By the early twentieth century, the issue that began to engross the historians was the changing character of the city's social life, and the conception of what ought properly to be included in an urban history drifted more and more into a description and justification of the culture of Kansas City. The writers began to grope for the "essence" of Kansas City's past, rather than for the "process" by which she had matured into metropolitan stature.

In 1900 even Griffith went to some pains in his history to distinguish the merits of economic expansion from the equally desirable virtues of increased civic amenity. For novelty, he had suggested that progress in the one did not necessarily mean an enhancement of the other. Kansas City's special urban quality, he claimed, partakes of "the spirit of the West." This spirit hovers over the city's past and present like a benign *genius loci*, which "saw the cabin fall and the palace rise." [36] Eight years later Whitney struck the same mystical note and assured her readers that the

"Western element knows no note of decadence" and that "the finality of Western history still lies in the distance."[37] And again, twenty years after this, Deatherage opened his voluminous history with a long poem invoking Manitou, who was identified as the tutelary spirit of the West.

This search for a larger context in which to set Kansas City's past is not limited to a simple identification with the merits of a particular section. Kansas City comes to be seen, rather, not only as a happily typical western metropolis, but as one that somehow represents peculiarly American characteristics. The city's own history becomes a nucleus around which increasingly larger sections of the country's history are wound, with the tacit implication that each illustrates the other. Griffith begins the process by devoting no less than one-fifth of his small book to the Louisiana Purchase and the Missouri Compromise in order to set the stage. Whitney, fumbling even more wildly for a usable frame of reference, begins her consideration of the city's Civil War era by discussing the Northwest Ordinance in detail. But Deatherage sets the record for diffuseness by opening his book with the discovery of America and literally does not reach Kansas City until page 347.

These strenuous attempts to overcome a narrow parochialism in the city's history and to extend its historical base bog down for lack of a conceptual vocabulary that could be used to relate the wider range of American history to local events. The authors press hard on their western metaphor, and the occasionally grotesque disproportion and irrelevancies in their works reveal an honest but unavailing effort to produce social history as sound and as sharp as the economic history written earlier. The uses to which material on the Santa Fe trail is put offer a compact example of this kind of changing emphasis. In Miller the trail figures as an economic issue, and he is interested in it solely in that connection. Case, who follows him, deals with it in much the same way, but he occasionally graces his account with anecdotes of adventure in the prairie commerce. Whitney, on the other hand, devotes thirty pages to the romantic associations of the subject, as an exemplification of life in the Old West, and barely mentions the business transacted; Deatherage follows Whitney's lead in the matter.[38] The effect, in the end, is to create an entirely amiable but unmistakable sentimentality designed to enhance sentiment of place by manipulating the emotional implications of data. This tactic, in the end, submerges the legitimate importance of the Santa Fe trail in the city's economic history.

Since 1930 the identification of the city's history with that of the nation and the statement of its essential urban attributes have been more gracefully expressed. Garwood, writing in 1947, claims that Kansas City's history "to a large extent has been a history of the country, in miniature, for the last one hundred years." Haskell and Fowler, three years later, warmly agree. "The history of Kansas City," they say, "in the last hundred years has paralleled with extraordinary fidelity the history of the United States. Many of the factors that shaped our life between 1850 and 1950 found local expression at the great bend of the Missouri." This emphasis, we think, reflects more than an exuberance of local pride; it stresses the notion that some of the main issues and central conflicts of American history found a crucial testing ground in the history of Kansas City. It is significant that the most recent history of the city, for example, turns to examine once again the factor of location, this time not to show that economic advantages are derived from the city's site, but to point out that Kansas City was in the path of at least two of the most important developments in American history: the Civil War and the settlement of the plains frontier.[39] And, it is implied, where the current of historical events ran most swiftly, the influence of those events was strongest, most lasting, and peculiarly telling.

So far, our review of the general course of the city's historiography has found a basically optimistic line, understandable in view of its roots in the booster tradition. But here and there, especially in some of the more recent works, a less sanguine note can be detected. In 1930 Ellis was musing whether it was wise to hope for continued increase in the city's population. Cities may forget, he warns, that "numbers alone do not constitute any proper criterion of comfort, culture, or permanent prosperity."[40] The unpublished M.A. thesis cited above [note 33] refers again and again to "Kansas City's worth" and to Kansas City's "just claims," in striking contrast to the high confidence that had characterized Spalding, Miller, and Case.[41] Perhaps this new mood, slightly represented as it is, may be due to the fact that the excitements of the city's first and most rapid growth are now muted. Garwood, more recently, suggests that "Probably the city today can be described as full grown, and for the time being somewhat quietly disposed toward the march of events."[42] This last would be indignantly scouted by many in the city, and it might be noted that Garwood is not a native; the strength of the historical tradition, with its origins far back in the first booster literature, is not so prominent in his book.

This written tradition, as we have outlined it, is essentially the success story of a city; it parallels closely the success story of Van Horn himself, who worked out most of its theoretical framework. It is easily accessible, its assumptions and its data, indeed, being the only ones that a more or less casual or hurried research is likely to encounter. Other local figures, whatever their reasons, have found themselves drawn toward different aspects of the city's history and have shown that much of what the written tradition takes for granted is in fact highly problematic. These divergent expressions, when they have been preserved at all, have taken the form of addresses to "old settlers'" associations, letters to editors, and unpublished reminiscences; they can be described, for contrast, as a sort of "oral tradition."

The leading source figure in the oral tradition was John Calvin McCoy. Son of the famous Baptist missionary, Isaac, he arrived at the site of the future city in 1830, almost a generation before Van Horn. He founded Westport, acted as secretary to the original town company, and engaged in large-scale business operations in the two towns before the Civil War.[43] Nevertheless, there was a more or less poetic vein in McCoy's character that seems not to have been satisfied with a purely business career. He did not stick consistently to the job of town-building; after putting up a store in Westport, according to his daughter, he soon realized "that he was not fitted by nature, or inclination, for a mercantile life" and withdrew from the enterprise. "You know," his mother once wrote of him, "he don't calculate closely about things, and promises too much. . . ." He was continuously involved in surveying trips and Indian matters, which took him west into the wilderness as well as east to Washington.[44] During the Civil War, McCoy, a southern sympathizer, had to leave Kansas City—significantly unlike Van Horn, who usually found himself able to roll with a punch. In 1863 McCoy corresponded with a Kansas City associate with whom he had business, proposing a meeting place outside the city. "I suppose," wrote this earliest of local pioneers, "it might not be safe for me to go to Kansas City."[45] Shortly after the war McCoy returned to Kansas City and engaged in real estate; he was never able to recoup his losses and died in 1889 in the care of relatives. Having withdrawn from history as participator, however, he re-entered it in the 1870s as bard-raconteur and spent his later years retelling and writing down the local history that he could remember.[46]

In brief, McCoy simply denied or ignored most of what came to make up the written tradition. His first contribution to a newspaper was called forth, he said, by an earlier article on local history that had included some misstatements; he did not specify what they were. His account, as would be characteristic, dwelt on the direct, personal quality of experience, rather than on its broad economic meaning. On his arrival at the site, he wrote, the ground was "clothed with dense primeval forest— the still, quiet solitude interrupted only by the barking squirrel, the howl of the wolf, the distant baying of the hunter's dog. . . ." Subsequent progress did not please McCoy; he sighed "for the good old days of genuine disinterested honesty . . . when one might lie down to sleep without fear of having his throat cut, his pockets picked, or the socks stolen off his feet."[47] His letters are studded with unpleasant imagery when the reference is to industrial growth: locomotives always screech, the city is always raucous ("Plutonic bellowings . . . as if old Nature had a stomach ache"), and morality tends to deteriorate in it. In pleasant contrast, the "dense, primeval forest" and it denizens recur time and time again.[48]

McCoy cut in behind Van Horn's "heroic age" with a "golden age" of his own. He wrote and spoke a good deal about the Indians and the French, on which Miller and Case had been almost totally silent. His major concern was not with pedantic correctness in small details; what he wanted was to preserve certain elements in the city's history that appeared to be rapidly vanishing into oblivion. When Miller's history appeared, McCoy praised it as containing much "historical and statistical information of great value." Nevertheless, he quickly added, "the facts I have written . . . are not touched upon in that work."[49] Earlier than this, he had already noted the appearance of a number of good statistical compilations relating to the city's growth, "but this," he said, "is only a part of the past history of Kansas City. . . ."[50]

Although the early town builders had been his intimate friends, McCoy pays them little heed in his reminiscences. Far from being heroes of enterprise, he wrote, they were "not disposed to risk much in the experiment, and did very little to push the town."[51] As far as prophetic insight was concerned, McCoy denied that there had been any. That the early businessmen were actually creating the basis for an urban center "never entered into their calculation." Many writers had asserted that Kansas City's greatness was predicted early in the course of events; but McCoy counters: "not a particle of foundation in fact has that assumption." Had anyone actually ventured upon predictions of this kind in the early days, he would have been laughed to scorn and his prophecies marked down as "the idle vaporings of a demented intellect." As for Spalding, that young man had written his material "as a puff for the young town, and the stereotyped fraud has become history."[52]

The historians of the written tradition could not, of course, ignore McCoy's writings; all of them quote from him one or more passages about the "dense, primeval forest" or else his account of the 1844 flood. But their purpose is to set off all the more dramatically the constructive energy of the town-building enterprise and never to call into question the value of the enterprise itself, as McCoy did. Interestingly enough, his standing as a founding father of the city was hardly alluded to in the written tradition until 1947, when Garwood identified him as the "principal founder" of Kansas City.[53]

There were other contributors to the oral tradition, men and women whose memories were cast in the same vein as McCoy's. Some of their narratives are preserved in a typewritten folder of "Pioneer Recollections" in the archives of the Native Sons of Kansas City. Apart from McCoy himself, the most prolific contributor was Daniel Geary, who had held office in the city government in the Civil War period. Geary could not remember the 1830s and 1840s, but he never failed to point out failures to predict accurately the course of events in Kansas City in the 1850s and later. "I might also recite many interesting incidents," he wrote once, answering a request for information about the war, "but I have observed that wherever I attempted to . . . only yawns were elicited which indicated lack of interest." Apparently, people preferred to get their history out of books, and as to the existing written histories of the city Geary simply remarked that they "might be classified as 75% absolute fiction, 20% exaggeration, mixed with a substratum of 5% truth."[54]

Obviously, there is more than one "past" in Kansas City. The written tradition —with its success story of prophecies redeemed, boldness vindicated, and the city itself a continuing testimony to triumph over the wilderness—exercises an almost hypnotic influence not only over its historians but in the city's present-day publicity. But historical traditions easily become a tangle of vested metaphors, blocking inquiry into the very questions they offer to solve. The conflicts between and within the traditions we have called "written" and "oral" mark a range of questions that remain open for new investigations and fresh judgment. It is quite clear that adequate local history can be written in terms of neither stereotype.

Perhaps the most important suggestion to emerge from our examination, however, deals not with the adequacy of Kansas City's historical traditions, but rather with their effect upon and their place within the general history of American culture. Nineteenth- and twentieth-century local history comprises an enormous body of literature in this country; the attitudes and presuppositions enshrined in this literature offer potential rewards to historical investigators. To some extent, what people believe about the history of their locale may shape their notions of how they ought to live in it and of the values they may hope to realize in their community. If, as Charles and Mary Beard once wrote, "the history of civilization may become an instrument of civilization itself," the course of American urban historiography may have operated in the formation of "urbane" and local attitudes.

NOTES

1. "Escape from the past is scarcely more possible for a community than for an individual. New growth is ever occurring but generally as an outgrowth of vital traditions or latent capacities. . . . If the community's tradition (its own story, its history) is then part of its character, the history of its historiography is an important chapter in the story of its cultural development"—Blake McKelvey, "A History of Historical Writing in the Rochester Area," *Rochester History* 6 (1944): 1.

2. See Henry Nash Smith, *Virgin Land: The American West as Symbol and Myth* (Cambridge, MA, 1951). To Smith's chapter on Gilpin may be added Gilpin's own basic contribution to the debate over the nature of the West: *The Central Gold Region* (Philadelphia, 1860). Gilpin's map of his projected "Centropolis" is reproduced in the *Kansas City Star*, May 26, 1901.

3. Meigs County (Ohio) *Telegraph*, June 27, April 25, 1850; the volumes of this paper edited by Van Horn are in the Kansas City Public Library. Where not otherwise indicated, biographical data on Van Horn comes from the sketch in Theodore S. Case, *History of Kansas City, Missouri* (Syracuse, NY, 1888), 432–40. There is a small but valuable collection of Van Horn papers in the Archives of the Native Sons of Kansas City.

4. Pomeroy, Ohio, February 27, 1854, Van Horn papers, Native Sons Archives.

5. Address at merchants' Christmas dinner, 1857, "Railroads and the Press—Twin Brothers in American Progress and Development," quoted in William H. Miller, *The History of Kansas City* (Kansas City, 1881), 79.

6. To I. Cartwright, Kansas City, February 27, 1858, Van Horn papers, Native Sons Archives.

7. *Western Journal of Commerce*, May 24, 1860.

8. Ibid., June 25, 1860.

9. *Kansas City Enterprise*, December 22, 1855. On the effort of the Kansas City leadership to remain "neutral" during the Kansas conflict, see James C. Malin, *Grassland Historical Studies*, vol. 1 (Lawrence, KS, 1950), 102–18.

10. See the interesting sketch of Van Horn (who is not named) in Albert D. Richardson's *Beyond the Mississippi* (Hartford, CT, 1867), 27–29.

11. Case, *History of Kansas City*, 434–35.

12. Manuscript of memorial address on Milton J. Payne (n.d., 1890?), Van Horn papers, Native Sons Archives.

13. Westport was then four miles from Kansas City; it has since been absorbed into the metropolis. Biographical data on Charles C. Spalding comes from an obituary in the Boston *Daily Advertiser*, January 20, 1877, supplied by the Boston Public Library, and from a valuable sketch by James Anderson, appended to the facsimile reprint of *Annals of the City of Kansas* published by Frank Glenn (Kansas City, 1950).

14. Charles C. Spalding, *Annals of the City of Kansas*, fifth and sixth unnumbered pages after the frontispiece; about a dozen copies of the original, printed by Van Horn and Abeel in 1858, are known to have survived. We have used the Glenn facsimile edition cited above.

15. Spalding, *Annals*, 10–14, 16, 70.

16. The only known biographical sketch of William H. Miller is in *The History of Jackson County, Missouri* (Kansas City, 1881), 816, 817. Miller's *History of Kansas City*, in addition to the separate publication cited in these notes, appears in this volume, pp. 373–632.

17. Miller, *History of Kansas City*, 15–16; Elizabeth Butler Gentry contributed a lively sketch of the early Westport social life (a subject that Miller ignores) in Carrie Westlake Whitney, *Kansas City Missouri: Its History and Its People*, vol. 1 (Chicago, 1908), 641–63.

18. Spalding, *Annals*, 9–10.

19. Miller, *History of Kansas City*, 72.

20. Miller's concluding chapter is "Kansas City—Why She Is and What She Is." In it, he reviews factors that seemed decisive in the city's growth, noting the apparently unlimited resources of the "new West." Despite its youth, Kansas City's supremacy in its region was clearly secure. "Since, therefore," Miller continues, "Kansas City already so largely controls the trade of this vast area, and since its intense and speedy concentration here is assured . . . it manifests that her growth will be measured by that of the country. It remains only for us to review the resources of the country and compare them with those of districts commercially tributary to the great cities of the world, to arrive at some idea of what Kansas City must become" (p. 249). History and prophecy were as inseparable as two sides of the same coin.

21. Ibid., 6, 7.

22. Ibid., 110.

23. Ibid., 111. See Roy Robert's prefatory note in Henry C. Haskell and Richard B. Fowler, *City of the Future* (Kansas City, 1950), 5: "but for the daring, the vision, and the faith of a handful of men, the capital of this great empire might just as well have been St. Joseph, Leavenworth, or even Independence. All three had a head start over the scrawny little village that sprang up at the mouth of the Kaw."

24. Miller, *History of Kansas City*, 247.

25. The best biographical sketch is in H. L. Conrad, ed., *Encyclopedia of the History of Missouri*, vol. 1 (New York, 1901), 517–19. It is difficult to say how much of his history Case actually wrote; his preface credits the assistance of compilers and remarks that he has subjected their work to strict inspection (p. 4).

26. Case, *History of Kansas City*, 3.

27. Ibid., 28.

28. Ibid., 60–61.

29. Ibid., 55, 58.

30. William Griffith, *History of Kansas City* (Kansas City, 1900). The Kansas City directory for 1900 identifies Griffith as associated with the firm that published his book; the same firm published other local history material and may have commissioned Griffith's book as one for which a substantial local sale was expected.

31. Griffith, *History of Kansas City*, 49.

32. Ibid., 106–107.

33. Whitney, *Kansas City Missouri*, 641–63; Charles P. Deatherage, *Early History of Greater Kansas City* (Kansas City, 1928); Roy Ellis, *A Civic History of Kansas City* (Springfield, MO, 1930); Darrell Garwood, *Crossroads of America* (New York, 1948); Haskell and Fowler, *City of the Future*. To these may be added an unpublished M.A. thesis: Alice Lanterman, "The Industrial Development of Kansas City" (Northwestern University, 1939). For examples of plagiarism referred to above, see Miller, *History of Kansas City*, 236, passage beginning: "The school year of 1868–9 . . ."; Case, *History of Kansas City*, 115, same words; Griffith, *History of Kansas City*, 75, same words; and Whitney, *Kansas City Missouri* (1), 306: "Of the school year of 1868–1869 . . ." See also Miller, 45, beginning: "There was no municipal government . . ."; Case, 198–99, beginning: "A circumstance occurred . . ."; and Deatherage, 375: "There was no municipal government. . . ." Again, see Miller on the Panic of 1873, 147: "the effect of this panic . . ."; Case gives the same passage without acknowledgment, 92–93 and again with acknowledgment, 284–85.

34. Haskell and Fowler, *City of the Future*, 61.

35. William Allen White, *The Autobiography of William Allen White* (New York, 1946), 212.

36. Griffith, *History of Kansas City*, 102.

37. Whitney, *Kansas City Missouri*, 9.

38. Miller, *History of Kansas City*, 21–26; Case, *History of Kansas City*, 33–36; Whitney, Kansas City Missouri, 149–79; Deatherage, *Early History*, 293–323.

39. Garwood, *Crossroads of America*, 11; Haskell and Fowler, *City of the Future*, 15.

40. Ellis, *Civic History of Kansas City*, 36; on page 148, Ellis remarks that "the strategic location of Kansas City" funneled into it a fine assortment of riffraff, "quite as much of the flotsam and jetsam of society as will any street in America [present] . . ." Thus does geographical advantage return to plague the local historian!

41. Lanterman, "Industrial Development of Kansas City," 2, 54, 130.

42. Garwood, *Crossroads of America*, 321.

43. The most complete biographical sketch of McCoy was itself "oral," a memorial address delivered before the Jackson County Historical Society, "John C. McCoy, Pioneer, and the Early History of Jackson County," by W. C. Scarritt. It was printed in the *Kansas City Times*; an updated clipping is in the John C. McCoy Scrapbook in the Archives of the Native Sons of Kansas City. In addition to this sketch, the present account generalizes from newspaper items, 1855–1860, and letters in the Isaac McCoy Letterbooks, Kansas State Historical Society, Topeka.

44. Mrs. Nellie McCoy Harris, "Memories of Old Westport," in *The Annals of Kansas City*, vol. 1 (Kansas City, MO: Missouri Valley Historical Society, 1924), 466. Christiana McCoy to Isaac McCoy, April 20, 1840, Isaac McCoy Letterbooks; John C. McCoy, "Survey of Kansas Indian Lands," *Collections of the Kansas State Historical Society*, vol. 4 (1890), 300–302, lists twenty-two surveying trips between 1830 and 1855.

45. To P. S. Brown, November 11, 1863, in Native Sons Archives.

46. An extensive collection of his "letters to the editor" and addresses are preserved in the McCoy Scrapbook [cited above in note 43].

47. McCoy Scrapbook, 2 (*Kansas City Daily Journal*, February 15, 1871).

48. *Kansas City Daily Journal*, February 22, 1888; McCoy confessed that he had no interest in economic history: "we will not waste time or space now to tell what everybody knows of the . . . dozen or more great iron bridges—the speeding cable trains, the screams and crash of a thousand trains. . . ."

49. *Kansas City Daily Journal*, March 19, 1882.

50. Ibid., January 1, 1881.

51. Undated *Journal* clipping, McCoy Scrapbook, 7.

52. *Kansas City Daily Journal*, November 18, 1883.

53. Garwood, *Crossroads of America*, 23; it has been noted above that Garwood cannot be considered an authentic bearer of the written tradition; he devotes more of his text to Frank and Jesse James than to the coming of the railroads to Kansas City.

54. Geary to W. L. Campbell, January 12, 1915, in "Pioneer Recollections" folder, Native Sons Archives.

Chapter Fourteen

A Manifesto:
The Defense and Illustration of Local History

Introduction

This "Manifesto" was written as the introduction to Guy Thuillier's *Aspects de l'economie nivernaise au XIe siècle* (Paris, 1966), and it appeared in *Annales, E.S.C.* 22 (January–February 1967). The title of Leuilliot's article refers to a sixteenth-century manifesto, explains translator Patricia M. Ranum, that defends the "French language by maintaining that it is the equal of all other languages and a suitable vehicle for the noblest themes. . . . Hence, in this article, Leuilliot's aim is to defend local history as a valid historical discipline and to indicate ways in which it can be improved."

Leuilliot presents six principles: that the economic history of a locality is related to our contemporary problems; that local history is qualitative; that local history requires flexibility; that local history becomes the history of a sector; that local history must be related to daily life; and that local history is differential history. These principles are accompanied by thorough explanations and illustrations. Leuilliot also discusses ways in which he believes local history must change. His illustrations and his defense are exceedingly important to every person dealing with the presentation or the writing of local history.

The translation of the work that appears here is reprinted, with permission, from Robert Forster and Orest Ranum, eds., *Rural Society in France: Selections from the Annales Economies, Societies, Civilisations* (Baltimore and London: The Johns Hopkins University Press, 1977), 6–21.

Paul Leuilliot, "A Manifesto: The Defense and Illustration of Local History," in Robert Forster and Orest Ranum, eds., *Rural Society in France: Selections from the Annales Economies, Societies, Civilisations* (Baltimore and London: The Johns Hopkins University Press, 1977), 6–21.

* * * *

L'avenir tel que le concevait un homme du passé fait partie importante de notre histoire.   —Paul Valéry, *Cahiers*

Guy Thuillier proposes that we attempt to establish a few principles concerning local history. Indeed, such principles ought to be and deserve to be part of a clearly defined theoretical framework. While the works of local scholars have become more numerous, such scholars are unable to formulate a method, much less develop a policy, for their local history. Once again referring to historians, Paul Valéry wrote that "their own doings"[1] get away from them. Marc Bloch was one of the few historians who was concerned about "doing" history—in this case local history—and by implication, about "doing" research itself.[2] He was concerned with the pursuit of research strategies, a pursuit that "has scarcely made any noteworthy progress despite the fact that logic has been applied to the organization of knowledge for centuries. . . . As a science, [research procedures] are still in the baby-talk stage," as Le Lionnais recently remarked.[3]

On the matter of what principles to follow when doing local history, I should like at the outset to venture one observation: the principles in question are autonomous and as a result run contrary to those applicable to general history as it is studied in schools and universities. Naturally, general history should not neglect or be disdainful of the work of local historians, who are not overly fond of manipulating partial curves, who do not even like to deal with series of statistics, and who are less interested in cycles than in micro-details, village "events," or the daily life of their town. Those "contemptuous pedants," as Bloch called them, are only interested in European or world or quantitative history. To this, local historians might reply as Auguste Jal did a century ago in his preface to the *Dictionnaire critique de biographie et d'histoire* (1864): "I confess, in all humility, that I am one of those people who enjoys probing into *those wretched matters*, as our brilliant minds have called them. I am short-sighted, and minute details are just right for my eyes—I mean my myopic mind. I am interested in a mass of microscopic facts that arouse pity in those historians and critics who are said—and who proudly make the same claims about themselves—to have the wings and eyes of an eagle. *De minimis curo*, as compared with the praector, ancestor of those fortunate and clairvoyant individuals. . ." So the struggle to do local history is not new. Let me add, in passing, that local historiography has yet to be done, that the names of local scholars are quickly—too quickly—forgotten, even when, as sometimes happens, their works are purloined. For local history is very important, quantitatively; it even represents the major part of the historical bibliography of France.[4] In view of its undisputed importance, local history has a right to claim autonomy. In this manifesto expounding the doctrine of local history, several principles seem of prime importance.

First principle. Local economic history of the nineteenth century leads into the present; it is related to our contemporary problems, our present-day preoccupations. First of all, local economic history permits us to discern a number of constants, a number of fundamental characteristics of the present situation, such as the repeated economic failure of certain businesses. The economic development of France necessarily requires this historical perspective; tomorrow's problems must be seen in terms of the century. One must take into account traditional aptitudes, available manpower, certain activities that often have long been carried on in a specific region, different types of regional growth, a locality's tendency to be thrifty and to store things up or to favor (or reject) a Malthusian spirit of enterprise. All these "current events" have repercussions upon the future.[5]

Regional economics—a new discipline[6]—must rely heavily upon local history, which provides not only documentation but also methods of approach, just as earlier in this century geographers in the French school of regional geography, such as Albert Demangeon and Jules Sion, had to rely upon history in their studies of the provinces.[7]

Therefore, it is appropriate and essential to begin at once studying the regional history of the past century—say, 1880–1985[8]—so that it may be used in government plans for the future that are now being drawn up. The predictions of economic planners are also an inseparable part of history, for Marc Bloch referred to history's role as a predictor in *The Historian's Craft* at a time when the techniques of economic planning had not yet been created. Indeed, this "century-long" history can be of great value in indicating future actions. Thus, Thuillier's history of the decline of the *faïence* industry might lead to a suggestion that this artistic craft be revived by establishing a trade or technical school or by giving grants to artisans. Made prudent by history, the government administrator will find himself on firmer ground. In the end, politics is inseparable from economics,[9] which is in turn influenced by history when it comes to making forecasts for the next twenty years. Urbanism is a perfect example of this—pardon me for not going into obvious details—for urban growth remains linked to historical constraints. Moreover, doing the history of the period 1880–1985, for example, would require that background work be done at the local level, in view of the vast amount of printed and archival materials to be consulted.

But local history is not solely concerned with immediacy. Its methodology is *régressive*, or "retrogressive," in the sense in which Bloch used the word.[10] Thus, the local historian, by definition rooted in a very specific bit of territory, moves from the present back to the past. This is also true for agrarian history, for financial history, and for the history of technology.[11] Thuillier provides fine examples of this in his work dealing with the *"lèpre de l'embouche"* [the conversion of wheatfields into pastures for fattening livestock]; the history of banking and insurance; and the development of metallurgical skills in the Nivernais region of which he is so fond, a region that has long been known for its metallurgy. The local historian is able to use his observations, and at times even his professional knowledge, about the present when interpreting documents of the past. Such is the case with the notary studying his minutes or the inspector of public records (two cases specifically mentioned in Thuillier's study of communities). It is obviously preferable to know all about the functioning of today's banks before beginning a study of the history of banking. Thus, a continuous circulation, an interpenetration that eventually bears fruit, is established between analyses of the present and those of the past. Now, "this faculty of understanding the living is, in very truth, the master quality of the historian."[12] This contact with the here and now gives local history its characteristic stamp, explains its vigor, and makes it important to people today.[13]

Second principle. Local history is qualitative, not quantitative; whether we like it or not, it cannot be conveyed by statistics.

This is true in part because figures lose their meaning on the local scale. If great care is not taken, figures are all too often incorrectly interpreted. In most cases statistics have intentionally been distorted at the local level. This is true in Nivernals for vineyards; for faïence, through the collusion of the manufacturers; and for forges. Production figures are also distorted by cheating on the part of the workers (a memorandum dated 1795 tells of the "customary abuses" committed by forge workers), as well as by distrust on the part of the owners, who fear being taxed on the basis of the products included in their lists. The complicity of some and the indifference of others—indeed, a general indifference—make these recorded figures very dubious. For example, the average prices of bread were often calculated in different ways; in like manner, neither the average prices of wheat for the various departments of France nor the average market prices are very reliable figures.

As far as agriculture is concerned, it is especially difficult to obtain good statistics, even today. Hence, agricultural statistics can only be used with great caution. Local history should strive to be critical of statistics rather than use them as the basis of overly assertive conclusions. It should try to perceive the discrepancies in order to interpret general curves; should try, for example, to note the discrepancy between the market price and the actual price received by an individual farmer. Let me add that in the case of long-term phenomena, during the period in question transformations may have occurred in structures that are understood to varying degrees and that are all too often poorly understood.

A recent article by Désert bears this out as far as sown fields, the price of meat or butter, and agricultural wages are concerned.[14] "The prefect [the head of a French department] acts upon the principle that the subprefects have undervalued or overvalued certain parcels of land, and he makes corrections (based on what criteria?). The subprefects have exactly the same attitude toward information sent to them by municipal governments. The result is an increasingly inflated total as one moves up the administrative hierarchy. . . . It is essential that these statistics not be viewed as true economic records. The peasants in the Calvados region of Normandy continually lied to the government all through the century, or else they refused to cooperate at all. Fear of increased taxes; fierce individualism; or simply the inability to answer questionnaires, or at least certain questions included in them owing to the unfamiliar vocabulary used—I am specifically thinking of agricultural units of measure—are among the possible explanations of their attitude. We have evidence of this open or hidden hostility throughout the nineteenth century."[15] And further on in the same article: "Let's say you can easily obtain the price of meats from market quotations or from hospital archives. Does that price accurately reflect the price of cattle on the hoof? I don't think so." We must also distrust price records for markets in the chief towns of the various arrondissements. "How can one really believe that, with the exception of the month of June 1839, the cost of a kilogram of butter purchased at Falaise never varied between January 1838 and December 1849!" The same extreme caution must be applied to data gathered about wages; for indeed, since very little data are available about agricultural wages, "the ideal would be to discover accounts of farms. But how many farmers in that day did regular bookkeeping?"[16] Désert has expressed the problem in a nutshell.

Moreover, local history must work with qualitative information, with unreliable statistics that are only useful as corroborating evidence. In the case of demography, birth and death rates are undoubtedly less important than an examination of the causes of mortality—malnutrition, poor hygiene, poor housing, occupational illnesses, and the "intermittent fevers" caused by the many marshes of Nivernais that had not yet been drained.[17]

In like manner, it seems less important to work out for a twenty-year period the "average price" of a product such as iron or coal than to evaluate the different components of this average. The average price for coal might be influenced by the prices of coal of poor or uneven quality.[18] The variations in the production of the different qualities of iron can partially explain variations in the curve as a whole. Likewise, in regard to wages, one must take into account wage variations according to occupational categories (as can be seen in the rural mine at La Machine) and the method of payment, particularly what part of the wages went for such workers' expenses as candles or repair of equipment (in the same coal mine).[19] The manner in which wages were paid is also important, for the employer might pay in copper coins,[20] or he might withhold one liard per franc,[21] and so forth.

In short, when working on the local scale the historian writing a monograph about a business or a region must reconstitute an economic mechanism as precisely as possible, rather than measure statistical variations. Besides, we know that prosperity-depression cycles do not mean the same thing from one region to another or from one business to another. Statistics cannot indicate these differences, which in part result from the extremely variable influence of a specific sector of the economy and, in the case of businesses, from the unequal volume of investments.

The best example in support of giving local history a qualitative orientation might be bread. For certain historians the prime concern has been to measure the price curve of wheat as revealed in rapidly changing market prices; yet a history of bread would show that it is more important to learn what really went on by ascertaining, among other things, the amount kept by the miller (either in money or in kind), how honest the miller was about the quantity, how he affected the quality by mixing flours, or how much bran was included—all ways of cheating that increased whenever there was an economic crisis. Other important factors were the cost of the bakers' supplies, which could not fail to influence the cost of bread, and fraud by bakers when they cheated on the weight of a loaf of bread or on the quality of the bread, which declined markedly during periods of economic crisis. To this must be added sales on credit; the way selling was conducted and how sales were affected by the *taille* and by coins made of bullion; technical difficulties involved in establishing the bread tax, which all too frequently was done in a rather approximate fashion; and the role played by private ovens, a role that varied from region to region and even from town to town according to the price of wood.

These are among the factors that should be included in a detailed study, which in turn should permit a more judicious interpretation of general curves. Such research and interpretation can only be significant on the strictly local scale. Indeed, on the national scale it is almost impossible to make anything but generalizations. The existence of "growth poles," of "dynamic" industries, and the variable importance of "innovative investments" in spurring regional growth explain the frequent discrepancy between regional and "general" economic conditions.[22]

Third principle. Local history requires a certain flexibility, for it is a loosely knit history compared with the often quite rigid sort of history found in doctoral dissertations. The dissertation must deal with a very specific period and cannot overlap the past and go back to the "origins"; it especially cannot overlap the future in order to "follow" the development of a given sector that is the subject of the research in question. In the end, in order to adhere to the outline of this "master-piece" that gains him entry into the profession, the author of the dissertation must also exclude certain other complementary sectors from his purview.[23]

The same is true for dates and for the way in which the subject is planned. As far as dates are concerned, it is hardly possible to do anything but look back from the nineteenth to the eighteenth century when going back to the "origins" and to "follow" developments up to the present. Despite the title of his book, I do not criticize Thuillier for having called to mind the origins of major industries in his chapter on Louis Le Vau's unfortunate speculations at Baumont-la-Ferrière [in the 1660s], nor for having included a memorandum on forests [in 1735] or on the state of forges in Nivernais circa 1770.

Dissertations dealing with regional studies rarely follow the thread up to the present. Nor are they free to delve at will into especially interesting sectors, which, although relatively small on their own, would unbalance the dissertation as a whole.[24]

Now, we should not hide the fact that such dissertations have a great influence upon local history, for in a way they impose a model that local historians feel obliged to imitate. Some lose heart when confronted with such an undertaking. It goes without saying that this influence should be neither abusive nor exclusive. I believe that local history requires a high degree of flexibility in approach and execution; it is the history of the individual—meaning by "individual" both the company and the municipality or, strictly speaking, the region. Depending upon the characteristics of this small region, the sector being studied and the period being considered will of necessity be different, and the chronological limits of the setting will be blurred if not altogether out of focus. As a result, local history cannot build carefully planned edifices; it must in a sense be modulated to conform to the imperatives of its subject. Thus, we are obliged to accept this flexibility: this would avoid the very evident wasted efforts of those local scholars who are either virtually wearing themselves out trying to imitate these "models" or else falling back, perhaps in despair, upon subjects that are too fragmentary. Recognizing the autonomy of local history means at the same time giving it the freedom of movement it needs.

Fourth principle. Thus conceived, local history becomes the history of a sector and, consequently, the history of structures viewed in terms of sectors (and products). After—but only after—this indispensable analytical groundwork has been laid does synthesis become possible.

The specific problems of a given sector should be studied in depth—for themselves, in a way; then certain constants or permanent elements can be discerned on the basis of certain given products. For example, technical and commercial problems relating to vineyards can be studied in order to reveal certain permanent elements, of yesterday and of today; and in all probability the unchanging element will be the vinedresser's propensity for preferring quantity to quality in his vineyard, as Robert Laurent has shown.[25]

Such a study of problems according to sectors would undoubtedly permit us to break with our preconceptions and eliminate the traditional prejudices of history in order to grasp instead psychological mechanisms and,[26] at the same time, to discern the variable and basic mutations that permit us to go beyond the local situation and make undisputed generalizations: for example, that the very slow spread of the bank note until 1914 resulted in the development of credit. The same is true for agrarian history and for the history of technical knowledge.[27]

Such a study of sectors offers more than one advantage over general history: it is easier to comprehend a sector, and doubtlessly to comprehend it better as well. Sometimes, for lack of a "model," the local historian must invent a method of approach for a particular problem; for local history this method, based on selective elimination, may differ from the method appropriate to general history, for the simple reason that a history of a sector must develop its own original hypotheses for discovery and inquiry. Obliged to work from life, the local historian cannot deduce his history *a priori* on the basis of a few general ideas; he must *invent* his subject in the strictest sense of the term. Such is quite commonly the case for those fields that have until very recently been scorned by university-based research.[28]

I can only deplore the dearth of autobiographies and memoirs by local historians that could reveal their methodology and, in most cases, their professional knowledge of a subject as well. We must return to the historian's craft as revealed by Marc Bloch, whose position is very similar to that of Paul Valéry, and to my own position in this manifesto.

Fifth principle. Local history must become increasingly concrete and must become related to daily life and to actual procedures involving technical skills and credit, the history of material life (food, shelter, and hygiene), and medical and social history, as well. Let me quote Bloch again: "Who believes that electrical companies have no archives, no records of power consumption, no charts of enlargement of their networks?"[29] The history of the spread of electrification has yet to be done.

But in addition to being concrete and material history, local history is the history of the invisible aspects of daily life, of things that cannot be seen, such as contraceptive practices; it is the history of things that are given, that do not have to be talked about—though so much the better if they are—such as money and its less visible confrere, thrift (we have only to remember how new French five-franc pieces became scarce shortly after their recent minting)[30;] and it is the history of the durable, of things that last over the years, of age-old traditions, or folklore, if you prefer to call that. Here local history overflows into the history of mentalities, of attitudes toward life, death, money, and innovation.[31]

That sort of history can hardly be done in Paris or in any other very large city, for it requires an intimate knowledge of a locality and of its people, the personal experience of local and provincial life that outsiders only rarely possess. Let me also emphasize that this sort of history attracts a local clientele composed of local notables. Thus, the history of medicine is of interest to physicians, and the history of technical skills attracts engineers, to the degree that these histories deal with a town or a small region and are buttressed by a solid and durable local patriotism that still shows a spark of life.

My definition of the principles of this concrete history has undoubtedly not been defined sufficiently or thoroughly enough, and the methodology to be used may still seem vague. Moreover, local history as I have portrayed it is surely a privileged branch of history. It is not isolated, as if it were made up of erudite speculations, of pure abstractions; instead, it is involved with the present and thus facilitates our understanding of the profound mutations that have occurred since the nineteenth century. It is significant that among such "witnesses for the common people" as

Nadaud, Sand, and Guillaumin, Fourastié includes Le Play's two monographs that deal with the miner in the argentiferous lead mines of Pontgibaud and with the agricultural laborer of the Morvan region. "His monographs are of greater importance than his opinions. Indeed, they describe the real situation of European families so carefully and precisely *that some of them should be included in the course work of our high schools.*"[32]

As evidenced by the authors I have mentioned, this is the true vocation of local history, which cannot be isolated in a sort of ghetto, for it is part of life. Most historical works are conceived on a national scale, and few if any are specifically local studies. If carried out on the basis of the principles of this manifesto, the local history I envisage will become involved with the history of the material and technical structures of daily life; for example, the history of problems involving water in both city and countryside, or the history of bread that I have already mentioned.

Sixth principle. Local history is differential history. It must therefore attempt to measure the discrepancy between developments as a whole and developments within a particular locality, and also to measure the differences in the rhythms of these changes. As a result, it will be able to provide specific information about the level of economic development or about the banking organization within a region, and also to discern the level of any given "regional" technical skill—for example, metallurgy or textiles.[33] This permits us to verify, appraise, and even measure how slowly technical knowledge spread and the degree of psychological resistance it encountered.

This differential history is of course particularly difficult, especially since the levels of development in other regions and the general evolutionary pattern are still relatively unknown. But such an analysis of differences will surely bear fruit; such differences in growth rates depend to a considerable, if not a major, degree upon nonmeasurable psychological or sociological factors stemming from daily, undiscernible history—such as population decline resulting from birth control, a very new subject of research and still poorly understood.[34] It is no less difficult to perceive a weakening in the spirit of enterprise, for example, as a result of tensions that might arise in a manufactory. The study of the causes of growth or of decline would surely be of major interest to the economist.

There are certainly other principles applicable to local history. Local economic history, written by local scholars, can briefly—and provisionally—be defined as a history that is concerned with the present, a history that is qualitative, a history with a "flexible" time scale, a history of sectors that studies daily life, a history that is essentially differential. This doubtlessly is how we should interpret Lucien Febvre's remarks about the knowledge of our provinces and minor cities during the Restoration. "It would be extremely interesting for us to know the situation of each of our provinces during the very interesting period 1820–30, a period when they still retained most of the traits of their distinct and traditional personalities on the eve of the great inventions that would change the appearance of the old world by overturning the whole established system of relationships."[35]

Although for various reasons the fact often goes unnoticed, local or regional history necessarily has a different orientation from that of "general" or national history; its concerns and methodology are also quite different. Its ambitions are *a priori* limited, for one of its basic tenets is a temporary refusal to make syntheses at a time when too few valid studies exist. It claims to be work that is being carried on while waiting for future regional or general works. This is the real basis for the work of local scholars, whose *raison d'être* lies in willingly and humbly doing the needed background research, working, in the words of Lucien Febvre, as good craftsmen who make possible *grande histoire* [that is, general as contrasted with local history].

University research—more prestigious, more centralized (a good part of it centered in Paris, despite an increasing number of dissertations being defended in provincial universities), based upon the doctoral dissertation written in accordance with the "principles" and directions of a mentor, and well funded—cannot, figuratively speaking, crush local research. Yet in many ways it influences local history by proposing, if not imposing, its "models" and the accompanying methodology, as well as its "fashions."[36] Think how hard it is for a provincial to consult documents in Parisian collections, even though the National Archives in Paris will lend its documents to departmental archives. How can a local scholar thinking of working in the National Library in Paris manage to thread his way through the maze of manuscripts, given the inadequate collection of manuscript catalogs? The local scholar has usually had no formal historical training and absolutely no opportunities to learn critical methodology. Often doing his history after business hours, he frequently receives the very disheartening impression that he is writing marginal history that will be looked down upon since it is being done far from the centers of innovating trends. He generally works alone, often without the help of the usual traditional associations—*a fortiori* the university—and owing to these circumstances and to his isolation, he does not keep abreast of the most recent work, since he is far from good libraries. But that is another problem.

Years ago Charles Morazé stressed this separation: "A minor historian has a larger public than the major specialists of the same period. Who is at fault? The public? The writer? The discipline? I will answer that question without the slightest hesitation: the discipline. The breath of life has not yet been breathed into it, so it has done nothing to take advantage of the public's taste and to make use of these efforts, which are often disinterested and which are always useful."[37] These are indeed major obstacles; yet the local historian today plays a very important role. As Morazé's judicious remarks indicate, the scientific, university-based sort of history is cutting itself off from its public and shutting itself up in its ivory tower, so the public is trying to satisfy its craving for history in a different manner.[38] It is significant that reviews of historical works in the press are scarce and that historical journals are read almost exclusively by "professionals."[39] A dangerous and very regrettable separation and divorce. Is local history perhaps to play the desirable role of mediator?

First of all, in such an event local history would indeed assume the primordial function of diffusing knowledge, while maintaining in the provinces the taste, and the feeling, for history. Here we are touching upon a much debated problem, recently brought up among the learned societies,[40] some of which are unquestionably much less active than others.[41] Yet these societies have led some individuals to choose the historian's craft. We must also deplore the failure to stress local history in our school curricula, official policy notwithstanding. The successful efforts of the educational services of the departmental archives, now active in about forty French departments, should be implemented throughout France, and these services should be granted adequate funds. More good textbooks on local history should be published (and kept by the pupils).[42]

Second, local research deserves to attract more attention, since it is breaking ground in barely cultivated and even virgin fields. The local historian, who has so much freedom of movement in his research, is freed from university "fashions." As a result, the innovative role of local history should not be neglected. Take as an example the works on the agrarian history of Poitou by Paul Raveau, supplemented by those of Dr. Louis Merle.[43]

Third, the local historian, rooted in his very concrete and precise territory, often ends up comparing general history and its long-term theories with his own strictly local problems. A certain number of local histories of the French Revolution probably resulted from a desire to compare the actual situation in a specific area with political or economic theories; that is, from a desire to verify the Revolution on a local scale. Sometimes it turns out that nothing at all happened, or virtually nothing.[44] In my own case, I recently asked myself, "What exactly was a Jacobin? or a man from Colmar?"—citing Georges Pariset, who observed that "one of the characteristics of the Revolution is that local life is infinitely diverse and that the histories of even the smallest cities and regions are never identical."[45]

In a sense, this is experimental history. Local history, defined as a science of the individual and the particular, seems to serve the authentic and definite function of restructuring history by creating at the outset a critical distrust of tenets, of theories that are always more or less inaccurate for lack of local monographs.[46]

In short, the moving spirit behind such monographs seems less systematic and more "liberal" than similar work done within the university system. Devotion to detail, which has so often been denounced and criticized, is not necessarily synonymous with narrow-mindedness. Perhaps not enough heed is paid to the working hypotheses, methods, and intentions of local scholars, or to their publications, which are not circulated very far afield. Yet Marc Bloch used to pay very close attention to local and provincial journals, and Lucien Febvre reprinted in his *Annales, E.S.C.*, an article that had caught his eye in a journal dealing with the region of Montbeliard. I shall conclude this "defense" by briefly suggesting a few ways to strengthen local history, which is too often misunderstood and whose concerns are, in my opinion, quite different from those of general history.

First of all, we must give it pedagogical help. In most cases, the local historian has trained himself on the job, so to speak, and has learned history as he went along. He needs a research manual that can supply adequate methodological "instructions" about research and writing and about the numerous catalogs of such national archives as the National Library in Paris. He also needs guides to the departmental archives—which archivists have fortunately begun to provide—not to mention a general record of all archives.[47] In addition he must be provided with regional bibliographies, bibliographies specializing in the different "sectors," and publications of various documents of general interest.[48]

Next, meetings or colloquia must be organized. The annual National Congress of Learned Societies could with profit be expanded to include sessions devoted to methodology. In addition, professors holding chairs of local history in provincial universities should be provided with sufficient funds to make sure they can effectively fulfill their advisory functions. Above all, financial help must be given to the various learned societies. The fact that financial reasons prevent local historians from publishing their work has had a marked effect upon the amount of research being done in certain provinces. If these societies no longer had to beg for funds, they could once again earn the respect due their renewed activity.

Lastly, it should be possible to organize certain activities involving the diffusion of information and the coordination of projects for the field as a whole. There is no question that local studies should be encouraged; but they should also be made available through discussions on radio and television, and reviews in the local press. This information must be as widely diffused as possible, for local history can provide documentation for a host of individuals: geographers, sociologists, and economists, for example. This diffusion should be carried out either by centers for the history of a sector—such as the Iron Museum at Nancy, the museum of printed fabrics at Mulhouse, or the Museum of Banking and Books at Lyon—or by the university-based centers of regional history, which, as I have mentioned, are inadequately funded, if they exist at all. As far as coordination is concerned, the improvement of basic research procedures would lead to joint activities in certain sectors. Learned societies already exist and could act as coordinators. The creation of regional commissions for technical archives has been suggested along the lines of the departmental committees for the economic history of the French Revolution. Thus, a certain amount of help could be given to local history, and there is little doubt that university-based research, which reaps many of the rewards stemming from the efforts of local historians, would as a result be greatly helped.[49] It is not enough to try to make a clear definition of method; an attempt must be made to help, direct, motivate, and launch a veritable policy for local history. At the end of this "defense," if I were to anticipate history and make predictions, I would ask, "What should—and what will—be the place of local history and the role of local historians in 1985?"

NOTES

1. Paul Valéry, *Cahiers* 21: 424.

2. Marc Bloch, *Apologie pour l'histoire, ou métier d'historien*, Cahiers des Annales 3, 5th ed. (Paris, 1964). English translation by Peter Putnam, *The Historian's Craft* (New York, 1964).

3. F. Le Lionnais, "Science et politique nationale," *Revue politique et parlementaire* (July–August 1965).

4. I quote the homage paid the late J. Joachim, of Delle, long the "dean of Alsatian historians," in Jean Suratteau's recent dissertation, "Le departement du Mont-Terrible sous le régime du Directoire" (1965): "During my frequent visits to [Joachim] I would always come out equipped with a mass of precious and irreplaceable information . . ." (introduction). A "local historian" of the department of Pas-de-Calais recently wrote me: "A certain number of these village scholars have acquired world renown, among them my poor Edmont, who died penniless after having teamed with Gilliéron to create linguistic geography. . . ."

5. Thus, Guy Thuillier contrasts the routine apathy and technical stagnation of the faïence workers of Nevers with the spirit of enterprise shown by the iron-masters of Nivernais. His chapter on the paper mills of Corvol-l'Orgueilleux is equally revealing. On the Vespa works of the A.C.M.A. (1950–1963), see below. Likewise, for the distant antecedents (chiefly during the Second Empire) of the Alsatian textile crisis, especially in the Vosges Mountains, see my "Action syndicale dans le textile du Haut-Rhin," *Revue de l'action populaire* (February 1965): 171–80.

6. The Institut de Science Economique Appliquée has published the debates of the Association de Science regionale de langue française. For example, *Structure et croissance régionale*, Colloquia of 1961–1962, Cahiers of the I.S.E.A., *Economie régionale*, suppl. 130 (October 1962). See also J. Martens, *Bibliographie de Science économique régionale*, Cahiers of the I.S.E.A., no. 125 (Paris, 1962); and Rene Gendarme, *La region du Nord* (Paris, 1954).

7. Jean Chardonnet (*Géographie industrielle*, vol. 2 [Paris, 1965]) includes history in his study of the conditions of industrial work. Conversely, geography can provide certain working hypotheses for the historian. Another example of having recourse to history is the work of sociologist Placide Rambaud, *Les transformations d'une societé rurale, la Maurienne (1561–1962)* (Paris, 1965), and her earlier *Economie et sociologie de la Montagne: Albiez-le-Vieux-en-Maurienne* (Paris, 1962), for which I wrote the preface. In the introduction to her latest book, Rambaud writes: "A historical event, a land register, a statistic are above all important because they are a condensation of social forces, the secret crystallization of a

complex network of decisions, of daily life that would be even more difficult to grasp without them. They are the stabilized replies made to countless efforts. To ask questions of a statistic amounts to asking questions of a man. . . .Their value gives them a formal identity, and the identity of these statistics is not the same in different epochs, nor do they all have the same value for social investigation . . ." (p. 13).

8. See *Reflexions pour 1985* presented to the Guillaumat Commission. Indeed, the mimeographed reports of Ducros and Fraisse on the regionalization of the French economy in 1985 are of great significance, as is Professor Bernard's *L'homme en 1985: Aspects physologiques et médicaux*. Guy Thuillier is also interested in social and medical problems of the past in Nivernais.

9. This was pointed out in the *Journées d'études*, a study of political forces in eastern France (Strasbourg, 1964). See my "Reflexions d'un historien a propos de l'Alsace," *Bulletin de la Societé industrielle de Mulhouse* 4 (1964): 13–20, and especially my *Recherches sur les forces politiques*, Cahiers de l'Association Interuniversitaire de l/Est (Paris, 1966).

10. Bloch, *Historian's Craft*, 45–47.

11. A. Birembault has written a thought-provoking study, "Quel bénéfice le technicien peut-il retirer de l'histoire?" *Revue de Synthèse* 37–39 (1965): 181–268. The technician answers the question of what he can learn from history by using both history and his own professional recollections. For him, "the detailed history of a technical skill and its diffusion requires the previous completion of regional studies" (p. 213).

12. Bloch, *Historian's Craft*, 13.

13. In one sense, the local historian is a person trying to "do the history" of his profession or trade; the physician does the history of his hospital; the insurance broker studies the development of insurance in his city or region; the manufacturer studies the history of his business. Behind this research lies a sense of ownership that calls to mind Saint-Phlin in Maurice Barrès's *Appel au soldat*.

14. G. Désert, "Les sources statistiques de l'histoire de France" (Basse-Normandiee, xixᵉ siecle), *Annales de Normandie* (March 1965): 22–52.

15. Examples cited for 1818, 1837, 1855, 1873, and 1888, ibid. 51, n. 22.

16. Désert, *Annales de Normandie* (March 1965): 28, 34, 37, 44, 51.

17. See the recent study by Pierre Pierrard, *La vie ouvrière à Lille sous le Second Empire* (Paris, 1965), which seems to indicate a favorable trend. Thuillier discusses both typical diet and medical and social problems in this book.

18. Accounts of 1859 for the coal mines at La Machine.

19. For similar deductions (for light, motor, etc.), see Pierrard, *La vie ouvrière*, 201.

20. See Guy Thuillier, "Pour une histoire monetaire de la France: le rôle des monnaies de cuivre et de billion [*sic*]," *Annales, E.S.C.* 14 (January–March 1959): 65–90, and the second part of this preface.

21. Pierrard, *La vie ouvrière*, 201.

22. The relationship between the "cycle" and investments are still not very clear. For the effects of such factors, see François Perroux, *Les techniques quantitatives de planification*

(Paris, 1965), which offers a fair number of working hypotheses for the historian (especially on the role of innovation).

23. For example, the remarkable dissertation of Pierrard, *La vie ouvrière*, scarcely went beyond 1870 and not much before that. On the other hand, a great merit of Maurice Lévy-Leboyer's *Les banques européennes et l'industrialisation internationale dans la première moitte du XIXe siècle* (Paris, 1965), lies in its having gone back to the period 1750–1770.

24. The history of insurance is often omitted from financial histories, as is the history of food from social histories, especially as far as workers are concerned.

25. Robert Laurent, *Les vignerons de la Côte-d'Or au XLXe siècle* (Dijon, 1957).

26. Such is the case for the psychology of the metallurgical worker; see J. Vial, "Louvrier métallurgiste français," *Droit Social* (1950): 58–68.

27. J. Courtin, *Transformations de l'économie et de la vie dans une commune rurale de la Limagne, Saulzet depuis 1914*, which deals with the shift from sickle to scythe; see also, by Courin, "L'invention en metallurgie (et ses conditions)," *Revue d'histoire économique et sociale* (1949): 233–73. Coutin is completing a dissertation on French metallurgy from 1814 to 1864. I must also cite André Thuillier, *Emile Martin (1794–1871)*, a publication of the Chamber of Commerce and Industry of Nevers and of Nievre, 1964.

28. Simply think of the notarial archives. See P. Massé, "A travers un dépôt de minutes notoriales," *Annales historiques de la Révolution français* (1953): 297–315.

29. Bloch, *Historian's Craft*, 66–67.

30. Y. Gaillard and G. Thuillier, "Sur la thesaurisation," *Revue économique* (September 1965).

31. See Robert Mandrou, *Introduction à la France moderne: Essai de psychologie historique (1500–1640)* (Paris, 1961); English translation, *Introduction to Modern France: An Essay in Historical Psychology* (New York, 1976); and Mandrou, *De la culture populaire aux XVIIe et XVIIIe siècles* (Paris, 1964).

32. See especially Françoise Fourastié and Jean Fourastié, *Les écrivains témoins due peuple* (Paris, 1964), 343–66. Le Play described refining in Nivernais in 1843.

33. See, on this subject, Pierre Léon, *Les techniques métallurgiques dauphinoises au XVIIIe siècle* (Paris, 1961).

34. See Y. Hilaire, "Les missions intérieures face à la déchristianisation pendant la seconde moitie du XIXe siècle," *Revue du Nord* (January–March 1964): 51–68.

35. Lucien Febvre, *La Franche-Comté*, Les régions de la France (Paris, 1905), 64. I used this passage as a motto for my *L'Alsace au début du XIXe siècle*, vol. 2 (Paris, 1959).

36. For example, no detailed catalogue has been made of the Holy de Fleury collection, which is , however, of great importance for the history of the French provinces. I refer the reader to my article, "Problèmes de la recherche, II. Catalogues et bibliographie de l'histoire de France," in *Annales, E.S.C.* 19 (November–December 1964): 1147–56.

37. Charles Moraze, *Trois essais sur histoire et culture* (Cahiers des Annales 2, 1948).

38. On the current state of affairs in the world of history, I see the study by R. Kaes, "Les ouvriers français et la culture (enquéte 1958–1961)," 1962, mimeographed, Editions Dalloz.

The chapter "Curiosity about the Past: History" (pp. 203–12), reveals that 61 percent of workers show some interest in history, 53 percent of non–trade-union workers are interested, as is 70 percent of the managerial staff. A sociological study of familiarity with history by social group would probably reveal unusual regional differences.

39. See the maps in J. Hassenforder, *La diffusion du périodique français* (histoire et géographie), a publication in the Centre d'études économiques (1957).

40. See my article "Problèmes de la recherche, III. Pour une politique des Sociétés Savantes," in *Annales, E.S.C.* 20 (March–April 1965): 315–26. Among the letters received on this subject, I would like to quote a passage dealing with learned societies: "Their members have a terrible failing: independence. They believe neither in prejudices, orders, nor intrigues; they have neither supple backbones nor weak characters. Too bad! But they do have knowledge and experience; they are not seeking personal advancement; and the sacred fire burns within them. Our universities can mass-produce archivists and holders of advanced degrees; once they receive their sheepskins they delve into facts, monuments, texts, and seek data from us. We must be indulgent with them; we will help them save time, twenty years of patient, unpublicized, accumulated labor, accessible to all comers. . . ." At the same time this correspondent noted the existence of nine or ten learned societies within the department of Pas-de-Calais alone. I also wish to point out the *Actes* of the first two colloquia of the presidents of learned societies, held at Lyon in 1964 and Nice in 1965, and published by the Comité des travaux historiques et scientifiques (1965–1966).

41. The Societé d'agriculture, sciences, et arts de la Sarthe publishes both memoranda and a monthly bulletin. The Amis du Viel Annecy have just published an issue of *Annesci* (vol. 11, 1964) devoted to R. Blanchard's account of changes occurring in their city (1954–1962). The *Revue du Bas-Poitou et des Provinces de l'Ouest*, (March–April 1965), which is also concerned with current events, published Y. Chataigneau's "L'avenir de la France et la région de demain"; and as early as 1961, it published J. P. Soisson's "Difficultés et espoirs de l'action régionale. Deux ans d'expansion dans les Deux-Sevres (1958–1960)."

42. See Baudot's report to the Archives group of the national government's Fifth Plan. We also need handbooks in local history for adults. Paperbacks have been performing such functions in Germany and England but have not yet had much effect in France. I would, however, like to cite G.-B. Cabourdin and J.-A. Lesourd, *La Lorraine (histoire et géographie)* (1960), published by the Société Lorraine des études locales dans l'enseignement public, and the *Bulletin* of that society, which began a new publication series in 1956; A.-G. Manry, R. Seve, and M. Chaulanges, *L'histoire vue de l'Auvergne* (1951–1959), a three-volume publication of the educational services of the Department Archives of Puy-de-Dôme; and H. Forestier, *L'Yonne au XLe siècle (1800–1848)* (1959–1963), a three-volume work published by the Departmental Archives of Yvonne, with an introduction by J. P. Rocher.

43. Paul Raveau, *L'agriculture et les classes paysannes dans le Haut-Poitou au XVe siècle* (Paris, 1926), and *Essai sur la situation économique et l'état social en Poitou au XVe siècle* (1931). Dr. Louis Merle, *La métairie et l'evolution agraire de la Gâtine poitevine de la fin du Moyen Age à la Revolution*, which fortunately has become a part of the collection *Terre et hommes* (Paris, 1958).

44. Such was the case in a village of the Morvan. See the conclusions drawn by A. Thuillier, "Semelay de 1793 à 1795," *Actes du 87ᵉ Congrès National des Societés Savantes Poitiers, 1962* (1963): 233–68.

45. Paul Leuilliot, "Si J'avais à récrire les Jacobins de Colmar . . .," *Saisons d'Alsace* 9 (Winter 1965).

46. Pierrard, *La vie ouvrière*, 8. When discussing G. Duveau's pioneering dissertation, "La vie ouvrière en France sous le Second Empire" (1946), Pierrard noted that "this classic work, which has been criticized for being based on too few sources and sources of debatable reliability, is especially ignorant of matters in Lille."

47. This is the goal of the Archives group of the Commission de l'Equipement culturel du Vᵉ Plan. See also the reports of J. Richard and J. Vidalenc on archival catalogues. The reports of this group, for which Guy Thuillier was the general secretary, will soon be published.

48. I am thinking of the reports of the Procureurs généraux, which provide rich documents on many questions. The Commission d'Histoire economique et sociale de la Révolution français has published in its bulletins various studies by M. Reinhard on the population during the Revolution and the Empire (1959–60), and by M. Bouloiseau on emigration (1961).

49. With the exception of the "Que sais-je?" collection (which has some very fine books), no collection dealing with provincial history has been planned since the war. Good guidebooks to local history intended for laypeople are very scarce. But the need exists, and I believe that such books would find numerous buyers. In fact, histories of Bordeaux, Besançon, and Lille are now in press.

Chapter Fifteen

A Sense of Place:
A Historian Advocates Conceptual Approaches to Community History

Introduction

Shelton Stromquist, previously coordinator of the Office of Local History at the State Historical Society of Wisconsin, now teaches history at the University of Iowa. He has carried with him to Iowa his interest in labor history, publishing in 1987 *A Generation of Boomers: The Pattern of Railroad Labor Conflict in Nineteenth-Century America* (Urbana: University of Illinois Press) and in 1993 *Solidarity and Survival: An Oral History of Iowa Labor in the Twentieth Century* (Iowa City: University of Iowa Press).

Stromquist's interests are academic and local, a blend he writes about in this essay, where he advocates the need for local historians and writers of local history to understand the wider context in which their research exists—important for museum personnel creating an exhibit, speakers discussing local topics, and those teaching or creating materials for the classroom. He understands, however, that local history also needs to "transcend the specific constraints that exist and establish a rapport with the sources of a community's past."

A sense of place, Stromquist cautions, is where the historian will find that which is consistent within a community and that which has changed. "The elaboration of that sense of a distinctive and unique place continues to be a defining objective of the local historian," he writes. "The objective is most tellingly achieved not by isolating the story of a community's past but by defining a context that makes it stand out in bolder relief."

Shelton Stromquist, "A Sense of Place: A Historian Advocates Conceptual Approaches to Community History," *History News* (April 1983): 17–20.

This essay is reprinted, by permission, from *Perspectives* (Spring 1982). It also appeared in *History News*, April 1983, pp. 17–20.

* * * *

History viewed through the prism of community and family institutions has developed a wide appeal. Set in familiar surroundings and peopled by individuals whose surnames are known, local histories address in a direct and personal manner a large segment of the population.

But this strength of local history is directly related to its major weakness. Often lacking a wider context or a comparative dimension, local history fails to identify and explain important social and economic changes that ultimately define the uniqueness of a place. We learn the names of community leaders, but not their social backgrounds nor their networks of influence. We see the grand march of community institutions—the fire department, the schools, the churches, the mills— but not the subcommittees based on class and ethnicity that deeply influenced the consciousness and behavior of people in the community. We witness the progressive development of a community to its present level of well-being, but miss the periods of economic adversity, important social divisions and conflicts, and the competing value systems and agendas that people have had for the community's future.

Anthropologist Anthony F. C. Wallace introduces his history of Rockdale, Md. *(Rockdale: The Growth of an American Village in the Early Industrial Revolution* [New York, 1978]) by noting that "it is not a community with a conspicuous history; none of its residents achieved national prominence during those forty years that I studied . . . it was not particularly unique in its industry or its society. It initially attracted my interest because I lived there and was curious about the old mills and tenements that lined the creek at the bottom of the hill." Wallace goes on to recount his fascinating journey into the community's past—his discovery that communities, however small, are never isolated from the wider historical changes that surround them and that, to understand the community's past, we must "have some grasp of the social processes going on around it." He also discovered, to his surprise and delight, a "plot" in the community's history, "an organized structure of conflict . . . that has made the work a poignant chronicle of struggles between well-intentioned men and women all striving toward a better age." Wallace's experience could serve well as a paradigm for local historians seeking to discover and communicate the history of their communities.

The defining attribute of local history is its attempt to capture and convey the uniqueness of a place in time. That finely tuned sense of place, nurtured by direct experience and familiarity with a particular physical environment and its people, makes a local historian particularly well situated to identify the special qualities of a community. For a thoughtful discussion of these attributes of community studies, see Kathleen Conzen's "Community Studies, Urban History and American Local History," in Michael Kammen's *The Past before Us; Contemporary Historical Writing in the United States* (Ithaca, 1980).

A local focus and attention to community uniqueness can, however, lead to an excessive and exclusive preoccupation with the peculiar and unique. It can produce a litany of "firsts" and bizarre occurrences that lead nowhere, explain nothing, and place a community's past in no context. Uniqueness can be defined only in context and comparison. Without points of reference outside the community, history is, in Wallace's phrase, "flattened out." It becomes the vehicle for a too-often stereotypical account drawn from unconsciously adopted assumptions about the way things were "way back when," with names and dates grafted on to locate that history in a particular place.

The task of the local historian, then, is to approach research and writing with sensitivity both to the uniqueness of the place and to the context that makes precise definition of that uniqueness possible. Local historians operate in a world that is different, in significant ways, but not unrelated to the worlds of other historians. It is worth noting the distinctiveness of the local historian's motivation, audience, and externally imposed constraints.

Local historians are motivated by a desire to tell the stories of communities that they are connected to, to interpret the lives of people familiar to them, and to articulate those qualities that make a place special. The initial purpose of their study may be to provide a focus for community celebration or to promote the place to the wider world.

Whatever its objectives, local history is produced for a local audience, an audience that is centered in the place itself and—to a greater or lesser degree—radiates outward. Local historians must anticipate meeting critics of their work on the street or in the grocery store. Many will judge their work—not necessarily by the standard of scholarship employed, but by the extent to which it conforms to the unconsciously transmitted and fragmented legacy that they know, or imagine, as the community's history, and by whether the names of their parents and grandparents are favorably mentioned. The audience for a piece of research and writing always acts as a constraint of some sort on the historian; but for the local historian, that constraint is particularly immediate and visible.

There are other constraints, as well. Rarely does the local historian enjoy unlimited time and freedom to travel, to consult the sources necessary to the study. The way historical records are generated and saved makes it inevitable to consult archives, libraries, depositories, and persons located outside the community, sometimes at great distance.

Ultimately, the local historian, like any other historian, must transcend the specific constraints that exist and establish a rapport with the sources of a community's past. The poignant "structure of conflict between well-intentioned people," if it surfaces from the sources, must find its place in the historical account. It makes the community, in human terms, a richer, more complex, and more interesting place to live.

There are some general guidelines for doing local historical research that historians must keep in mind. These guidelines should indicate how local historians think about historical communities and should help to define strategies for conceptualizing and researching their histories.

First, the researcher must establish a dialogue between the unique and the general. Research should be preceded by some general reading in the history of the region and on the social and economic processes that impinged on it— industrialization, immigration, settlement, modernization. Thinking about such general phenomena sensitizes the local historian to the broader significance of specific events in the community being studied. Of equal importance is the examination of the history of other communities in the state and in other states—communities both similar and dissimilar to the one that is the researcher's prime interest. The qualities that make a community distinctive cannot be known unless its history is seen in relation to the history of other communities.

A second guideline for community research is to develop a set of ordered concepts, a conceptual scaffolding, that helps to define the significant aspects of a community's past that warrant investigation. Without some method for defining what is significant, we are left with a mass of factual data, a historical catalogue. An essential part of this task is the judicious selection of data that makes sense of the past, that conveys both the subjective experience of people in the past as well as the process of historical change that they may have only imperfectly understood. J. H. Hexter, in *Doing History* (Bloomington, Ind., 1971), has suggested a "reality" principle as a test for the historian's reconstruction of the past; it should be "the best and most likely store that can be sustained by the relevant extrinsic evidence."

In the same article, social historian James Henretta suggested that this reality principle cannot be satisfied "simply by ascertaining the 'facts.'" He argues that the primary task is developing an "explanatory scheme that penetrates to the heart of their reality."

A third guideline, recommended by Henretta in "Social History as Lived and Written," suggests that there are several modes of thought for reconstructing the past and making sense of it for others. History as lived and much history as written are essentially chronological. One thing follows another. Because chronology parallels our own historical experience, it is very natural way to understand the past, at one level. However, if our concern is not simply to recount what people experienced and what they understood about what they experienced, but rather to explain the course of events and to identify larger forces that the historical actors may have been only dimly aware of, we must employ other modes of thought.

One alternative approach involves the manipulation and analysis of "hard" empirical data in order to identify important social patterns or community characteristics. Community growth and differentiation can in some sense be measured by growth in population and in the economic statistics of trade and production. The people of a community can be systematically observed as they passed before the eyes of the census-taker who recorded certain characteristics—their age, marital status, occupation, birthplace, and literacy. If we reorganize by category the information that census-takers recorded, we can analyze the age structure, occupation distribution, and ethnicity of that population; we can see how those characteristics of the community's population changed, over time (at least at ten-year intervals); and we can relate one characteristic to another (the age distribution of Poles as compared to Swedes, or the proportions of unskilled laborers among the Welsh and the Irish).

These empirical observations suggest many questions that historians may or may not be able to answer. For example, why did a community grow steadily until 1890 and then precipitously decline in population for the next two decades? Why was there a disproportionately large number of young, unmarried, native-born men in the community from 1870 to 1880? Why was the rate of home ownership higher among unskilled Irish laborers than among the better-off German skilled workers? The hard, empirical data suggest these questions. Some of the questions are important, others are trivial; some can be answered with certainty, others cannot. The data lack the flesh and bones of real people, distinguishing people by group rather than by individual characteristics. The use of such data requires certain assumptions about the significance of ethnicity, class, property ownership, or age. Using those assumptions to connect group characteristics to individual and group behavior creates a great opportunity for error.

Another mode of thought used by historians to reconstruct the past helps put abstract characteristics back into a workable historical framework. By examining the historical record for patterns of historical change and individual and group behavior, historians can develop conceptual models. Communities are classified according to certain characteristics based on regular patterns of growth. From those growth patterns, certain "types" of communities are derived. Those community types are then used to compare and explain the growth of other communities. One consequence of this process is the continual refinement of the typology to account for increasing numbers of community variations.

This conceptual mode of thinking is directly related to the analytical. It assimilates and makes sense of data. At the same time, it continually confronts a historical record of infinite variation. Each new pattern or model defined is almost immediately challenged by historical data that it does not perfectly explain. At the same time, these patterns help to suggest questions that deserve answering, characteristics that are important, and a general context for community history that makes the history of a particular community stand out in high relief.

The local historian must be aware of these alternative modes of historical investigation and the data they employ. He or she must be prepared to use each as it helps to sustain "the most likely story" of the community's past.

Local history begins with a very concrete sense of its subject. Communities are anchored in space; they are actual places, usually with well-defined limits. This definition of community in terms of place lends itself to a holistic conception of community. The community is physically delimited from the surrounding communities; it is one place. If, however, we think of community not simply as a place, but as a set of relationships, then our sense of the community as one whole begins to change.

People in the community are not only citizens of that town—they are neighbors and members of congregations; they work in a variety of settings and have relationships formed there; they belong to unions or chambers of commerce, fraternal associations, and social clubs; and they think of themselves in a variety of ways: as members of a family, an ethnic group, a class, a religious group. For most people, there is some hierarchy of identities by which they define their relationship to other people; those hierarchies are quite different, from one individual to the next; and they change, over time. Ultimately, we have a community that looks more like a collection of communities.

As we try to reconstruct the history of a place into a comprehensive record of the people and what made their lives distinctive, we find ourselves dealing with the vast majority of people that normally do not occupy a place in histories, local or otherwise. Take a walk down any block alongside the census-taker for 1880 and see whom you meet. Even for historians well versed in their own communities, the strangers far outnumber the familiar faces. There are tradesmen, domestic servants, day laborers, housewives, children, itinerants, industrial workers, and artists—most of whom left the community before much could be recorded about their lives. But they and people like them were active and vibrant parts of the "communities" in the town while they were there. Most did not succeed, in the popular sense of that word. They did not pay for their places in the subscription history of the community. They rarely, if ever, saw their names in the paper. They did not hold political office or assume a leadership position in their lodge or church. But they worked; most of the men in the nineteenth century voted; they belonged; they procreated; they may, on occasion, have protested. They were both passive and active agents of their lives and, in that sense, of the place where they lived. In thinking about the history of a community, we must to some degree take account of their lives.

Simply providing a catalogue of the people and organizations in a community's past is a far cry from giving an account of its history. The history must reflect an understanding of causation; it must capture the sense of the community as a changing, dynamic entity. To do that, the local historian must look not simply at the lives of individuals or formal groups, but at the social process—the pattern of informal relationships and the effects of changes in one aspect of community life on changes in others. The coming of a railroad, the closing of a factory, the splitting of a congregation, or the fight to control the sale of liquor were the consequences of forces external and internal to the community. Each in turn set off other kinds of social and economic changes in the community. The historian's task is to provide the explanatory links between events.

The basis for historical explanation must derive from an adequately described context of community growth and change. That description rests on an understanding of the general economic, political, and social history of the period and a sensitivity to those external factors that may have shaped the community's history. It also rests on the quality of the concepts that the local historian uses to identify important aspects of community change and the critical questions that must be answered about the development of the place. Finally, good historical explanation can grow only out of the marshaling of historical data appropriate and adequate to answer these critical questions about a community's past.

Let us suggest in very broad strokes what some of these critical questions about a community's past might be. All communities offer some record of economic change and adaptation. Periods of growth in population and economic activity alternate in some unique configuration with periods of stagnation or even decline. How can these patterns of economic change be accurately described and explained? What were the effects of these changes on different groups of people in the community and on the general character of the place?

People in the past moved in and out of communities with great regularity, but they also created "islands of stability," subcommunities of people with similar backgrounds, occupations, or levels of well-being, according to Richard S. Alcorn, in "Leadership and Stability in Mid-Nineteenth-Century America: A Case Study of an Illinois Town," in the *Journal of American History Quarterly* (April 1977). There was a pattern in the flux and stability of historical communities. We must ask who came to the community and why? In what groups did they congregate? How did organized groups influence the development of the community?

People brought culture in their baggage when they moved to a community. They brought a set of beliefs, social rituals, norms of behavior, and aspirations. The way those cultures intermingled in a particular setting and the pressures on individuals to adapt or resist cultural change left an indelible mark on the history of communities. What major ethno-cultural groups were important in the life of a community? What tensions or conflicts as well as adaptations resulted from their interaction?

Finally, communities organized from the beginning to conduct their own affairs. Participation and influence were rarely distributed evenly across the population. Many social groups lacked direct access to the informal structures of decision making so prevalent in community affairs. Some groups—like women—lacked access to participation in formal political processes as well. What were the sources of power and influence in community life? What were the issues and organizations that mobilized people to exert political influence through established channels or through popular protest?

These sets of questions are not necessarily ones to be definitively answered in the course of studying the history of a community, so much as they are meant to give shape to the inquiry. The depth of inquiry that they imply suggests that a "total" history of a community, like that of a society, should come at the end of a process of investigating numerous more narrowly focused—but not insignificant— questions. Attempts at synthesis of that total history of a community need not necessarily wait until all the research is in or all the questions adequately researched. But, by the same token, attempts at synthesis should not preclude or discourage the essential work of careful investigation into specific aspects of a community's past. The existence of several very fine journals published by county historical societies provides an ideal vehicle for promoting this kind of research. Some examples are the Maniotwoc County Historical Society's *Occupational Monographs*, published quarterly; and the Milwaukee County Historical Society's *Milwaukee History*, published quarterly.

Some conventional wisdom about the history of nineteenth-century communities argues that important functions of small community life gradually were taken over by institutions of fairly large scale and that the more traditional, place-oriented notion of community declined in functional utility and significance. Works by Thomas Bender, Robert H. Wiebe, and Samuel P. Hays explain this position in some detail.

Clearly, many community institutions have been divested of some of their functions by large-scale institutions. The plethora of local newspapers, small-scale producers, and retailers serving strictly local markets, and the autonomy of local government come immediately to mind as examples. Today, even in small, rural communities, metropolitan newspapers and mass media, regional shopping malls, and specialized manufacturing for distant markets are facts of life; local government is enmeshed in a web of state and federal regulations as never before.

However, as historians of a community are able to demonstrate, there are important ways in which a historical sense of place infuses small-town life and neighborhood communities. The continuing functional vitality of community life has the same opaque quality that much local history has, when viewed from the outside. The story is ultimately about specific people, their families, their relationships, and the unique qualities that their collective life as a community manifests.

The elaboration of that sense of a distinctive and unique place continues to be a defining objective of the local historian. That objective is most tellingly achieved not by isolating the story of a community's past, but by defining a context that makes it stand out in bolder relief.

PART V

Rx for Local Historians

. . . in trying to guide local historians into the paths of righteousness and away from the amateurish imbecilities that often marked much of their work in the past, I am in danger of "taking all the pleasure out of local history."

—W. G. Hoskins, *Fieldwork in Local History*

Chapter Sixteen

How Not to Write Local History

Introduction

H. P. R. Finberg was educated at Oxford and for many years was head of the Department of English Local History at the University of Leicester. He published several English local histories himself, trained a number of scholars who went on to produce local histories, and encouraged the writing of English local history.

Finberg is associated with the Leicester school of historians who believe that a community smaller than the nation has a history that deserves to be studied for its own sake: that local history is not written only as a training exercise for historians who will go on to do greater and more important things, nor is local history important only for what it can contribute to national history. The Leicester school of local history seeks to have historians re-enact and portray the origin, growth, decline, and fall of a local community.

This essay, which his widow recalls that Finberg had a great deal of fun writing, details all the ways one should *not* write local history. Finberg's rules are important for local historians everywhere—at least those people determined not to write local history in the "usual flat and tedious" manner.

This work is reprinted, by permission, from H. P. R. Finberg and V. H. T. Skipp, *Local History, Objective and Pursuit* (Newton Abbott, England: David and Charles, 1967), 71–86.

* * * *

Anyone who wishes to avoid writing local history will find it perfectly easy to do so: he has only to switch on the radio or television; or he can just go to sleep.

H. P. R. Finberg, "How Not to Write Local History," in H. P. R. Finberg and V. H. T. Skipp, *Local History, Objective and Pursuit* (Newton Abbott, England: David and Charles, 1967), 71–86.

For present purposes, however, let us assume that somebody, somewhere, wants an occupation of a quasi-intellectual nature, and feeling no call to engage in some generally respected and lucrative pursuit, is determined at all costs to write the history of a local community. It is for his sake that I write; I shall try to show him how to reach the standard of performance that is expected of him: in other words, how to achieve that monumental flatness, tedium, and lack of acceptance which has been the hallmark of local history as too commonly practiced.

It may be objected: "What need is there of teaching on this subject? The shelves of every big library creak under a dead weight of books, almost every one of which is a model of the way not to write local history. With so many exemplars to guide him, how can the beginner possibly go wrong?"

There is force in this contention. On the other hand, it is possible that our student might waste a certain amount of time hesitating over the choice of models. Moreover, while native genius may have saved the authors of those books from the need of taking thought, mere ordinary talent must be improved by study and practice. For these reasons it may be useful to set forth one or two general precepts, making explicit the principles which have guided the hands of the masters in this dim field of study. I ought perhaps to add, in the spirit of the novelist who declares that every character in this story is fictitious, that when I speak with less than entire respect of our predecessors, I am referring mainly to local historians who are already dead, though I may inadvertently include one or two who still move and breathe and are unaware how dead they are.

The first rule to be laid down is one that admits of no exception. Since fortunes are not made by writing local history, the writer's impulse can only proceed from a genuine enthusiasm for the subject, and the rule is: TO ASSUME AN EQUAL ENTHUSIASM IN THE READER. In his single-minded devotion to the *genius loci*, the historian finds an endless fascination in every aspect of his chosen theme, and he takes it for granted that his readers will approach it in the same spirit; or rather, in his modesty, he assumes that nobody will read his narrative unless he cares about the place at least as much as the writer does. This assumption is usually correct; and it has the further merit of being immensely labour saving. A historian who feels himself under an obligation to woo the interest of as many readers as possible, including people who have never set foot in the parish, will have to take thought about his narrative; and, as we all know, there is no pain like the pain of thought. He will have to introduce some order, art, and method into the work, to exercise a modicum of selection and compression, to polish up his literary style. But the golden rule I have enunciated will save him all this trouble. No need to shape his narrative, to give it a beginning, a middle, and an end; no need to enliven it with graphic touches, to season it from time to time with the salt of irony, to work on the imagination and sympathies of the audience. He can go straight ahead, spilling the contents of his notebooks pell-mell over the page, never pausing to ask himself whether he is becoming a bore. Addressing himself only to an imaginary company of like-minded enthusiasts, he goes on adding yet another to the long list of local histories which only the most pressing curiosity will impel anyone to read.

Now since our historian is by definition an enthusiast, and since he obviously depends on some other source for his livelihood, he will have scant leisure for comparative study. Even if he has any curiosity to spare for other parishes and other counties, it never occurs to him that some places are more significant historically than others, and that his own village may not need to be portrayed at the same length as an ancient market town or a big manufacturing city. Thus the element of comparison is lacking; he never knows what is peculiar to his own parish and what is common form. He finds that the churchwardens from time to time spent money on the destruction of vermin; that vagrants were driven out of the parish with all convenient speed; and that under the later Stuarts the parson was obliged to certify that deceased parishioners were buried in woollen shrouds. Happily unaware that the same things were being done in parishes all over the country, he naturally communicates these exciting discoveries to the reader, who, let us hope, will be equally uninformed.

Odd creature as he is, the local historian is sufficiently human to have his likes and dislikes; in fact, he is often a crotchety character. And since he cannot hope to erupt into print very often, he treats the history of his town or village as a heaven-sent opportunity for airing his crotchets. Every now and then he peppers its pages with fiery little outbursts against Henry VIII or Oliver Cromwell or the pope. This certainly gives the book a semblance of animation, but unfortunately it is not of a kind that really exhilarates the reader. He also has his antiquarian preferences: a passion for Gothic architecture, perhaps, which leads him to describe the church at unconscionable length, while never sparing a glance for the Georgian manor-house or some uniquely interesting farmstead.

An even more fruitful source of tedium is the landed gentry. Many a so-called history seems to have been constructed on the principle that nobody ever lived in the parish but the squire and his relations. Dr. Joan Wake, that doughty champion of local studies at their best, remembers overhearing a conversation between two elderly gentlewomen in Northamptonshire. The village of Isham happened to be mentioned; whereupon one lady asked: "Who's living at Isham now?" To which her friend replied: "You know quite well that nobody has ever lived at Isham." An overpowering interest in the class to which the historians themselves belonged, or would have liked to belong, has cast a genealogical blight over English local history from which it is only now beginning to recover.

Then a feeling for romance, impelling the writer to fill his pages with picturesque or sentimental anecdotes, can do wonders in putting the reader off. The ghost of the white lady who flits about the manor-house; the underground passage alleged to lead from the priory to a nunnery some five miles off; the bed that Elizabeth I or Charles II may have slept in; the local skirmish between Cavaliers and Roundheads; the minor cases of bad language, assault, and bloodshed recorded in the manor court rolls: if enough space is given up to trivialities like these, the writer can be sure of leaving out the topics of most interest to an intelligent reader. In the history of a Cheshire village published a few years ago we read of a secret tunnel and a murdered nun. "She was murdered," says the writer, "because she broke her vows and married." We naturally wonder who did the deed, her husband or the abbess; but on this point curiosity remains unsatisfied. "It is not known what the date of the tragedy could be," he tells us candidly, "but her habit was black."

Most historians naturally feel more at home in one period than another. Two excellent local histories, Robo's *Medieval Farnham* and Fowler's *Medieval Sherborne*, make no pretence of carrying the story down into a period with which the authors felt unable to deal sympathetically. Contrast this with two other works, both of great merit in their different ways: Hine's *History of Hitchin*, and the more recent *History of Birmingham* by Gill and Briggs. Here the first thousand years or more are disposed of in about fifty pages, after which the writers settle down to write in earnest about the last century or two, which is all they really care about. A FORESHORTENING OF HISTORICAL PERSPECTIVE is one of the most common failings. It besets national as well as local history, notably in the Oxford History of England, which sets out to cover some nineteen hundred and fifty years in fifteen volumes, and devotes eight volumes to the last four centuries. The truly great local historian, when he appears, will deal faithfully with all periods.

Not so the chronicler for whom I am prescribing. He will probably begin by quoting the Domesday reference to the place; or perhaps he will first describe a round barrow and an earthwork which he incorrectly declares to be a Roman camp. Then the Domesday passage; and there is no better way of unnerving the average reader at the outset than to hurl a chunk of Domesday at him, without any explanation of its terminology or so much as a hint that scholars are not altogether certain what some of the entries mean. Next, perhaps, a page about the church, and one on the descent of the manor; after which, having scampered through the first thousand years or so in fewer than a dozen pages, the writer settles down to regale the public with his gleanings from the parish registers, family papers, and the local newspaper, interspersed with anecdotes about the local worthies and unworthies, and finishing perhaps with a detailed account of the festivities got up to celebrate a royal jubilee.

This distortion of the time-scheme is usually defended on the ground that it is natural for a historian to write more fully when his materials become more abundant. Natural, indeed, it may be; but history is not a natural pursuit: it is a science and an art. The mere accident that records have survived in plenty does not by itself invest a subject with historical significance. Of all the reasons which may impel a man to undertake a piece of historical research, the fact that documents bearing on the subject are abundant and accessible ought to weigh least. In reality, people who advance this plea only do so because their conception of historical evidence is an unduly narrow one. They are thinking too much about written and printed documents, not enough about farm names and field names and parish boundaries; not enough about the shapes and sizes of fields, the roads, the hedges, the visible pattern of settlement and cultivation. There is plenty of material for reconstructing the early history of a local community if only they would go out of doors and look for it. And seeing that the earlier centuries were in fact the formative period in the life of most local communities, there is no excuse for shirking this essential part of the historian's task.

Even when documents are plentiful, however, a really accomplished bungler will contrive to overlook them. The Reverend Roderick Dew comes to mind here as a conspicuous example. In his *History of the Parish and Church of Kilkhampton*, in Cornwall, he lamented that "the early churchwardens' accounts have not been preserved, and many ancient writings dealing with the church and church property have disappeared." Mr. Dew was rector of Kilkhampton from 1908 to 1940. In 1948 his successor found in the vestry a rusty key which fitted the lock of an iron safe standing in the south-west corner of the church. The safe had been there, visible to all, as far back as the church cleaner could remember, and she was getting on for ninety. It proved to be crammed with parochial documents, including a fine set of churchwarden's accounts. It may be added that if Mr. Dew had looked into Dugdale's *Monasticon*, that rich quarry for historians, he could have found a valuable clue to the history of Kilkhampton in the Saxon period. On the same page Joseph Fowler would have found—in fact, he did find—an equally valuable clue to the early history of Sherborne. He found it, and made nothing of it; so appreciation of his book must be qualified by the criticism that although he devotes a chapter to the pre-Saxon history of the place, he has missed a vital link in the evidence. It must be added that his ample quarto, which is full of topographical detail, includes no map, so that for readers who do not enjoy the privilege of living in Sherborne, many pages are completely unintelligible.

This brings us to another sovereign rule for the type of local historian we have in view. DON'T PROVIDE A MAP; or if you do, see that it is not drawn by professional cartographer. Draw it yourself, or get it drawn by a friend who likes drawing maps. No matter that your or his idea of lettering would disgrace a class of infants. Make sure that several of the places named most frequently in the text are omitted from the map. Then let the blockmaker reduce it so drastically that most of the names become illegible; and finally let the binder insert it into the book in such a way that it tears every time you open it.

Many a local historian, sooner than face the exertion of shaping his facts into an ordered narrative, contents himself with printing the documents and leaving them to speak for themselves. Instead of a local history he produces a collection of raw materials. Even this admits of judicious mishandling. If you provide a transcript or translation which may justly be suspected of inaccuracy; if you leave out bits which you think unimportant, without giving any indication that you have done so; if you omit to state whether you are reproducing the original document or someone else's edition of it; then, in addition to presenting the materials in an undigested form, you will have done your best to rob them of any value to the trained student and the professional historian.

Some compilers pay homage to the muse of history after their fashion by serving up the contents of their notebooks in a kind of substitute for narrative. Each fact is presented in a paragraph quite unconnected with the paragraphs before and after, or connected only by some transparent thread like that phrase which came so readily to the pens of the young women who used to write the chapters on monastic life in the Victoria County Histories. Finding in the bishop's register two complaints against a monastery, with perhaps the better part of a century between them, the author gives the substance of the first denunciation, then opens a new paragraph saying: "Things were no better eighty-five years later." It need hardly be said that such a thin coating of narrative, far from making the mixture really palatable, only helps to set the reader's teeth on edge.

A word must be said, too, about the erudite person who thinks it unnecessary—if he thinks at all—to render the jargon of bygone centuries into plain English. His pages are sprinkled with final concords, assizes of novel disseisin, inquisitions post mortem, fines and recoveries, writs of *Monstraverunt*, and the like. Here is another rule, then, complementary to the rule enunciated at the beginning of this discourse. ASSUME THAT THE READER IS ON A PAR WITH YOURSELF, not only in enthusiasm for the subject, but also IN ACQUAINTANCE WITH THE TECHNICALITIES. He ought to feel pleased and flattered; unfortunately, so perverse is human nature, he very seldom does.

The rule which bids us omit no triviality has for its corollary and counterpart that other rule bidding us EXCLUDE ALL THAT MATTERS. Faithful to this principle, the bungler is as maladroit in his silences as in anything he actually says. He gives the reader to understand that in what he calls the middle ages the village soil was cultivated under the open-field system; but where the fields were, whether there were two or three or more, what crops were grown, what stock was kept: on these topics he has not a word to say, and the suspicion arises that what he does say about the open fields is merely repeated from the textbooks. He mentions, without a flicker of curiosity, that "in some ancient records the place is styled a borough," but leaves you guessing how or when it acquired that status, whether it was coextensive with the manor, and how it was governed. Changes of incumbent, he remarks, were unusually frequent in the sixteenth century, but he omits to say which parson, if any, was evicted as being too fervent a papist, and which because he was too extreme a protestant. He states that the common fields and pastures were enclosed in 1786, but whether this left the mass of inhabitants richer or poorer, and whether the population went up or down in consequence, remains obscure. The local industries come and go without a word of explanation. The history of a Lincolnshire parish, recently published, gives not the slightest hint that land may have been gained in past centuries by reclamation from the sea, or lost by coastal erosion, though the author has seen erosion taking place in his own lifetime.

A word or two now on the subject of references. The obvious and simple course of not giving any has much to commend it, to the publisher if to no one else, for footnotes are so expensive that he groans every time he sees one, and feels more keenly than ever that he has taken the book on against his better judgment. The reader, on the other hand, likes to have some clue to the evidence on which the work is built, and the author for his part is not as a rule unwilling to furnish it, for although references put him to a certain amount of trouble, they also provide the best possible opportunity for displaying his erudition. Here again the problem resolves itself into that of seeming to provide what is wanted but not really doing so. Even in the works of reputable historians examples of this technique are to be found. I once wasted the best part of a day in a vain attempt to follow up a footnote reference in Round's *Feudal England*. It consisted of the single word "Hermannus." The catalogue of the London Library gives twenty-one different authors named Hermann or Hermannus; and by the time I had looked up their dates in various works of reference, eliminated those who were not early enough, and ransacked the works of the remainder, darkness was beginning to fall. It was only some weeks later, through the kind help of a correspondent, that I discovered how the footnote ought to have been worded: it should have read "Migne, *Patrologia Latina*, CLVI, col. 983."

On another occasion, while reading H. S. Bennett's *Life on the English Manor*, I was forcibly struck by the statement that monastic landlords from time to time "caused their serfs"—to do what?—"to marry free women with inheritances." Feeling naturally curious to know more in detail how the abbots contrived to practice this refined form of cruelty, I endeavured to follow up the author's footnote, which consisted of the one word "Walsingham." This presumably meant the St. Albans chronicler Thomas Walsingham, but the eight volumes of his works printed in the Rolls Series threw no light on the subject; so I wrote to Mr. Bennett for more information. He replied that while our country was at war he was not in a position to consult his notes. Thereupon I appealed to Dr. Coulton, editor of the series in which Mr. Bennett's work appeared, and a redoubtable stickler for accuracy. Thanks to his good offices, it was presently established that reference should have been made, not to Walsingham, but to *Rotuli Parliamentorum*, III, p. 319. And when I looked it up, it did not tell me how, if I had a serf, I should set about "causing" him to marry an heiress; it only said that when such marriages took place, as occasionally happened, they slipped through a loophole in the Statute of Mortmain.

Apart from the obvious course of giving no references at all, or giving the wrong ones, there are other ways in which they can be used to baffle the reader. One of them is the simple trick of quoting "Smith, *op. cit.*," thus forcing him to search through the undergrowth of perhaps a hundred and fifty pages before he can tell which of Smith's works is being cited. A more subtle device is to use printed sources, like the *Calendars of Close Rolls* and *Charter Rolls*, but to cite them in such a form as to suggest that reference is being made to the original manuscripts. This effectually deters most readers from following the reference up. It sometimes happens that a writer will give abundant and correct references to support what he has to say about the battle of Hastings or the dissolution of the monasteries or some equally well-known event, while giving none at all for the more striking and unusual incidents in the local scene. Or he will cite a manuscript without saying where he found it ("From a court-roll of the manor we learn" so and so), or without indicating its character ("a manuscript volume in the possession of Mr. X"). He will quote a work in many volumes without specifying volume and page. Mr. L. J. Ashford, in his otherwise excellent *History of High Wycombe*, goes even further. On p. 285 he quotes an unprinted document with no other reference than the words "Public Record Office." The usefulness of such a footnote can be measured by recalling that the number of documents in that repository, according to the estimate of their official custodians, approximates to fifty million.

What has been said here about references applies also, *mutatis mutandis*, to the index. The obvious course of providing no index at all has many precedents, particularly in the work of foreign scholars. One French academy set out to print and publish the whole series of papal registers, and did actually print about a score of them; but for all the use they have been to students they might just as well have remained unpublished, for hardly any of them are indexed. The concept of an index, in fact, as we understand the term, has found no secure lodging in the Gallic mind. But in this country we like our books to have an index; so it may be as well to make a show of giving the reader what he wants. One sure method of letting him down is to get your wife or a friend to make the index for you. Another is to give about fifty page-references under one entry, without any classification or sub-division. The entries may be confined to personal names, omitting place names; or vice versa. These are the more obvious inadequacies. A really subtle practitioner will improve upon them. The index he provides will look exhaustive, will in fact be so in all the minor entries, and only prolonged use will reveal that some of the most important references are missing. For a crowning touch, he can add a note apologizing for any shortcomings, like the writer who at the end of five hundred closely printed pages gave what he rightly called a "limited index" and explained that it was "prepared under somewhat difficult conditions on board the *Queen Mary* between Southampton and New York."

I have left to the last the most important matter of all. Hutchins, writing a monumental history of Dorset in 1773, remarked: "Works of this kind are of all others least capable of any advantages of style." How wholeheartedly most local historians have agreed with Hutchins on that point is plain for all to see. Moreover, in these days, when a torrent of letterpress roars past us day and night in full spate, and every other sentence is an outrage against one literary canon or another, it is easy enough to write badly: a bad style is in the very air we breathe. It does not take long to discover that one grand object of the contemporary prose-writer is NEVER TO USE ONE WORD WHERE YOU CAN POSSIBLY USE FOUR. A single illustration will suffice. I quote it from a meritorious recent work on suburban history. The writer wished to make the point that if a speculative builder believed house-building likely to bring in fat dividends, he might be tempted to build too many houses; if not, he would build few or none. Our historian put it in this way: "The profitability of house-building, and therefore of the supply of new houses, depended among other things on the alternative earnings of the capital used in it, and this meant that the provision of suburban houses could either be retarded for lack of capital which had been put to more profitable employment elsewhere; or, conversely, it could be expanded far beyond current needs when idle capital was put to what was considered safe use."

It will be noticed that the structure of this passage rests upon a foundation of impersonal abstract nouns. The figure of the moneyed man, contemplating his swollen bank-balance and pondering how best to employ his spare cash, is completely hidden from view under a cloud of verbiage. This too is in strict accordance with contemporary practice. A crude statement, such as "Balbus built a wall," is not acceptable in this day and age. Anything sooner than give the impression that history is concerned with human beings. The living, breathing Balbus, the fellow-creature with a mind of his own, must be got rid of at all costs, reduced to a statistical abstraction, an economic trend. The historian who consistently adheres to this great principle may well find it leading him on to higher things. He may end by quitting the lowly plane of history for good and soaring into the empyrean of Sociology, a subject, incidentally, which is much better endowed.

No one who can drive a pen or bang a typewriter should find any difficulty in following the simple precepts enunciated in the foregoing pages. And though success in any literary undertaking is not a thing which can be guaranteed, I believe there is a fair chance of it for the local historian who faithfully and consistently applies the principles I have ventured to lay down for his guidance. If he does this, he can be reasonably confident that his work will be as uninviting to the general reader as exasperating to the well-informed, and that when it has joined the older local histories on the shelves, it will gather as much dust as any of them.

Chapter Seventeen

The Local Historian:
His *Occupational Hazards* and *Compensations*

Introduction

This view of local history was devised by Professor John Caughey, who presented this talk in Pasadena, before the History Guild of Southern California, on December 30, 1942. It is a remarkably fresh essay, despite its age.

Caughey looks at some of the assets local historians have and the hazards inherent in those assets. He points out that local documents, often a treasure of information—and relatively unknown outside the area they treat—also lead local historians to focus their research narrowly. He notes that because a local historian lives in the community about which he or she writes, there is often a degree of self-censoring, or protection of community topics. He looks at the question of bias and the writing of local history. Professor Caughey also discusses the relationship of local history to the discipline of academic history.

John Caughey was a professor of American history at the University of California at Los Angeles and author of many books about California and the American West.

His essay was first published by the Pacific Coast Branch, American Historical Association, *The Pacific Historical Review* 12 (March 1943):1–9 and appears here with permission.

* * * *

The title of this paper implies that there is something about the local historian which sets him apart from the ordinary or real member of the profession. Perhaps it implies that in a gathering of historians, the practitioners of local research should

John Walton Caughey, "The Local Historian: His Occupational Hazards and Compensations," *The Pacific Historical Review* 12 (March 1943): 1–9.

be as readily distinguishable as, let us say, the poodles at a dog show. Whether the breed has identifying characteristics, such as a microscopic habit of the eye, or an untraveled look, I hesitate to affirm. Nevertheless, it is certain that the local historian is a well-known and established variety, and that he possesses traits, habits, possibilities, and limitations that are, at least in part, peculiar to him.

By local historian, incidentally, I mean to comprehend those who treat of state or region as well as those who deal with a fraction thereof. Purely quantitative considerations would seem to indicate such a course. A part of one state may well be larger than the entirety of another, and a single state may outbulk an accepted region. For example, the historian of Los Angeles, when he appears, will find that his subject dwarfs Rhode Island, and the historian of California must cover more ground than the historian of New England. Furthermore, there is a commonality of problem and method, of opportunity and danger, that all these less-than-national historians must face.

Those who confess to being local historians will probably insist that the occupational hazards outweigh the compensations, and that the pitfalls into which one may tumble are greater than the eminences to which one may aspire. I do not propose, however, to budget five minutes to rewards and twenty-five to penalties, or to attempt any other sharp segregation of pros and cons. The two are interwoven. Failure to grasp an opportunity is common cause for falling into error, and the attainment of success is often achieved by alert avoidance of hazards.

Of all the arguments for local research the most persuasive is doubtless that the materials for it are conveniently at hand. In California we have two great repositories, the Bancroft and the Huntington libraries, where one can consult almost every title listed in the bibliographies of California history. A half-dozen other libraries have notable collections, and scores of others are adequate for the investigation of wisely selected topics. Beyond this, anyone who possesses the thirty-nine volumes of Hubert Howe Bancroft's *Works* has the digested equivalent of a voluminous collection, superior to the best libraries available on several less fortunate states. The State Library and the Bancroft Library are strong in newspaper files; the Bancroft has a wealth of manuscript material on the Spanish, Mexican, and early American periods, and the Huntington Library, with some early manuscripts, is rich on the middle and late nineteenth century. Other manuscripts and newspapers are in humbler quarters. The only known file of the Inglewood *Star*, for instance, belongs to the Inglewood Historical Society; for the Coronel Papers one should go to the Los Angeles County Museum, and for the Bixby Papers to the Palos Verdes Library.

Furthermore, there are additional materials in county and city archives, in the possession of title companies, railroads, oil companies, land companies, and other business concerns, and in private hands. These materials are for the most part uncatalogued, and usually they have not been tagged as historical, yet it is from them that many chapters of the state's recent history must be written. The essential point is that a local researcher, though ordinarily he would do well to repair to the Bancroft or the Huntington, can usually find quantities of material closer at hand.

The hazard that attaches to this advantage is that one may forget that not all California has been corralled within the state. The investigator of almost any phase of the Spanish period will find that the documentary trail leads to the archives in Mexico City, Seville, and Madrid. Forty-niner letters and diaries are constantly cropping up in the East, and eastern libraries often bid for collections which include important Californiana, as Yale University recently did with success for the superlative Mark Twain collection of the late Willard S. Morse.

A companion virtue of local research is that one can get close to the subject. A national or a world historian, if he has the traveling instinct of an Eleanor Roosevelt or a Wendell Willkie, may see much of the world. Yet it is doubtful that his knowledge of the natural setting of his chosen subject will compare with the local historian's. A Californian will be mindful of the climatic influences that hovered over the participants in local development. He can view the terrain on which they operated, and oftentimes can find it relatively unaltered. Since the more important action is crowded into the recent past, the chances are excellent that he will be able to interview some of the participants, or at least to get testimony from persons who knew them in the flesh. Thus Bancroft gathered hundreds of statements from forty-niners, from veterans of the War with Mexico, pioneer settlers, earlier American residents, citizens of Mexican California, and oldtimers who dated back to the Spanish regime. Similarly, today's investigator of the Epic campaign, of the Lincoln-Roosevelt reform movement, or of the Boom of the Eighties could gather firsthand information to supplement the manuscript and printed testimony.

The benefits of being close to the subject also include awareness of results. Modern California contains reminders of the Japanese problem of a generation ago, of the earlier and repeated demands for transportation improvement, and of the controversies between the sections of the state.

Inherent in this closeness to the subject is the hazard of bias. I am not sure that local historians are guilty of greater partiality than students of the Trojan War, the Spanish Inquisition, the conquest of Mexico, or the origins of the first World War, but the temptation is certainly present. Examples could be cited of colored accounts of the Spanish missions, of John C. Frémont, of the San Francisco Vigilance Committees, and of the Associated Farmers. The bias of which the local historian is most often accused is that of inordinate pride in his state or region. The California booster has long been a recognized type, and naturally his spirit has infected the writing of California history. Herein the damage may after all be slight. I do not argue that California merits boosting, but merely mention the standard antidote of ridicule, good-natured or otherwise, that is poured on promotional history, even when it is a sober recital of facts.

A more serious error to which the local historian is prone is that of provincialism, in my opinion his deadliest peril. Superficially the term "local history" may seem to call for concentration on the purely local, but in most instances it is totally unrealistic to look only as far as the county or state boundaries. For example, no one will understand the Spanish administration of California unless he considers it in connection with the practices and problems of the empire as a whole; no one can explain California's admission to statehood without integrating this step with the other elements of the Compromise of 1850; no one can get the full picture of the work of the California Fruit Growers Exchange unless he examines its nation-wide arrangements for marketing. California has had its quota of nearsighted chroniclers, who acted as though the state had existed in a vacuum. Bancroft as the scope of his *Works* indicates, had a much broader view, and other writers, particularly in the last quarter-century, have shown awareness of the wide horizons that the subject demands. The local researcher who keeps this perspective will avoid the worst pitfall of provincialism and will find that local history, paradoxically enough, is broadening.

Local history is often used to illumine the course of national experience or world affairs. Thus one may study California politics of the fifties to learn about techniques of vote-getting and boss rule, or study the development of the Southern Pacific as an illustration of the rise of big business. Studies such as these yield a profit, but they do not provide a full view of local history. At the other extreme is the attitude that local history's essential function is to take note of local peculiarities, of deviations from the norm, and of elements that are unique. Rather more of our state history has been cut to this pattern, though occasionally with a reminder that Californians of a given generation shared in the experiences and aspirations of Americans in general. Since California history is written primarily for American readers, it may be proper to assume some understanding of the setting in national history. The local scene, however, is only partially reflected in a narrative that disregards so much that is orthodox American rather than peculiarly Californian. For example, we all know that Californians are often more concerned about the outcome of national rather than state elections, yet except for 1860 and 1912 our state histories cannot be counted on to record or analyze the presidential vote of the California electorate.

Between the definitions of local history as "a small-scale model of national or global history," and as "a narrative of peculiar and unique experiences," choice is neither easy nor comfortable. As with all dilemmas the solution seems to demand a bold grappling with both horns. Parts of local history move inexorably in the rhythm of the nation or the world. Thus the American acquisition of California was an expression of Manifest Destiny, and thus the problems of capital and labor in twentieth-century California dovetail with those of the nation. Other parts are unique—the gold rush, our Orientals, our motion picture industry, and much of our agriculture—and no attempt to treat them as average samplings of American experience will do them justice. The truth embraces both these definitions, and the local historian must weave his fabric with both warp and woof. Too often it has been only woof, or provincialism, or, so far as outlanders are concerned, triviality.

The sword of censorship is a greater menace to the local than to the national historian. In part this arises from proximity to his subject and from dependence upon local sources of support and upon a local printer. Furthermore, a local pressure group is more easily organized than a national one, and has greater prospect of success. There are a few famous instances of United States historians running afoul of censorship, but usually a censorship exerted by a local faction or chieftain such as Big Bill Thompson. I have never heard of a researcher being warned away from a national or larger topic because it was "loaded with dynamite." Within my limited experience, however, several such instances have occurred in the field of local research. I recall the phrase that research on the San Francisco Graft Prosecution would be "premature." I recall disapproval of a research proposal on the ground that it might offend a particular religious group. I recall a tempest over a historical document spread upon the pages of a local journal, a subsequent change in the editorship of that journal, and the suppression of the remaining installments of the document. In the realm of local history, censorship is an existent reality.

More significant than the fact of censorship are the impulses that promote it. One of these obviously arises because the readers as well as the writers of local history find themselves close to the subject, if not right in it. They have a natural desire that they, their fathers, their grandfathers, and their friends shall be given favorable and prominent mention. The usual expression and exploitation of this impulse is in the mugbook—the local history to which are appended biographical sketches that have been bought and paid for. The mugbook, of course, is an inversion of censorship, an application of external pressure to determine what shall be published, rather than a dictation of what must be suppressed. On occasion this same impulse has produced outright censorship; for example, when the choleric David S. Terry demanded certain changes in Bancroft's *Popular Tribunals.*

Another impulse to censorship derives from the fact that the average person, though chary of claiming expertness in medicine, engineering, law, or dentistry, can easily convince himself that he is an authority on local history. Living in a place supplies the observant person with bits of historical knowledge, and if family and friends help with traditive testimony, a certain amount of historical expertness can be soaked up from the environment. In community after community some oldster who "remembers when" is pointed out as knowing the entire history of the place.

The disingenuousness of the professional historian, the Ph.D. in history, contributes to this appropriation of authority. For history is the least mysterious and least cloistered branch of learning. It has no secret techniques of theory or apparatus; it has no special vocabulary. It is the one discipline whose most advanced findings are set forth in everyday speech and purport to be addressed to the multitude. This unpretentiousness requires the professionals to be better historians. It encourages them to sound reasoning and to clear expression. It also has opened the door to historical research and writing on the part of such gifted men as Francis Parkman, Theodore Roosevelt, James F. Rhodes, Albert J. Beveridge, George Fort Milton, and Carl Sandburg. Yet in the field of local history, there is at times an undue willingness on the part of the nonexpert to pass on the merits of historical studies. Our society has expressed in legislation its reluctance to have untrained persons build bridges, practice law, fill teeth, or doctor sick cats. Yet individuals with virtually no training in history volunteer to prescribe how local history shall be written.

The researcher in local history has the consolation that several publication avenues are open to him. California, for example, offers the quarterlies of the California Historical Society and the Historical Society of Southern California and the yearbooks and occasional publications of several county and local associations, all of which are devoted entirely to California history. Other historical journals, such as the *Pacific Historical Review,* the *Hispanic American Historical Review,* and the *Mississippi Valley Historical Review,* are more or less open to California contributions. In addition, there are journals of more popular vein, such as *Desert, Westways,* and the *Pony Express Courier,* which regularly accord some of their columns to local history. Eastern book publishers have developed a certain tolerance for California history subjects, and there are local publishers, such as the University of California Press, Stanford University Press, the Arthur H. Clark Company, the Grabhorn Press, the Colt Press, Ward Ritchie, and the Huntington Library, ready upon occasion to issue California books. A seminar of mine not long ago saw the majority of its reports into print, using such media as the Historical Society of Southern California *Quarterly,* the California Historical Society *Quarterly,* the *Pacific Historical Review,* the *Alumni Magazine* of the University of California at Los Angeles, and the Inglewood *Shopping News.* I mention this last, not only in genuine pride, but also in hopes that it will point the way to other stimulating outlets for student papers on local history.

Looking at the darker side, one notes that the circle of potential readers is more limited than for the national or world historian. California histories remind me of a remark attributed to one of the Marx Brothers turned author. "All my books," he ruefully reported, "are first editions." I happen to know that a high school text on the state's history, a work whose reputation is purely local, has sold more than 20,000 copies, which means several printings; but, so far as I am aware, no *History of California* has gone into a second edition.

Also on the darker side is the limited market for the specialist in local history. California history is rather generally taught in the fifth grade and in high school. It is offered in most junior colleges and appears in the course list in several of the four-year colleges. Almost never does it constitute a full teaching program, and usually it is regarded as an incidental course to be handled by someone whose principal duty and specialization is in United States history, Hispanic American history, English, or physical education. The prospective teacher therefore should be warned to prepare to handle something in addition to California history. The Ph.D. candidate will not need that warning, for, even if his dissertation is in California history, most of the requirements for the degree will lie elsewhere. To the best of my observation, a dissertation in California history, though no great help, is no handicap when it comes to landing a job.

What effect continued specialization in local history would have on one's chances of rising in the profession is not so clear. The local specialist gives hostages to fortune. He forfeits any great likelihood of a call to Harvard, or Chicago, or any of the other seats of eastern learning. It is possible that this factor has something to do with the apparent reluctance of historians to devote themselves exclusively to research in California history. It is a curious and otherwise inexplicable fact that the leading authorities on our state's history and most of the professionals have been only part-time laborers in this vineyard. I can think of no other branch of history where part-time laborers are the rule.

Despite all these Cassandra-like warnings about the prospects for the researcher in California history, I extend a warm welcome to all who would dig in this soil. It is no private preserve. Anyone may enter. Much has been done, especially on the Spanish period and the early American era, but still more remains to be done. Portolá, Rivera, Neve, Borica, and Lasuén are as deserving of biographical study as were Serra, Crespi, Palóu, and Anza, on whom we have excellent appraisals. Chapman's thorough work on *The Founding of Spanish California* should be matched by a comparable work on the end of Spanish rule and on the secularization of the missions. Ogden's *California Sea Otter Trade* should have a sequel on the hide trade. Lives of Sutter, Marsh, Smith, and Reid should be followed by more adequate treatments of Larkin, Vallejo, Stearns, and Robinson. From Frémont and Starr King, we could profitably turn to such men as James E. Birch, David C. Broderick, and Sam Brannan; from the San Francisco Vigilance Committees to rural vigilante action.

Research possibilities are not yet exhausted on such familiar topics as the Spanish missions and the gold rush. The particular opportunity, however, lies in the American period and especially in its more recent portion. Works such as Daggett's *Chapters on the History of the Southern Pacific*, Stewart's *John Phoenix* and *Bret Harte*, Walker's *San Francisco's Literary Frontier*, Cleland's *Cattle on a Thousand Hills*, and Alexander's *Chaffey*, light up a few comers of this sprawling subject-matter, but the greater part is unexplored and uncultivated. There is room for good books on lumbering, on the cattle business after 1849, on whaling and fishing, on viticulture, on the grain ranches of Frank Norris' *Octopus*, on politics in the late nineteenth century. The mainstays of California's recent and current economy—oil, the citrus industry, moving picture production, the tourist business, and airplane manufacture—await their several historians. These and their companion social and cultural phenomena are perhaps less bizarre than the Franciscan friars, the red-shirted forty-niners, and San Francisco's volunteer firemen, but they go much farther toward explaining modern California, and they must eventually find recognition as the most significant chapters in local history. Their elucidation awaits researchers.

Lack of training in California history is no bar to entrance upon these tasks. The ideal perhaps is that most of this research should be done by Ph.D.s whose dissertations were on California topics. I say "perhaps," because some doubts exist that professional training is essential, or even helpful. We still lack proof that there is a positive correlation between graduate training in history and effective research and writing.

California history, at any rate, has been written principally by individuals without training, or by individuals trained to do something entirely different. The first local historian, Francisco Palóu, made his preparation through missionary work, Franklin Tuthill through journalism, and Theodore H. Hittell through law. Josiah Royce took a sabbatical from philosophy to write the California volume for the American Commonwealths series, and Irving B. Richman warmed to the subject of the province under Spain and Mexico by doing a history of Rhode Island and a monograph on one of the Swiss cantons. Most prodigious of all these volunteers was Hubert Howe Bancroft, the San Francisco book dealer who turned collector, publisher, and historian. Among his staff there was nothing approximating a Ph.D. in history.

Among the moderns consider the leading authority on California history, who pre-pared for this career by writing a dissertation on the free Negro in the ante-bellum South and by seven years' teaching of medieval history. Consider also the retired mining engineer who has written authoritatively on Drake, on Spanish voyages of the sixteenth century, on West Coast cartography, and on the bibliography of the Spanish Southwest and the Plains and Rockies. Also, I might mention a past presi-dent of the Pacific Coast Branch whose specialty is Scandinavian history but who has found time to publish on California sheep drives and horse drives and on an early phase of the oil industry. Another illustration is afforded by a young instruc-tor, fresh from New York by way of Harvard, who immediately upon arrival in the state began to supervise the writing of senior term papers in California history. Or—to make clear that these comments are not meant to be invidious—may I mention my own launching as a regional historian. Trained as a Spanish Americanist and innocent of any expertness in local history, I was, with one day's notice, placed in charge of three hundred students enrolled for a course in Pacific Coast history.

A field with such capacity for attracting and shanghaiing workers needs no sales talk. Nevertheless, I plead for more research all along the line and especially on the more recent phases of California development, that we may better understand our own position, and for the light that these local studies will throw upon national problems and world relations. California history has been rich in variety, in drama, in the ludicrous, in heroism and villainy. More than most local histories, it has influenced its bigger and more respectable cousins, national and global history. The researcher who elects this field will find that I have not exaggerated the pitfalls, obstacles, and hazards. I trust, however, that he will encounter correspondingly larger compensations.

Chapter Eighteen

How to Write a *Dull* Town History

Introduction

Not all commentaries about local history began as talks by academic historians or appeared in academic journals. Geoffrey Elan is the book review editor for *Yankee Magazine*, which receives many New England local histories for review. In this charming piece, Elan, who also writes columns about history, offers some comments about the genre of local history.

Elan offers three rules guaranteed to ensure that a local history will put the reader to sleep. He suggests that the history should be written by a committee, that it be all-inclusive, and that the author or authors make certain not to offend anyone.

Elan, Caughey, and Finberg touch upon many of the same issues—Finberg and Caughey in search of better history, Elan in search of better literature. All these essays hold lessons for anyone preparing to write a local history—and are a great deal of fun to read.

Elan's blithe commentary is reprinted, with permission, from *Yankee Magazine*, (March 1986): 169–70.

* * * *

We have about 700 town histories in our little Yankee Publishing Inc. library, and receive two or three new ones each month. I'm defining the term loosely here, to include histories of counties, regions, valleys, parts of towns, churches, neighborhoods; perhaps it would be better to call them local histories. They generally have three things in common: They are written by amateur historians, they do not achieve wide readership, and, alas, they are unreliable and stupefyingly dull.

Geoffrey Elan, "How to Write a *Dull* Town History," *Yankee Magazine* (March 1986): 169–70.

I intended to discuss how to write a good town history, with examples. The trouble is, there are not many examples, and they tend to defy classification; that is why they are good. The failures are all very much alike, and that is why they are bad. So, based on the principle that we learn more from our errors than from our triumphs, and on the fact that I have had more experience with the former than the latter, here are Elan's Infallible Instructions for Writing a Dull Town History.

1. *It should be written by a committee.* That way more of the town will be involved in the project, and different viewpoints will he represented. This will result in renewed civic pride and a bland pudding of a book without a point of view. As the old joke says, an elephant is a horse put together by a committee.

Committees have produced some great works. The King James Bible was written by a committee. It shows. See the "begats" in Genesis, and the endless itinerary of the Israelites in Numbers, both faithfully reproduced in most town histories. It might be argued that the purpose of a town history is to tell who begat whom and where they traveled and lived in their lifetimes. My response is that those are records, not history, and there is a difference between the archivist and the historian. History is story, not facts. What we remember of history (including the Bible) is the story it tells, not the lists of names and places. A committee, however, finds it easier to pile up facts than to tell a story. This leads into the second rule, which is . . .

2. *Don't leave anything out.* An extreme example of this is one history that begins in the Paleozoic Era, when "fishes swam where Chicopee and Holyoke people now walk." *Holyoke-Chicopee: A Perspective* by Ella Merkel DiCarlo ($11.95, Main Poland Road, Conway, MA 01341) bubbles with personalities and appealing stories. But the extinction of the dinosaurs in the Connecticut Valley, the plagues that swept the area clean of Indians, and the color of the wig worn by the proprietress of a notorious house of ill fame all get equal billing. There may be perspective, but there is no proportion.

Another example of the reverent reporting of trivia comes from *The Book of Heath* (Paideia Publishers, P.O. Box 343, Ashfield, MA 01330): "September 14, 1885: Due to the increased price of the rental of telephones, Preston Baker, the Misses Maxwell and George Bemis had theirs taken out."

Sandwich: A Cape Cod Town ($21.50, 145 Main Street, Sandwich, MA 02563) is 572 pages long, counting index, bibliography, genealogical charts, lists of subscribers, and other shilly-shallying. The author, R. A. Lovell, Jr., writes with the gravity and individuality of the classic town historians of the 19th century. l think he's done a splendid job, but he complains that he was forced to "prune greatly what we would wish to relate. . . ." It is the duty of the historian to prune away the inessential facts and avoid what E. B. White called the mistaken notion that everything is important. To do so, however, would be to violate Rule #3 . . .

3. *Don't offend anyone.* A section of *Durham, New Hampshire: A History 1900–1985* ($25, Phoenix Publishing, Canaan, NH 03741) begins with the words,

"With no intention of slighting anyone," then rattles off a lengthy list of persons who helped out the Town Recreation Committee (see Rule #2). Such a list belongs in the Town Report, not in the town history.

A more common application of this rule is not to rock the boat by injecting elements of history that are at odds with the accepted local myths. This can take the form of selective amnesia, as in *Fitzwilliam: The Profile of a New Hampshire Town, 1884–1984* ($16, Phoenix Publishing, Canaan, NH 03741), which lists all the sextons of the past century in a five-page chapter on cemeteries, but gives one line to a community of several hundred Italian stoneworkers and their families who worked in the quarries. On the other hand, Renee Garrelick, author of *Concord in the Days of Strawberries and Streetcars* ($17.50, Concord Historical Commission 350th, Box 535, Concord, MA 01742), is to be commended for reporting the stoning of Irish and Italian laborers in that town along with warm memories of wildflower-decorated "school barges" and town baseball teams.

Paul Maureau probably made no friends in Masardis, Maine, by writing with candor and sympathy in *The Masardis Saga* ($10.95, TBW Books, Day's Ferry Rd., Box 164, Woolwich, ME 04579) about the pleasures of visiting hunters, or "sports," of the late 19th and early 20th centuries: "I have heard many tales of women who made extra money on their backs, if they happened to be pretty and friendly. They would have been unmarried or widowed women, I suspect. When you remember that dollars were scarce in this part of the world, you can hardly blame them for making hay while the sun shone." But he made a town and a time come vividly, humanly alive.

And that, I suppose, is what marks a good town history for me. There is no story without conflict, the spark of life that leaps from the clash of flint and steel, old ways and new ideas, immigrant and Establishment. The embodiment of this approach to local history is *Far Out the Coils* ($15, The Tashmoo Press, RFD Box 590, Vineyard Haven, MA 02568) by Henry Beetle Hough, who died last June on his beloved Martha's Vineyard. The book is subtitled, "A personal view of life and culture on Martha's Vineyard," and it manages to pack so much history, insight, humor, indignation, and love into 128 pages that it fairly quivers in the hand.

I think it was John D. Rockefeller who once listed three rules for getting rich. The first was to start work early in the morning, the second was to work late into the night, and the third was to find oil. The lesson for town histories in Rockefeller's parable is that earnest efforts and good intentions are not enough. If you want a good town history, you have to find oil: a Henry Beetle Hough, a Paul Maureau, a Gladys Hasty Carroll; a Spindletop lurking in the library.

Chapter Nineteen

Local and Community History:
Some Cautionary Remarks on
an Idea Whose Time Has Returned

Introduction

This essay by David Gerber was published in 1979, just as local history was gaining new popularity, brought on in part by the Bicentennial celebration of the American Revolution; by the preservation movement; and by the rise of interest in ethnicity, in gender, in history from the "bottom up"—an era that saw the publication of books extolling smallness and home-grown skills. As that movement swelled, David Gerber, professor of American history at the State University of New York at Buffalo and a specialist in ethnicity, wrote the following cautionary piece.

Written primarily for teachers of history, this essay is, nonetheless, important for local history administrators as well, and for anyone interested in researching and writing local history.

Gerber's commentary is reprinted, by permission, from *The History Teacher* 13 (November 1979): 7–30.

* * * *

Local and community may well be one of the fastest growing popular intellectual pursuits in the United States today. At a time when history languishes in the schools, many Americans are engaged in separate searches into their "roots"— writing histories of their towns, families, ethnic communities, and parish churches. Though the particular enthusiasms and interests which comprise this phenomenon are diffuse and as yet without a common voice, we may still speak with accuracy

David A. Gerber, "Local and Community History: Some Cautionary Remarks on an Idea Whose Time Has Returned," *The History Teacher* 13(1) (November 1979): 7–30.

of the existence today of a popular local and community history "movement," for, as this essay is to argue, there seems to be a core of attitudes, emotions, and goals common to the participants. For historians and history teachers, this popular movement suggests new opportunities to establish their discipline's primacy in the popular culture and imagination. But more importantly, history teachers may now utilize with renewed vigor and increased acceptance familiar local and community material in pursuit of the historian's highest and ultimate concerns—to bring objectivity and analytical rigor both to the study of the broad, inclusive sweep of change and to the on-going effort to create a comprehensive synthesis of human experience.

It is difficult for history teachers, accustomed to apathetic, vocationally minded students or declining enrollments, to avoid getting caught up in this enthusiasm of the popular culture and letting some of the popular cultural influences enter their teaching. This enthusiasm itself can only be quickened, as it has been for me, by encounters with today's occasional student who comes to history eagerly, after some recent exposure to popular local and community history. But these very temptations and enthusiasms require that we look closely into the nature and consequences of this new trend. As I shall suggest, an unexamined plunge into the current modes of popular local and community history may have classroom consequences which are, because of their tendency to present students with a false view of themselves and an incomplete view of the past, unproductive and even negative.

At present we lack a serious analysis of the origins and development of this contemporary popular involvement with local and community history.[1] Instead we find a proliferation of how-to and do-it-yourself books[2] which, while useful in dozens of practical ways, place their emphasis wholly on technique and method, to the neglect of the more difficult, qualitative problems of cultural ideology and historical conceptualization. Moreover, there has been little effort to place in apposition this popular cultural trend and the increased scholarly interest over the past two decades in local and community history. An important consequence is that teachers of history lack perspective not only on an influential popular trend which might be affecting their students' attitudes toward the past, but also on the relationship of that trend to their own formative academic training.

This essay will address the possible benefits and the often unanticipated but quite real problems for historical studies and history teaching in the current upsurge of interest in local and community history. First, however, I want to present a perspective on today's interest in popular local and community history through an analysis of similar movements in the past. Following that, some general guidelines will be suggested by which teachers might utilize local and community history effectively in the classroom without surrendering themselves to the pitfalls in the popular trend.

It is easy to exaggerate the uniqueness of the present interest in local and community history. The study of small, functional spatial units of human settlement (such as neighborhoods, towns, cities, etc.) and of social solidarities and affinity groups within and among such localities (such as social classes, races, sexes, ethnic, family and kinship, religious, and voluntary groupings, or parts and combinations of them, sharing common concerns and characteristics and a sense of common identity)[3] is, of course, hardly new. Nor is the contemporary practice of analytically juxtaposing a single locality and an individual community within it without precedent. Historians, amateur and professional alike, have always seen the utility of examining an aspect of the past from the perspective of the smallest possible social and spatial units. What is new is the present converging of academic and popular interests in local and community history. This is because the current popular enthusiasm has arisen at a time when local and community history have attained unprecedented legitimacy among academic scholars. The coincidence of these two developments explains the great extent to which many academic historians are presently involved in various cooperative and advisory relations with popular historical institutions and organizations. In the past, such close working alliances on this scale would have been most unlikely.

The depth of this change becomes more apparent if we review the differing perspectives from which academic and popular historians traditionally viewed local and community history and each other. Formerly local and community history were largely the province of amateurs, antiquarians, fileopietists, and genealogists, whose combined interest in family achievement, ethnic defense, parochial local issues, and historical memorabilia brought scorn from academic scholars. Yet, to the non-academic, the academic scholar seemed guilty of a type of reverse parochialism. Academic historians were largely preoccupied with what they believed to be "the big picture." The locality and the individual social group within it were often seen as merely provincial, part of a small tradition which contrasted unfavorably with what the anthropologist Robert Redfield called "the great tradition" of cosmopolitan values and high culture.[4] Reinforcing this orientation was the tendency of academic historians to synthesize the past around events involving the gathering and use of power.[5] War, politics, diplomacy, and high finance, and the interactions between them, held center stage. Though it was recognized that Podunk voted, paid taxes, and sent its sons off to war, the action still seemed always to be in the halls of Congress or the President's office. Podunk's citizens and its amateur historians might well be excused if they came to feel that their concerns were left out of this type of written history.

Much has changed in professional scholarship in the last few decades. For generations the process of synthesis was governed largely by a standard paradigm: history as the study of past politics, of struggles for power between contending cosmopolitan political, diplomatic, and economic elites.[6] But attacks on this paradigm have come from two directions in the post-World War II period. First, members of traditionally nonelite groups (women, blacks, Jews, Catholics, "New Immigration" ethnics, etc.), which have historically lacked access to power, have entered the historical profession. They have brought with them the need and desire to pursue new questions forged of their own worlds and experiences—slavery, poverty, ghettoization, disfranchisement, discrimination, foreignness, and disorienting social and geographical mobility. Second, the appropriation of concepts and methods developed by social science, but tailored to history's needs, has provided historians with ways of researching, understanding, and organizing the history of conventionally inarticulate groups, which usually have failed to leave behind them significant amounts of written evidence. In consequence of both of these developments in scholarship, complex and ramifying new concerns, such as social integration, pluralism, class formation, and cultural hegemony, have been thrust into the center of our historiography. Though the concept of modernization has influenced many contemporary historians, no single paradigm has emerged to replace the moribund old one. Indeed, history today has few orthodoxies. Instead, history has come increasingly to see itself as the sum total of human social development over time. Its legitimate purview has become almost anything, for it has recognized that since all historical phenomena are directly or indirectly linked in their causes, content, or consequences, all historical phenomenon have the potential to transform our understanding of the past and of ourselves.[7]

We are consequently confronting a view of history which does not allow the past to be synthesized, as it has been traditionally, by great events. As historians have become more familiar with social science, they have come to think instead in terms of social process. Synthesis is now routinely guided by analysis of underlying, inclusive forces and movements of change—urbanization, etc.—which involve to differing degrees all groups and individuals within a society in all their varied social activities. The relationship between social process and local and community history will be addressed in the final section. The point is that dynamic, multifaceted processes like industrialization involve such levels of complexity that, for practical reasons alone, historians are led to examine them in the most retrievable units of analysis. Which is to say that it is easier to study the impact of industrialization in one city among one group of people than to study its impact upon everyone in society.

A fresh insight into the shaping of past American societies has complemented this practical dependence on localities and communities as units of analysis and research. In the twentieth century, thanks to the development of a truly national communication and transportation network and of national marketing and franchising, we have become a more or less integrated nation, in which local and regional differences play a declining, though not a disappearing, role. In the more distant past, this was not the case. Like their counterparts in other pre-modern and modernizing societies, pre-twentieth century Americans oriented their lives more around their locality. To be sure, Americans of earlier centuries were involved in markets which spanned regions and indeed continents, and they did develop various types of national or patriotic traditions. But they were certainly more isolated physically from one another, and they had a dimmer sense of the nation as a whole. Probably, too, a sense of place was a much more acutely developed aspect of consciousness among earlier Americans than it is with most of us today. Such appraisals of American social development have led eminent scholars like Robert Wiebe to insist upon the central role of the locality in their efforts to conceptualize the nature of American development in previous centuries.[8]

While historians have thus been moving toward local and community history through various developments internal to their discipline, the lay public has embarked on its own course in the same direction. It has already been noted that we do not have any serious analysis of this movement within the popular culture. Lacking such an analysis, it is particularly tempting to dismiss the popular trend as little more than a fad, or as mere nostalgia, and to give no further thought to understanding it. To the extent that the trend has been commercialized, as for example by the recent Bicentennial celebration, it has been faddish and nostalgic. But at the same time, it is more. Its origins lie deeper in the American experience than the Bicentennial, in the traumas and dislocations of American life in the mid-twentieth century. The rapid socio-economic mobility and cultural conservatism of post-World War II American society yielded in the 1960s to violent political upheaval and disorienting cultural rebellion. These, in turn, yielded in the '70s to economic decline, cultural introspection, and a sharp loss of confidence in the nation's goals and in its Vietnam- and Watergate-haunted leadership. In all of this, amidst challenges to deeply held beliefs and aspirations, where has the individual stood? What has there been to hold on to? As our sense of national mission and national uniqueness declines, where do we find what is best in America and how do we identify with it?

The Bicentennial presented an opportunity to give form to such questions, but hardly brought us very far in answering them. Individual Americans, however, have been attempting to find their own answers, and their search has led them back into the past. For many there is a faith that the answers lie in a rediscovery of their "roots." They seek, in other words, an emotional and spiritual return to the presumed security of the most elemental units of life—church, neighborhood, family and kin, ethnic group, etc. They find a source of strength and inspiration in the study of the history of the family, for time and again history seems to prove that in the face of holocausts and heartburnings what is elemental survives.

This is certainly not a profound reading of the past—or the present. It is ahistorical to the extent that it obscures the impact and experience of change on the past's own terms. Under any circumstance, it seems not to wish to acknowledge that today the elemental units of life themselves are probably less independent of the world around them than ever before.[9] That people come to rediscover the past in search of ways to relate to the present is surely not novel. And that the history they write under such circumstances often bears the stamp of their passions, enthusiasms, and preoccupations (and thus varies greatly in quality) is not surprising. What is most important for our purposes is that it must be the task of historians and teachers of history alike to tap all of the vast potential which lies in the current upsurge of interest of the lay public in local and community history. But this should not be for the sake of reinforcing the pronounced tendencies toward cultural consolation, romantic ethnicity, and sentimental populism in today's popular trend. Instead teachers of history in particular must employ the best work of both today's popular and academic local and community historians, to bring students and the public generally into a more objective understanding of the forces which have shaped American society and culture. Without an effort to shape serious goals, the current local and community history movement is likely to prove either as ambiguous in its contribution or as ephemeral as its various predecessors. History will then have lost an important opportunity.

It is necessary to analyze these predecessors, for by comparing and contrasting the various waves of popular interest in local and community history we may gain adequate perspective on the nature of the current trend. The three previous significant developments—two in the nineteenth century and one during the Great Depression of the 1930s—have also been products of rapid and confusing change. Yet they have differed enough from one another in their social constituencies and ethos that only one of them, that of the 1930s, resembles ours today.

Native white Protestant elites initiated the two nineteenth-century movements.[10] We find the first of these elite-inspired efforts centered in early and mid-nineteenth-century New England, a region experiencing declining economic and political power and cultural prestige as the American Revolution receded into the past and as newer, wealthier regions emerged to the West. Plagued by their section's (and hence their own) status anxieties, native white Protestants were also threatened in the 1840s and 1850s by the massive influx of poverty-stricken, Irish Catholic, peasant immigrants. Under these circumstances, affluent descendants of the Pilgrims (and a large number of others who wished they had the same genealogy) became increasingly conscious of their sectional, ethnic, and family history. They founded socially exclusive, historically oriented, patriotic societies and equally exclusive local and state historical societies, which they then dedicated to the preservation of the archives and memorabilia of their class. They wrote town histories which extolled the supposed virtues of the world their ancestors had created and which credited that world with giving rise to our Revolution.

Stepchildren to this New England movement were similar, though fewer, activities and organizations among native white Protestants in the cities and towns of the mid-Atlantic region and of the Old Northwest. In the former, rapid population and economic growth and massive Irish and German immigration menaced traditional patterns of power and status. In the latter, on the other hand, pioneering elements within the eastern, native white Protestant diaspora felt the need to create local historical traditions (and hence roots for themselves) and to secure the cultural hegemony of the East in rapidly developing areas, which were then emerging from wilderness and frontier social conditions.

Still later in the century, another local and community history movement, larger in both scope and scale than its predecessor, emerged among native white Protestants. It was prompted by the nation's Centennial celebration, the dislocations resulting from industrialization and urbanization, and the beginnings of a yet more massive influx of more exotic immigrants from eastern and southern Europe. This movement also created socially exclusive historical and patriotic societies. But even more significant are the volumes and volumes of county history it left behind. These county histories remain to this day a staple item in the bibliographies of historians (amateur and professional alike), students, and genealogists.

The nineteenth-century movements celebrated a world which was white, male, Protestant, bourgeois, acquisitive, individualistic, self-reliant, and even when urban, deeply rooted in rural and agrarian feeling and memory. They defended values and virtues thought lacking among the emergent groups outside their own ranks—freed slaves, foreigners, Catholics, Jews, restive workers, insistent feminists, etc. Thus both movements were informed by a vision of the good society which was out of touch with an increasingly pluralistic social order and with urban, industrial, and corporate realities. Yet emanating from stable, higher status groups of prestigious and articulate, native stock Americans, these movements naturally had some influence upon our American self-concept. Their ethnocentric and class-bound conception of our national past helped to create an elitist historical mythology which continues to provide justification for the hierarchical tendencies in American society. At the same time, however, these popular movements were not alone in creating that mythology. American professional historical scholarship, which slowly emerged in the last quarter of the nineteenth century, confirmed the same viewpoint. The first generation of academic historians, heavily comprised of Anglo- and Germanophiles influenced by germ theories of civilization, set as its goal the discovery of the distant Anglo-Saxon origins of idealized American institutions.[11]

The third wave of popular interest in local and community history came in the 1930s. Not surprisingly, the depression decade produced a different ethos for local and community history. There came an upsurge of populist sensibility and a leftward shift in popular political ideologies and practice,[12] which in turn led local and community history to values and themes that were the antithesis of those put forward by the previous elitist movements. Now the underclasses were celebrated, and the story was told of their bitter strength and resiliency in struggles for survival against the forces of oppression and exploitation. Cooperation, collective values, and folkish generosity, integrity, and wholesomeness were now extolled, and individualism, acquisitiveness, and materialism criticized.

A particularly vital component of this third wave existed among the out-of-work writers, artists, teachers, scholars, students, and countless others from all walks of life who were briefly employed by federally funded relief projects, principally the

Works Progress Administration. These WPA workers produced a distinguished series of inexpensive local and state guide books with a strong historical orientation, a number of equally inexpensive, mass-marketed popular histories and social documentaries based on transcribed interviews-in-the-field with ordinary folk such as ex-slaves, and a striking, often commemorative, public art, which still engages the eye in courthouses, post offices, and other public buildings.[13] In contrast to the socially exclusive organizations and elite-oriented histories of the nineteenth-century movements, this was a public history, accessible economically, physically, and thematically to popular audiences.

The populist spirit of the depression decade's local and community history movement is particularly evident in WPA public art. Typically, a WPA-sponsored mural does homage to some local or regional epoch of economic development and social progress, and in so doing also celebrates the herculean labors of working class, often black and immigrant, men and women. They are often portrayed literally building America from the ground up—laying down railroad track, loading freight on the banks of some great river, plowing the fastnesses of the Great Plains, or excavating the foundation for a skyscraper of the metropolis.[14]

One purpose of this art was celebratory, for, in addition to their personal aesthetic goals, the WPA artists hoped to create a permanent memorial to those whose heroic labors in building America had seldom been fully acknowledged. But a number of the artists also hoped to evoke a political response to their art.[15] An art which celebrated the labors of the exploited common people of the past might also evoke in their descendants feelings of pride and anger and power. In turn, these emotions might themselves become the basis for political assertiveness in pursuit of reform or revolution.

It is not clear how the politics of this art, as it was visually perceived, struck most viewers during the Depression. Today, almost five decades later, I believe it evokes mostly bewilderment in viewers, the large majority of whom remember or have learned little of this art's origins. Its realism seems naive—at best, innocent and youthful, at worst, callow or puerile. On second glance, it may seem propagandistic, but certainly not a propaganda which seems likely to harm anyone, much less create disorder. In short, divorced from its times and its ideological foundations in the populism of the Depression period, this public art seems neither to inspire nor to inform. In comparison with the local and community history movements which preceded it, the 1930s movement appears to have had little lasting impact upon any segment of the popular historical consciousness.

Although today's local and community history movement shares populist attitudes with its predecessor of the 1930s, it also differs in significant ways with respect to motive, technique and method, and subject interest. Contemporary local history is not inspired by economic collapse but by a loss of faith in government, other social institutions, and national leadership which has caused many ordinary Americans to turn inward and search the past for strength and consolation.

Moreover, today we have what may be called a "democratization of technique and methodology." Among the nonacademic historians, writers, genealogists, historic preservationists, museum curators, producers of film, radio, and television documentaries, and many others who have been trying to give the movement direction and practical assistance, there appears to be a desire to demystify their own research techniques and methods and place them in the hands of the lay public. Experts themselves, they have sought to make near-experts of others through a profusion of do-it-yourself guides to genealogical research (itself once the lonely preserve of scions of the DAR and FFV and of Latter Day Saints congregants), to family, town, and ethnic history, to "reading" gravestones, to the use of statistics in local and community historical research, and to conducting oral history interviews with the noncelebrities around us who are not used to being interviewed.[16] These guides, most of which are now available in inexpensive pamphlet and paperback editions, have been accepted both in and out of the classroom. We might predict that the experts are fostering the rise of a new class of amateur historians and creating stiff competition for themselves. In contrast, the local and community history movement of the 1930s wished to give the past back to the people, but was not particularly concerned with having that history written by the people themselves.

History is too important to be left solely to the experts or, as the nineteenth-century movements wished, to social elites. It has no business developing Mandarin traditions which serve to remove it from popular comprehension and popular practice and ultimately to deny people access to their pasts. Yet it is also important to remember that specialized techniques and methodologies in themselves do not necessarily provide the most effective keys to the past. Indeed, history is intrinsically one of the most democratic of the disciplines for the very reason that in it specialized methods, techniques, and languages which are accessible to experts alone, are at most handmaidens of the art, but never the art itself. History, after all, owes its origins not to the academy but to preliterate bards, and much of the best written history still is characterized less by highly sophisticated methodology and technique, which is present in so much contemporary social science, than by the evocative and persuasive language of these ancient precursors. Moreover, even in this era of computers and electronic media, historical synthesis still remains more dependent on applied intuition, imagination, and common sense, informed by a previous immersion in published history and in the written records and material artifacts of the past, than on what, even by the loosest definition, may be called "science." Technique and method help us to organize data and perceptions we accumulate through that immersion. But neither can do the work of interpretation and generalization, upon which synthesis is built. Thus, while it is important to democratize methods and techniques, it is no less important to protect students and the public-at-large from the illusion that once one possesses them, the study of the past becomes an exact science and the past itself an open book.

Today's practitioners of popular local and community history are concerned with two frequently overlapping subject matter concerns.[17] First, they wish to write a history that is emphatically local—one which focuses on the smaller units of settlement. Regional, national, and international influences are more excluded from this view of the locality than in the popular local history of the past. In part, this exclusion is a consequence of the movement's populism: it seeks to write the history of ordinary people and thus is much less concerned, whether as heroes or villains of the local story, with elites possessing regional, national, or international influence and power. For example, a staple of nineteenth-century local history was a discussion of the men who had represented the local area in the national or state legislature. In much contemporary popular local history, one would be hard-pressed either to find mention of the legislature or to learn that the legislature had any impact upon local life.

Equally important, however, in explaining the nature of present conceptions of local history is that a chief concern of today's popular local history is evoking the subjective, emotional, and experiential aspects of social life and human interaction. People, ordinary and elite alike, thus are of concern not so much in terms of their objective social status, power, or wealth, but rather in terms of how they conceive of themselves and are perceived by those around them with whom they interact. This goal of evocation appears to these local historians as more likely to be fulfilled in smaller cities and towns and in neighborhoods, where the subtler aspects of culture are thought to be more conveniently researched by, and more psychologically accessible to, the researcher. The goal of evocation further suggests the reason why oral history is so frequently the basis of this work—to the extent that oral interviews and testimonies, often without any commentary or interpretation, are the only text in a number of recently published works of popular local history. As the WPA historians discovered in seeking ways to move the public to empathize with history's victims, letting people talk candidly about themselves and their neighbors is a surer way of creating an emotional, richly evocative response to the past than the scholar's analytical prose.

A second, and stronger, subject interest of popular local and community history today is immigration and ethnicity, particularly *white* immigration and ethnicity. This will come as no surprise to anyone familiar with the intensity of the 1970s' white ethnic revival, which is closely tied, in an informal alliance of both organizations and individuals, with the local and community history movement. It would be no exaggeration to say that what black history was to the '60s, white ethnic history has been to the '70s.

The interest in white immigrants and their ethnic descendants differs from the type of interest which the 1930s' movement manifested in the same social groups. The Depression Era popular historians saw immigrants and ethnics as vital components of a diverse American proletariat which shared, for all its subcultural fragmentation, common needs and a common history of economic hardship, cultural resilience, and individual and group struggle. The emphasis was on what united, to the exclusion of what divided. But ours is a period of economic scarcity and competition among groups, not of shared economic collapse. Moreover, large numbers of ethnics are already decades out of the working class. They have entered the broad ranks of the middle class. Although more comfortable and secure than their immigrant ancestors, they have also discovered that ethnic barriers continue to block the path to social prestige and national economic and political power. Perhaps then it was inevitable that the 1970s would come to a different perspective on immigration and ethnic history. Ethnic groups are studied not as components of a single class, but as distinct subgroups in society. Indeed, either directly or by implication, diversity, past and present, is usually celebrated, and all pressures toward homogenization looked at with suspicion. Moreover, while immigrant hardships are stressed, the emphasis is not so much on the exploitation of the foreigners' labor as on the more subtle cultural disorientation and social ostracism which have been (and are still being) suffered during painful decades of assimilation. This latter interest particularly lends itself to a concern for evoking the same subjective, emotional, and experiential aspects of the individual and group past which interests the new popular local history.[18]

From the viewpoint of both teaching and scholarship, this new concentration on a single locality and an individual ethnic group helps compensate for the past's preoccupation with the behavior, attitudes, and ideologies of cosmopolitan elites. Efforts at evocation, too, may be seen as an attempt to rescue the past from academic history, much of which has always been dry, monographic, and coldly analytical, and much of which now is often too technical and complexly conceived to be readily accessible to lay people. But just as in the case of the democratization of technique and method, these developments themselves are not without their own more dubious implications, particularly for the classroom teaching of history. The final section of this essay will examine these implications and offer some general guidelines for integrating the ideas and works of history of the new, popular local and community history into the curriculum.

An unfortunate by-product of the upsurge of black cultural nationalism in the '60s and of the contemporary white ethnic revival has been the legitimation of a public ideology which, in the name of some vaguely defined, presumably benign cultural pluralism, accepts racial and ethnic divisions within the population as good. This legitimation has been greatly reinforced by the 1970s' economic decline, which has intensified competition for scarce resources among racial and ethnic groups. In such a social context, teachers should be cautioned against adopting instructional methods and goals which encourage students to think of themselves and those around them solely in terms of competing racial and ethnic groups.

Many teachers unwittingly do encourage students to think this way. There are two principal ways in which this occurs in the classroom. First, teachers very often adopt a strategy for teaching about immigration and ethnicity which proceeds from one individual group to another, in one unit, for example, studying Irish-Americans, in the next Poles, in the next Mexicans, etc. This method does implicitly pay homage to worthy, pluralistic notions of fairness. At the same time, by its very nature, it accentuates differences—unless, that is, one adopts the technique of using each group's history to illustrate the common problems (immigration, the struggle for economic security, social assimilation, cultural change, etc.) of all lower status groups of foreign origin. In that case the common problems have become the center of the teacher's instructional goals, with the individual groups more a means of illustrating these problems. More direct and less repetitious methods could easily be found to accomplish these ends. I do not at all mean to suggest that differences have not existed (and do not continue to exist) between ethnic groups. We have only to look at language, religion, customs, and recent historical experience. But even such differences can be pedagogically organized under common experiential categories (work, religion, family, etc.), which suggest the essential unities of human concern and activity.

Second, teachers frequently seek to establish, as I once did, the relevance of immigration and ethnic history by first impressing upon students that each one of them is an ethnic. But what if the students resist that conclusion? At best, one may then drop the tactic as a false start—after having already created unnecessary confusions over personal feelings and attitudes. Or, at worst, one may choose to persist. It is disconcerting to hear teachers, as I have, boast that they were successful at "convincing" students that there was indeed something ethnic about each of them, though the students themselves had previously refused to concede feelings of Polishness or Italianness, etc., and had, in fact, identified themselves simply as "American." Such persuasion, however gentle or friendly, is a violation of the students' identities and personal integrity, not to mention a dubious exercise of the teacher's own authority. Moreover, it is based on assumptions which may be a violation of our own contemporary sociological reality. To be sure, ethnicity has been and continues to be an important basis of identity and group life in America. But students who do not see it as a key to understanding their own lives may well be reflecting the fact that there are other, often more powerful, identities, loyalties, and affiliations—for example, gender, social class, religion, age group—which cut across ethnic lines (and indeed even the less permeable racial ones), tying together people of otherwise diverse backgrounds. Then, too, there is our common American way of life, defined by the political and economic systems in which all of us participate in diverse ways, and our common American cultural values, which we share to the extent that seldom are our attitudes and actions wholly a mystery to other Americans with whom we interact.

Just as there is a need for subtlety and moderation in judging the importance of ethnicity in the present, so, too, must we use care in looking into the historical significance of ethnicity. Historical reality was no less complex than our contemporary one. Doubtless ethnicity had greater social salience in the past than it does today. But it is also true that in the past the ethnic groups shared common problems as a consequence of their foreignness and low status. These common problems lessened the uniqueness of any particular ethnic group's history. Moreover, other sources of social solidarity coexisted alongside ethnicity in the past, making claims upon the individual and group and lessening the impact of ethnicity. Indeed, evidence may be found from within the ethnic groups themselves. Each ethnic group was hardly ever lacking in internal, frequently quite bitter, divisions, which were the product of region of Old World origin, religion, social class, political alignment, and earliness or lateness of arrival in the New World.

A related note of caution needs to be sounded regarding the temptation to celebrate the high degree of ethnic diversity in the American past in the belief that ethnicity and diversity are somehow good in and of themselves.[19] Many of us today live in places where ethnicity (not only our own but others' too) is a resource we may consume with enjoyment in our leisure time. Often the only tempting restaurants around us are ethnic. Ethnic crafts present a pleasing alternative to the mass-produced plastic goods available to us in staggering volume. Ethnic fairs, feasts, and festivities make life more interesting, active, and spontaneous.

But this, it must be stressed, is only part of the story. In another guise, ethnicity has been a source throughout our history of individual and social tension. For the individual who has experienced prejudice and discrimination because of national origin, differences have often been social defects, and foreignness has been associated with low status, poverty, and social embarrassment. Even the much romanticized immigrant families of the past often had so much economic difficulty to put up with that tremendous strains were placed on family relationships. Moreover, the Old World patriarchal traditions of such families made many an Americanizing teenage boy and especially girl restive, and would doubtless be totally unacceptable to their Americanized teenage descendants today.

When we look at the history of society-as-a-whole, the same antiromantic visions of ethnicity confront us. In a society based upon competition for unequally distributed resources, ethnic identification and affiliation, spread out over dozens of groups with as many claims on jobs, residential space, schools, etc., have also been sources of tension, fragmentation, and not infrequently violence. (One has only to think, for example, of the use of immigrant strikebreakers in the past, and of the highly unpopular, but widespread, employment of very low-paid, illegal-alien workers today.) At the very least, our ethnic and racial diversity has made collective and cooperative behavior across ethnic and racial lines much more difficult. While the development of ethnic-oriented values and loyalties has helped to unify and strengthen groups in their competitive struggle for security, self-determination, and dignity, these same values and loyalties have also impeded the growth of a sense of the common good, a sense of "We-ness," necessary to tie Americans together in firmer patterns of mutual obligation and concern. This is by no means to say that those who value ethnic affiliation and loyalty have not been good citizens, or that they have acted or thought incorrectly. After all, ethnicity has been an important fact of American life, legitimized as a means of political and social mobilization and praised for its contributions to our culture by our own melting-pot ideology. It is to say, however, that such affiliations and loyalties have always been claimed at a price. And this, in turn, simply serves to remind us that in discussing ethnicity, as in discussing any other complex historical phenomenon, celebration is less the point than analysis.

Excessive concentration on ethnicity to the exclusion both of other, competing social groupings and identities and of the total social system into which all these groupings and identities are integrated, is but one example of the way parochialism threatens local and community history. Another and perhaps more self-evident example posing the same threat is a narrow concentration on the individual locality. To varying degrees and in varying ways in different historical epochs, regional, national, and international markets, social, political, and diplomatic realities, such as trade, migration, war, and territorial annexation, have impinged upon and influenced the individual locality. Thus, even while recognizing along with contemporary social historians the centrality of localities throughout much of pre-twentieth-century American history, we must at the same time remind ourselves that the history of a town or of a neighborhood may not stop at its borders.

Finally, a word must be said about the emphasis of the new, popular local and ethnic history on the emotional, experiential, and subjective aspects of social life, an interest which has been of great importance in the first place in producing this excessively localistic orientation. We have noted that to an extent this development is a legitimate and perhaps inevitable response to the tendency of academic history to take a wholly analytical stance, to concentrate on the objective rather than sub-jective, and to become too technical for the average layman. Evocation does indeed often produce a history which deepens our understanding of individual lives caught up in the impersonal forces of historical change, and in so doing perhaps deepens our capacities for empathy, an important goal of historical studies in the schools. But there are pitfalls in the contemporary methods chosen to achieve evocation, and these severely limit the quality of the past evocation allows us to recreate. Histories which are comprised largely or solely of oral testimonies, for example, often are profoundly evocative. But just as often they achieve their emotional impact at the expense of describing and analyzing the larger social context of the individual life history, which traditional historical methods, with their focus beyond the individual, are best at fleshing out. Then, too, oral history is the product of memory, and memory, even when drawn out by the most sensitive interviewer, is not history. It is less a question of memory being incorrect than it is of memory making no pretence of rendering a view of the past from outside the individual. Memory is subjective, personal, and idiosyncratic by its very nature. It lacks the ability, which analytical history possesses through critical standards for the examination of evidence and the scholarly apparatus of footnotes and bibliography, to provide checks on its own errors. Indeed, more often than not, memory doesn't know, cannot know, that it is in error.

But the problem is only superficially that of a method which depends on oral testimony, the admirable point of which is to allow ordinary people, wrong or right in their perceptions, to tell their own tale in their own way. The problem lies deeper, in the very nature of emotion and evocation, for both must severely test even the most mature scholar's objectivity precisely because they must pose an inevitable tension for the dispassionate and analytical state of mind upon which objective judgment depends. The answer is not, however, that we must have one sort of history or another. Rather we must confront the fact that each kind of history poses an inevitable problem for the other and find a method of mediation. Popular history should not give up its goal of evocation. But we do need more works of popular history which combine, say, oral testimony, aimed at evocation, with traditional historical analysis, aimed at an analytical description and explanation of the larger social contexts of the past beyond the individual, the small group, or the locality. Such a combination of methods and purposes to some extent allows for a cancelling out of the reasons for the difficulties the popular audience of students and others has in accepting academic history. But it does so in a manner which simultaneously provides a larger historical context qualifying the distortions and idiosyncracies of memory. At the same time, this combination of methods and purposes makes it more likely that the particular feelings and attitudes of the moment historians wish to evoke need not become as outmoded and mysterious to posterity as the WPA art of the 1930s has become for us; for there will be in popular historical works an analytical context to give evocation continued meaning and significance for the future audience.

In various ways all of the problems with the new popular local and community history underscore what is its most common fault—the failure to integrate local and community history into larger relevant social and spatial contexts. Without efforts in such a direction, local and community history, whether influenced by the ideas and published work of this popular history movement or of its predecessors, must always tend ultimately toward the parochial, ethnocentric, and antiquarian.

To take up the issue which thus confronts teachers: How can we frame classroom assignments and shape curricula in local and community history so that we do not lose sight of the symbiotic relationship between the general and the specific, the "big" and the "little" pictures?

Let us consider two generic types of uses of local and community subject matter in teaching history. The first of these uses local and community perspectives to illuminate epic events (whether they be recurring or nonrecurring), such as wars, depressions, national or state elections, assassinations, epidemics, or natural disasters. The course of such epic events is usually beyond the control of any individual locality or community, and the ultimate outcome often unrelated to any large extent to specifically local or community considerations. As a consequence, the strength of this approach appears to be more utilitarian than pedagogical. Because events, even when recurring, are not continuous through time, we do not get a picture of the full range of interactions between localities or communities and the world beyond them. In addition, because the localities and communities are responding to externally initiated events, they appear more or less passive in relation to forces outside them; thus we are denied a sense of the dynamic interactions between those forces and the communities or localities with which they interact. But, on the other hand, this approach does have a practical strength. It enables teachers to synthesize conveniently and comfortably certain standard events, around which they and most Americans have traditionally been taught to organize the national past, in a way that "brings home" those events—i.e., makes their epic quality more immediate without sacrificing too much of their drama.

The second type employs local and community perspectives in a different, and I believe superior, manner. Here the point is to analyze the interaction between various social processes, such as urbanization, industrialization, social mobility, or immigrant assimilation, and particular localities and communities.

Because the study of social processes ultimately demands a more profound confrontation with the complexity and interconnectedness of phenomena through chronological time than does the study of events, this approach has several relative strengths. Social processes are seamless and dynamic, continuously taking place and developing over long and indeterminate periods of time. Epic events may be either recurring or nonrecurring, but they are not continuous through time. Since one of the most accessible and desirable consequences of the study of history is the understanding of change and development over time, processes are indeed one of the most useful tools for teaching historical analysis. On the other hand, an excessive preoccupation with events may lead students to the conviction that history is a series of voids connected by wars, elections, and depressions. I am unhappy to have to report that most of the undergraduates today who enter my own history courses, after having had little or no history since high school, still view the past this way.

Social processes impact more generally throughout society than do epic events. Not all communities and localities may be deeply or lastingly influenced by an event such as the assassination of a president or a national election. But the study of social processes, such as a society's urbanization, if taken to its logical analytical conclusions, eventually leads us to formulate questions about all communities and localities within that society. After all, even the inhabitants of rural areas may be deeply touched by the development of urban markets for agricultural commodities, or by a tremendous expansion of the urban job market.

Though social processes occur generally throughout a society at a given time, they almost always vary to one extent or another in shape, content, and consequence from place to place and community to community within that society. This is part of their instructional value and fascination. They call out to us for comparison and contrast between communities and localities. In turn, such comparison and contrast may well give us acute insight into what is specifically and uniquely local to a particular place, or Italian-American, or Catholic, or working class, or suburban, etc. In contrast, because epic historical events are so often initiated or controlled outside the locality or community, there is a tendency toward a greater uniformity of outcome to these events among localities and communities.

When we study events, we logically are led into a search for their prime movers, who more often than not appear to be powerful and affluent persons at the center of government and politics, or the economy, or the military, etc. It is, of course, sheer populist romanticism to believe that the activities of elites are unimportant. But often left out of the analysis of the epic events elites appear to initiate and control are millions of ordinary people, without money, high status, and significant political power, whose labor, migrations, and votes deeply, but often quite subtly, influence the social processes which determine the larger direction of historical events.

The last point leads us to the final, and perhaps most important, reason why social process is the best working perspective for local and community historical studies. Social process provides the best framework through which to study the evolution of such central social issues as economic growth and development, the distribution of wealth and power, and social and cultural cohesion, all of which are vital to our students' lives as citizens and social beings with responsibilities for others as well as for themselves. Local and community perspectives not only make these issues themselves more accessible conceptually and imaginatively. They also provide a coherent basis for concrete understanding of the forces which daily influence the quality of life in the localities where we live *and* in those where others live, and within those communities in which we live *and* in those in which others live. Thus, local and community perspectives afford us the opportunity to use the "little" picture as a means to achieve empathy and to discover the "big" picture. In effect, we are given the opportunity to employ the potentially parochial for the sake of overcoming parochialism.

Today's popular local and community history movement will doubtlessly only be judged a success by historians of the future if it transcends the narrow and uncritical enthusiasms of parochialism. For only by moving beyond its own version of evocative, celebratory populism, which failed its 1930s' counterpart, will it be able to make a lasting contribution to American life. To be sure, without developing serious, analytical concepts and goals, popular local and community history may well make positive contributions to the quality of many individual lives, particularly by helping us to achieve the "roots" so many of us now seem to crave. As well, the evocative power of much of this contemporary popular history may make us all more feeling individuals. But limited even to such worthy goals as these, today's popular local and community history will not be able to accomplish a still greater purpose: to provide Americans with a more objective consciousness of their society's past, and hence with a means for reshaping our present and winning our future.

APPENDIX

There are so many guides and manuals to local and community history now, one hardly knows where to begin in listing them, let alone how to be fair in choosing among them. The following list is by no means definitive, but I believe the works are both representative of general interests and good in quality; included for the sake of teachers' convenience are some works which are aimed at students as well as the lay public.

1. Local history: Thomas E. Felt, *Researching, Writing, and Publishing Local History* (Nashville, 1976); Donald Dean Parker, *Local History: How to Gather It, Write It, and Publish It* (New York, 1974); James Robertson (ed.), *Old Glory: Pictorial Report on the Grass-Roots History Movement and the First Hometown History Primer* (New York, 1973); David Weitzman, *Underfoot: An Everyday Guide to Exploring the American Past* (New York, 1976); Ted L. Underwood, "Undergraduates as Historians: Writing Local History in a Seminar on Historical Research," *The History Teacher* 7 (November 1973): 19–23; David R. Goldfield, "Living History: The Physical City as Artifact and Teaching Tool," *The History Teacher* 8 (August 1976): 1–19.

2. Ethnic history and genealogy: Charles Blockson, with Ron Fry, *Black Genealogy* (Englewood Cliffs, NJ, 1977); Dan Rottenberg, *Find Our Fathers: A Guidebook to Jewish Genealogy* (New York, 1979); Gilbert H. Doane, *Searching for Your Ancestors* (New York, 1974); Jeane Eddy Westin, *Finding Your Roots* (New York, 1977).

3. Ethnic and family (recent ancestry, as distinct from genealogy's interest in distant ancestry) history: Jim Watts and Allen F. Davis, *Generations: Your Family in Modern American History* (New York, 1972, 2nd ed.)—a text for classroom use; David H. Culbert, "Undergraduates as Historians: Family History Projects Add Meaning to an Introductory Survey," *The History Teacher* 7 (November 1973): 7–17; Kirk Jeffrey, "Write a History of Your Own Family," *The History Teacher* 7 (May 1974): 365–73; David J. Russo, *Families and Communities* (Nashville, 1974); David Weitz, *My Backyard History Book* (Boston, 1975); Allan J. Lichtman, *Your Family History* (New York, 1978); David E. Kyvig and Myron A. Marty, *Your Family History: A Handbook for Research and Writing* (Arlington Heights, IL, 1978).

4. Oral history: Willa K. Baum, *Oral History for the Local Historical Society* (Nashville, 1974); Gary Shumway and William G. Hartland, *An Oral History Primer* (Fullerton, CA, 1973); Cullom Davis et al., *Oral History from Tape to Type* (Chicago, 1977); John A. Neuenschwander, *Oral History as a Teaching Approach* (West Haven, CT, 1976).

5. Excellent pamphlets and booklets for guiding both teachers and amateurs to local and community history research materials are published by the American Association for State

and Local History, 172 Second Avenue, North, Nashville, TN 37201. Two items in this technical leaflet series which are suggested by the text of this essay are: Sam Bass Warner, *Writing Local History: The Use of Social Statistics* (Nashville, 1970); and John J. Newman, *Cemetery Transcribing: Preparations and Procedures* (Nashville, 1971).

6. Excellent curriculum planning materials are available from the Family and Community History Center, Newberry Library, 60 West Walton St., Chicago, IL 60610. They are to be found in its series, "The Newberry Papers in Family and Community History," and cover many facets and methods of local and community history, such as oral history, media, folklore, material culture, and museums. The papers often contain sample syllabi for courses currently being offered around the country.

NOTES

1. But see the suggestive remarks of Judith Wellman, "Introduction" to *The First Women's Rights Convention, Seneca Falls, New York, 1848: A Sourcebook in Local, Social, and Women's History*, in *New Approaches in Teaching Local History*, Newberry Papers in Family and Community History, no. 78–5 (Chicago: Newberry Library, 1978), v–x and Tamara K. Hareven, "The Search for Generational Memory: Tribal Rites in Industrial Society," *Daedalus* 107 (Fall 1978): 137–49. I attempted to deal with related issues in "Haley's *Roots* and Our Own: An Inquiry into the Nature of a Popular Phenomenon," *Journal of Ethnic Studies* 5 (Fall, 1977): 103–107.

2. See Appendix.

3. As Raymond Williams notes in his excellent study of the usage of common political, ideological and philosophical terms, *Keywords: A Vocabulary of Culture and Society* (New York, 1976), 65–66, there is little agreement among scholars, philosophers, and social scientists on a precise definition of the elusive word "community." Two tendencies, according to Williams, are present historically in the definition of the word: "on the one hand the sense of direct common concern, on the other hand the materialization of various forms of common organization" (p. 66). The former definition would allow for the use of the word "community" to describe a group of young men who regularly meet at a certain street corner. The latter would use the word to describe, for example a *place* and might speak of an institution located at that place as a "community institution." The definition I have employed is, I believe, preferable because it encompasses a larger scope and scale of behavior, particularly in its ability to include informal organization. Furthermore, today the word "community" increasingly is intended, though without fully rationalized purpose, to suggest some sort of affinity linking, rather than a mere formal bond as, for example, would be likely shared by any two residents of the same city. Finally in the context of this paper, I felt it would be helpful to differentiate as fully as possible between the words "locality" and "community." Obviously, however, under certain circumstances, a locality can be a community.

Obviously, too, attempting to define either "community" or, for that matter, "local and community history" with a high degree of precision is destined to be a frustrating experience.

4. Robert Redfield, "The Folk Society," *American Journal of Sociology* 52 (1946): 293–308. Also, see his *The Little Community: Viewpoints for the Study of a Human Whole*

(Chicago, 1955) and *Peasant Society and Culture* (Chicago, 1956) for a further elaboration of this idea.

5. For the major statement of this viewpoint by a scholar surveying the historiography of the American past, see Thomas C. Cochran, "The 'Presidential Synthesis' in American History," *American Historical Review* 53I (July 1948): 748–59. For an important reformulation of the same idea by feminist historians, who are critical of the exclusion of women from most syntheses of the past, see Ann D. Gordon et al., *Women in American Society* (Boston, 1972), 6–7.

6. Jacques Le Goff, "Is Politics Still the Backbone of History?" *Daedalus* 100 (Winter 1971): 1–19, for an inquiry into the centrality of political history in past historiography and a call for the merger of political history with other subdisciplines. Also, see Cochran, "The 'Presidential Synthesis' in American History," 748–59; and John Higham, *Writing American History: Essays on Modern Scholarship* (Bloomington, IN, 1970), 157–74.

7. For important articles suggesting the scope and scale of these changes, see the special issue, *Historical Studies Today,* of *Daedalus* 100 (Winter 1971).

8. Robert Wiebe *The Segmented Society: An Introduction to the Meaning of America* (New York, 1915), 14–46.

9. The point is made skillfully for the particular context of the family, but with a wider applicability suggested at the same time, in Christopher Lasch's *Haven in a Heartless World: The Family Besieged* (New York, 1977).

10. For a good review of nonacademic local and community history in the nineteenth century, see David J. Russo, *Families and Communities: A New View of American History* (Nashville, 1974). My sketch is based on this work and: Barbara Miller Soloman, *Ancestors and Immigrants: A Changing New England Tradition* (Chicago, 1956), especially Chapters 1, 4, 5; Wallace E. Davies, *Patriotism on Parade: The Story of Veterans' and Hereditary Organizations in America, 1783–1900* (Cambridge, 1955); E. Digby Baltzell, *The Protestant Establishment: Aristocracy and Caste in America* (New York, 1964), 109–32; Leslie W. Dunlap, *American Historical Societies, 1790–1860* (Madison, 1944), Julian P. Boyd, "Historical Societies," in James Truslow Adams (ed.), *Dictionary of American History* 5 vols. (New York, 1940), vol. III, 33; "Historical Societies," in Oscar Handlin et al., *Harvard Guide to American History* (Cambridge, 1955), 13; Evarts B. Greene, "Our Pioneer Historical Societies," Indiana Historical Society *Publications* 10 (1931): 83–97.

A complex variation on the same relation between social status and movements to institutionalize the past is found in the creation of a few historical societies by various ethnic upper classes between 1880 and 1950; see John J. Appel, "Immigrant Historical Societies in the United States, 1880–1950" (unpublished Ph.D. dissertation, University of Pennsylvania, 1960).

11. John Higham, *History: Professional Scholarship in America* (New York, 1973 ed.), 158–70.

12. William E. Leuchtenburg, *Franklin D. Roosevelt and the New Deal, 1932–1940* (New York, 1963), 19–37, 95–117; William Stott, *Documentary Expression and Thirties America* (New York 1973), Parts II and III; Irving Bernstein, *The Turbulent Years: The American*

Worker, 1933–1941 (Boston, 1970); Arthur M. Schelsinger, Jr., *The Age of Roosevelt*, vol. III, *The Politics of Upheaval* (Boston, 1960), Part I.

13. Stott, *Documentary Expression and Thirties America*, 102–18, gives the most perceptive analysis of the local and community, populist focus of many WPA projects.

14. See, for example, the hundreds of illustrations of this public art in the excellent study by Marlene Park and Gerald E. Markowitz, *New Deal for Art: The Government Art Projects of the 1930s, with Examples from New York City and State* (Hamilton, NY, 1977), passim and text, 39–44.

15. Cari Chiarenza, "Form and Content in the Early Work of Aaron Siskind," *Massachusetts Review* 19 (Winter 1978): 828–29; Park and Markowitz, *New Deal for Art*, 8 14, 26–31, 79, 88–91, 96–97, 111, 114. Francis V. O'Connor (ed.), *The New Deal Art Projects: An Anthology of Memoirs* (Washington, DC, 1972) and *Art for the Millions: Essays from the 1930s by Artists and Administrators of the WPA Federal Art Project* (Greenwich, CT, 1973) are also recommended.

16. See Appendix.

17. For examples, see such works as Laurel Shackelford and Bill Weinberg (eds.), *Our Appalachia* (New York, 1977); John Baskin, *New Burlington: The Life and Death of an American Village* (New York, 1976); Reed Wolcott, *Rosehill* (New York, 1976); Tamara Hareven and Randolph Langenbach, *Amoskeag: Life and Work in an American Factory City* (New York, 1978); Michael Lesy, *Wisconsin Death Trip* (New York, 1973) and *Real Life: Louisville in the Twenties* (New York, 1976); Studs Terkel, *Division Street, America* (New York, 1967); Andrew M. Greeley, *That Most Distressful Nation: The Taming of the American Irish* (Chicago, 1972); Richard Gambino, *Blood of My Blood: The Dilemma of Italian-Americans* (New York, 1974); Irving Howe, *World of Our Fathers: The Journey of the East European Jews to America and the Life They Found and Made* (New York, 1976), Allon Schoner, *Portal to America: The Lower East Side, 1870–1925* (New York, 1967); Michael Novak, *The Guns of Lattimer* (New York, 1978); Theodore Rosengarten, *All God's Dangers: The Life of Nate Shaw* (New York, 1974); Ande Manners, *Poor Cousins* (New York, 1972); Harry Roskolenko, *The Time That Was Then: The Lower East Side: 1900–1913—An Intimate Chronicle* (New York, 1971); and Carol Kammen (ed.), *What They Wrote: 19th-Century Documents from Tompkins County, New York* (Ithaca, NY, 1978). There are also a large number of autobiographies now in print in which the experience of participation in an ethnic community and the personal sense of ethnic history are seen to play a formative role, among the best of these are: Michael J. Arlen, *Passage to Ararat* (New York, 1975); Maxine Hong Kingston, *The Woman Warrior: Memoirs of a Girlhood Among Ghosts* (New York, 1977); Richard Brown, *I Am of Ireland* (New York, 1974); and of course, though a variation of this genre, Alex Haley, *Roots* (New York, 1977).

18. On the ethnic revival: Michael Novak, *The Rise of the Unmeltable Ethnics: Politics and Culture in the Seventies* (New York, 1972), S. M. Tomasi et al. (eds.), *Pieces of a Dream: The Ethnic Worker's Crisis with America* (New York, 1972), Alfred Aversa, Jr., "Italian Neo-Ethnicity: The Search for Self-Identity," *Journal of Ethnic Studies* 6 (Summer 1978): 49–56; Richard Krickus, *Pursuing the American Dream: White Ethnics and the New Populism* (New York, 1976), Preface; Victor Grenne, "Old Ethnic Stereotypes and the New

Ethnic Studies," *Ethnicity* 5 (December 1978), 328–50; M. Elaine Burgess, "The Resurgence of Ethnicity: Myth or Reality," *Ethnic and Racial Studies* 1 (July 1978): 265–85.

19. A view criticized as unsparingly as briefly both by Gunnar Myrdal, "The Case Against Romantic Ethnicity," *The Center Magazine* (July–August 1974): 26–30 and by Orlando Patterson, "Ethnicity and the Pluralist Fallacy," *Change* (March 1975): 10–11. Also, see Irving Louis Horowitz, "Race, Class, and the New Ethnicity," *Worldview* (January 1975): 46–53.